August Wilson
and
Black Aesthetics

AUGUST WILSON AND BLACK AESTHETICS

Edited by
Dana A. Williams
and
Sandra G. Shannon

AUGUST WILSON AND BLACK AESTHETICS
© Sandra Shannon and Dana Williams, 2004

First published 2004 by
PALGRAVE MACMILLAN™
175 Fifth Avenue, New York, N.Y. 10010 and
Houndmills, Basingstoke, Hampshire, England RG21 6XS
Companies and representatives throughout the world

PALGRAVE MACMILLAN is the global academic imprint of the Palgrave Macmillan division of St. Martin's Press, LLC and of Palgrave Macmillan Ltd. Macmillan® is a registered trademark in the United States, United Kingdom and other countries. Palgrave is a registered trademark in the European Union and other countries.

ISBN 1–4039–6406–8 hardback

Library of Congress Cataloging-in-Publication Data
    August Wilson and Black aesthetics / edited by Sandra Shannon and Dana Williams.
        p. cm.
    Includes bibliographical references and index.
    ISBN 1–4039–6406–8
    1. Wilson, August—Aesthetics. 2. Historical drama, American—History and criticism. 3. African Americans in literature. 4. African American aesthetics. 5. Aesthetics, American. 6. Aesthetics, Black. I. Shannon, Sandra Garrett, 1952– II. Williams, Dana A., 1972–

PS3573.I45677Z57 2004
812'.54—dc22   2003068822

A catalogue record for this book is available from the British Library.

Design by Newgen Imaging Systems (P) Ltd., Chennai, India.

First edition: August, 2004
10 9 8 7 6 5 4 3 2 1

Printed in the United States of America.

CONTENTS

1

INTRODUCTION

Dana A. Williams

Since 1990 when he won his second Pulitzer Prize for Drama, August Wilson has been among the most well-received and critically acclaimed playwrights in American theater. In 1996, however, his writing of plays took a back seat to his politics when he delivered his now infamous speech, "The Ground on Which I Stand," before the Theatre Communications Group (TCG) in Princeton, New Jersey. Among other things, the speech articulated Wilson's position regarding the *appropriate* function of black art, particularly black theater; his firm stance against colorblind casting to accommodate multiculturalism initiatives; and his belief that black theater is alive and well but underfunded. In these instances especially, the speech voiced a number of assertions that desperately needed to be heard.

First, he writes that "race matters" and argues that it is "the largest, most identifiable and most important part of our personality."[1] As platitudinous as the phrase "race matters" is, it is, perhaps, one of the most significant of Wilson's assertions. If Wilson's speech was effective at all,[2] it was most effective in the sense that it forced Americans, once again, to think and to talk about race. As much as it informs and, in too many cases, controls society, race is still all too often not thought about or talked about by non–African Americans in meaningful ways. Robert Brustein's suggestion that there should be a statute of limitation on white guilt about its past inhumanity to man speaks volumes to America's denial of the significance of race to African Americans and non–African Americans alike in today's society.[3] But as Elmo Terry-Morgan so succinctly writes in *Black Theatre Unprecedented Times*, a special publication of *Black Theatre News*, "[...] the Black/White race war in America will not end peacefully until a critical mass of White folks acknowledge that racism is intricately woven into their cultural inheritance."[4]

The latter part of this statement—that "racism is intricately woven into [white people's] cultural heritage"—I would argue, is the very point that Wilson tries to make with his comments about theater subscriptions and about critics who write from the position of cultural imperialists. Notably, the subscription audience at theaters that mount Wilson's plays and other mainstream American plays alike is overwhelmingly white in more cases than not. And as long as the majority of subscription audiences are white, this privileged audience "holds the seats of [the] theatres hostage to the mediocrity of its tastes, and serves to impede the further development of an audience"[5] that is more likely to be attuned to the aesthetic values of non-white playwrights. Similarly, the white critic who writes from a position of privilege and through a belief system that adopts hegemonic values (with a white aesthetic as the standard to be met) does more damage to the growth of a diverse American theater than good. As Wilson suggests: "The critic who can recognize a German neo-romantic influence should also be able to recognize an American influence from blues and black church rituals, or any other contemporary American influence."[6] The absence of such an ability of a critic creates an unsurpassable disadvantage to the playwright who deviates from the mainstream or from the traditions with which critics are most famil-iar, particularly when these traditions and values privilege a white aesthetic over, say, a black aesthetic or for that matter a Latino, Native, or Asian American one. At least two questions that subsequently emerge from Wilson's speech and which stand in desperate need of answers are *how do past, present, and future traditions of black aesthetics penetrate a monolithic value system that draws almost exclusively from European or white ancestry?* And since this single value system is being held firmly in place, *do black plays,* consequently, *com-mand being judged by aesthetic criteria that, at the very least, recognize their worth or difference?*

Second, Wilson argues, "[t]here are and have always been two distinct and parallel traditions in black art: that art that is conceived and designed to enter-tain white society, and art that feeds the spirit and celebrates the life of black America by designing its strategies for survival and prosperity."[7] He contends that he and his art stand "squarely on the self-defining ground" of the latter tradition—a tradition he claims was birthed in the confines of the slave quar-ters as a source of survival and that reemerges as the "high ground of self-definition the black playwrights of the '60s marked out for themselves."[8] Buried within this rhetoric are some all-important inquiries—*Is the basic function of (dramatic) black art different from the basic function of (dramatic) white art? Must all high-end or quality black theater speak to the black experience above all else? When given a stage, can African Americans afford not to be socio-political? Can art provide an avenue to political and cultural power?* These seem to be the pressing questions that need to be answered before we can gain clarity about and adopt, willingly or grudgingly, a black aesthetic. And this aesthetic, though distinctly black, should and must meet an aesthetic cri-teria of excellence that assumes a posture of diversity, not sameness, and which incorporates into its standards and value system the contributions of all peoples rather than exclusively privileging only those of certain ancestry.

Third, much to the dismay of many black actors and any number of oth-ers, Wilson characterizes colorblind casting as "an aberrant idea that has never had any validity other than as a tool of the Cultural Imperialists who view American culture, rooted in the icons of European culture, as beyond reproach in its perfection."[9] Remove the totalizing and essentialist tone from Wilson's description of colorblind casting, and one is left to admit that colorblind casting did, indeed, emerge out of an initiative by cultural imperialists who, rather than adopt a real multicultural agenda, which would have included mounting more plays written by multicultural artists, instead, made a concession to impose a multicultural cast on a white standard. Principally, there is nothing wrong with an all-black cast of *Death of A Salesman*. But if it is mounted (in the name of multiculturalism) in lieu of a play that is truer to black experiences, for *Death of A Salesman* simply is not reflective of a general black experience, since few black men ever have the luxuries of the denials, delusions, and fantasies that Willie Loman experiences, then there is too much wrong with an all-black production of Miller's play to be ignored. If black actors are cast in white roles, no matter how *universal*, largely for the sake of ensuring the employment of black actors (rather than mounting a black play) and to ensure funding from agencies that require some level of commitment to multiculturalism (again, rather than mounting a black play), colorblind casting is ineffective. In both cases—an all-black cast of a white play or the colorblind casting of a black actor in a white role—cultural imperialism still prevails. The standard seeking to be met is still mainstream and white. It fails to acknowledge the worth of black culture, for a black play is still left unproduced. Instead, it would seem, only the white play and, hence, the white experience, is worthy of being integrated or mimicked.

It is also true of both instances that "[...] identity politics allows the focus to remain on difference rather than forcing the dominant culture to look at the structure of inequality and exploitation that actually lie at the root of the continued marginalization of people of in the theatre."[10] In short, when colorblind casting is implemented by mainstream theaters exclusively or even primarily for the benefit of receiving funds from agencies that demand multiculturalist practices of them, everyone loses—minority plays are not mounted; minority actors lose the benefit of exploring their own experiences; and audiences are denied the possibilities of learning about others and of experiencing aesthetic diversity and growth. Clearly, the potential detriment outweighs the minimal benefits of employing colorblind casting in the name of multiculturalism. This, of course, is only one side of the argument for or against colorblind casting. But it is a side that Wilson rightly asserts must be strongly considered when funds are being issued to theaters which perpetuate a white standard and negate the value and worth of all others. The question, then, becomes *when and under what circumstances is colorblind casting an appropriate and viable option for the continued development and growth of African American theater?*

Finally, and perhaps most importantly, Wilson issues a call to "black playwrights to confer with one another, to come together to meet each other face to face, to address questions of aesthetics" and, along with artists and actors, to "be the spearhead of a movement to reignite and reunite our people's positive energy for a political and social change that is reflective of our spiritual truths [...]."[11] In March 1998, the call was answered in the form of a weeklong summit, "On Golden Pond," of forty-five key figures in African American theater, one of whom was my coeditor, Sandra G. Shannon;

a daylong conference, which was open to the public; and a second summit convened during the 1999 Black Theatre Network Conference. Accordingly, the essays included in this collection attempt to address issues raised either by Wilson's initial speech or by the subsequent ideas and responses that emerged from the fruitfulness of the "gathering of the minds" at one or more of these venues.

The breadth of essays included here is among the collection's strongest points, and each, in its own unique way, advances contemporary thought about black theater, black aesthetics, black intellectual thought, or black arts. Accordingly, we have divided the collection into four parts—Part I: Black Aesthetics as Theory, Art, and Ideology; Part II: Black Aesthetics and Interdisciplinary Black Arts; Part III: August Wilson's Plays and Black Aesthetics; and Part IV: Interviews. This is followed by Sandra G. Shannon's Afterword. Included in the Appendix is Sybil J. Roberts's *A Liberating Prayer: A Lovesong for Mumia*.

Included in Part I is Mikell Pinkney's "The Development of African American Dramatic Theory: W.E.B. DuBois to August Wilson—Hand to Hand!" Pinkney's essay (chapter 2) thoroughly maps a chronological history of theoretical writings concerning African American theatre from DuBois to the present and explores what Pinkney argues are the five basic aspects or fundamentals of African American dramatic philosophy—protest, revolt, assertion, music, and spirituality—in seven periods or developmental eras: the Plantation or Slave era, the American Minstrel era, the New Negro Renaissance era, the Assimilationist era, the Black Revolutionary era, the Afrocentric era, and the New Age post-Revolutionary movement. Ultimately, he argues that Wilson's 1996 speech rearticulates the dramatic theories of DuBois, Baraka, and others, all of whom recognize and acknowledge black arts' unique spiritual nature.

Following Pinkney's historical overview of dramatic theory is Tracey Walters's essay (chapter 3), which argues for the inclusion of African American authors who work in classical traditions into a broader vision of black aesthetics. Focusing on Rita Dove's *Mother Love* and alluding to non-traditional playwrights like Adrienne Kennedy, Walters argues that Dove and any number of other African American writers who write in the classical tradition can also be rightly noted as writers who subscribe to a more liberal and variable articulation of black aesthetics. Though Dove clearly draws from classical mythology in *Mother Love*, careful analysis of the text, which Walters conducts, reveals both overt and covert references and allusions to black culture. Significantly, she points out that African American authors need not abandon nonblack traditions nor limit themselves exclusively to black cultural or literary traditions to be accepted as writers who make significant, though different, contributions to a working concept of black aesthetics.

In contrast to Walters, Georgene Bess Montgomery's "The Ifa Paradigm: Reading the Spirit in Tina McElroy Ansa's *Baby of the Family*" (chapter 4) offers a theory of reading select African American texts through a distinctly *Africanist* lens. In her essay, Montgomery argues that reading certain literary texts through what she terms the *Ifa Paradigm* provides readers with a significantly different and substantively more meaningful way of interpreting symbols and ideas in certain diasporic texts. Ifa, she explains, is an ancient African spiritual system of the Yoruba tradition. While some spiritual leaders argue that the idea of Ifa belongs specifically to the Yoruba people of Nigeria, Montgomery attempts to show how African belief systems resonate throughout the diaspora, influencing diasporic faith systems and, subsequently, diasporic literature. Her Ifa reading of Ansa's *Baby of the Family* thus offers a way of interpreting the "spirit" in the novel as an expression of a lesser-known aesthetic of diasporic blackness.

The final essay in this section, John Valery White's "Just 'Cause (or Just Cause): On August Wilson's Case for a Black Theater" (chapter 5), examines black aesthetics as ideology, particularly as black aesthetics relate to the politics Wilson expresses in "The Ground" speech. White critiques both Wilson's speech and the Wilson/Brustein debate for both men's attempts to define "authentic blackness," a futile pursuit, White argues, which "impoverishes the critical debate over the future of American theater and the role of black theater in that future." He insightfully points out that Wilson, instead of making the simple, though all-important point that there could be no American theater without blackness, is trapped in the rhetoric and politics of Black Nationalists' notions, which demand that he fight for the existence of something that already and simply *is* and *must be*. That Wilson chooses not to escape these politics, White argues, may very well slow the progression and enhancement of black theater more so than advance it since these politics distort the real issue—the need for more funding for continued and new black theater development. Ultimately, White contends that Wilson might have been more effective in his critique of the state of funding of black theater if he had simply said black theater should be funded more responsibly "just 'cause" doing so advances such a "just cause."

Part II of the collection opens with Harry Elam, Jr.'s " 'Keeping it Real' ": August Wilson, Hybridity, and Hip Hop" (chapter 6), which connects two seemingly disparate black art forms—rap and theater—and shows their relationship by pointing out that like hip-hop culture, which often demands its musical artists "keep it real" or "stay true" to the culture out of which the music was birthed, Wilson's politics demand that African American playwrights be true to African American culture and that they speak to the black experience especially if not exclusively. Elam contends that "analyzing the politics of rap in relation to Wilson's "The Ground" speech on and through the politics of rap produces a revealing reading of the power of visibility and the place of history, of cultural production as a site of resistance, of the politics of representation, of the seductive authority of commercialism, and of both the oppositional possibilities and limitations of "keeping it real." In short, Elam's essay explores the problematics and the potential of the politics of representation and the politics of *realness* by which both hip-hop culture and Wilson claim to be motivated.

In "Giving Voice and Vent to African American Culture: August Wilson's Black Aesthetics and Katherine Dunham's Fight for Cultural Ownership in

Mambo" (chapter 7), Dorothea Fisher-Hornung highlights the timelessness of Wilson's comments on the need of African Americans to create a means of protecting their cultural property and of declaring cultural ownership of their creations as she details Katherine Dunham's struggle for cultural ownership of the artistry (the film's dance choreography especially) she created for the 1954 film project *Mambo*. Fischer-Hornung likens Dunham, who was a dancer, choreographer, instructor, dance theorist, and anthropologist, to Wilson's Ma Rainey who, like Dunham, actively fights against having her voice and style co-opted by white culture.

Closing this section is Sybil J. Roberts essay (chapter 8) which offers a playwright and scholar's comments on the meaningfulness and vibrancy of theater activism as she experienced it while developing and producing the Mumia project—*A Liberating Prayer: A Lovesong for Mumia*—at Howard University. Noting that she drew from a rich tradition of black theater activism and aesthetics, including the ideologies of Barbara Ann Teer, Ntozake Shange, Abena Brown, and Robbie McCauley, to create *A Liberating Prayer* (which is included in the appendix), Roberts offers an articulation of her aesthetic and the aesthetic of others from the perspective of a theater practitioner who creates interdisciplinary performance rituals that address international issues of justice, peace, and sustainable "lifeways" by removing theater from the confines of the stage and its conventions to the street platforms of protest rallies and the like.

Each of the essays in part III of the collection offers new readings of Wilson's plays, focusing especially on aesthetic nuances of his texts. First is Reggie Young's "Phantom Limbs Dancing Juba Rites in August Wilson's *Joe Turner's Come and Gone* and *The Piano Lesson*," which examines Wilson's use of a black aesthetic—spiritual realism—in these two plays. Young's contention is that attempts to explain the surreal elements of *Joe Turner* and *Piano Lesson* as magical realism are, more often than not, misinformed. Instead, spiritual realism, as a distinct mode of black expression, he argues, is a much more effective way of reading such texts, particularly Wilson's, because they are "rooted in the culture of juba, ring-shouts, spirituals, and the blues, and share a cultural connection to Africa and not Latin America or Western Europe, except in incidental ways." Thus, he reads *Joe Turner* and *Piano Lesson* through the lens of spiritual realism as a New World African aesthetic that seeks to use rituals to offer characters redemption from the fragmentation they experience after being enslaved and exposed to Western religions.

Next is Tara T. Green's "Speaking of Voice and August Wilson's Women" (chapter 9), which argues that though women tend to have limited speaking presences in Wilson's overall dramatic canon, Ma Rainey from *Ma Rainey's Black Bottom*, Rose from *Fences*, and Risa from *Two Trains Running* are exemplary examples of the need for cultural ownership and voice that Wilson argues for in "The Ground on Which I Stand." Thus, it is his female characters who represent Wilson's perception and conception of art as an expression of African American culture, which struggles to be acknowledged and to be heard in a world dominated and controlled by a more powerful other.

Ma, Green argues, is very aware of the power her voice affords her and is empowered because of it. And though Rose does not come into her own voice until the end of *Fences*, Green astutely notes that she successfully injects her voice in the front yard rituals, reminiscent of Zora Neale Hurston's manly porch-talk, and, ultimately, comes to realize that her *self* is intimately linked to her voice. And Risa's lack of voice in *Two Trains Running* demonstrates the significance of African American self-definition and freedom and control of voice to success and to survival.

The last essay in this section, C. Patrick Tyndall's "Using Black Rage to Elucidate African and African-American Identity in August Wilson's *Joe Turner's Come and Gone*" (chapter 10), attempts to connect Wilson's politics with his art. In "The Ground" speech, Wilson calls for federal support of black art and theater to improve the black community in general. *Joe Turner*, Tyndall argues, is an example of how theater can be used to improve the community since the play functions as a healing tool both for its characters and for the community. Thus, Tyndall's reading of the play explores Wilson's use of black rage to re-create African American identity that has been complicated by white oppression.

Finally, in part IV, we have included two previously unpublished interviews that focus especially on Wilson's politics and his idea of black aesthetics. First is Yolanda Williams Page's interview with Charles Dutton (chapter 11), which reveals Dutton's thoughts on working with Wilson as a major character in three of Wilson's most successful plays—*Ma Rainey's Black Bottom*, *Joe Turner's Come and Gone*, and *The Piano Lesson*. Dutton also shares with Williams Page his thoughts about Wilson's politics and his call for the continued development of black theater as an entity distinct from mainstream American theater and as one that acknowledges the value, worth, and artistry of African American cultural creations. Second is my and my coeditor's interview with Wilson (chapter 12) where he talks candidly about the speech and its aftermath. He also comments on his idea of black aesthetics and on the future of black theater.

We are especially pleased to have included in the appendix Roberts's *A Liberating Prayer: A Lovesong for Mumia*, which makes its published debut here but which was first produced in 2001 at Howard University in Washington, DC. Though we had no intention of making this collection an anthology, it *was* our intention to reveal the meaningfulness of black theater and its potential, as Wilson notes, to "disseminate ideas, [. . . to] educate the miseducated, because it is art—and all art reaches across that divide that makes order out of chaos, and embraces the truth that overwhelms with its presence, and connects man to something larger than himself and his imagination."[12] So when Roberts offered us her comments on the meaningfulness and vibrancy of theater activism as she experienced it while developing and producing the Mumia project at Howard, it only seemed fitting that we should include the play as an appendix to the essay so that the power of black theater and its impact on those who experience it personally could be, at the very least, made known and available to all.

As we initially conceived this project, my coeditor and I sought to publish essays that aggressively investigated the wide variety of issues Wilson raised in "The Ground" speech. We successfully resisted all urges to include essays that dealt only with Wilson's plays or that sought to uphold his ideas as expressed in the speech. Instead, we are confident that we have provided a range of ideas and interpretations, all of which challenge scholars to reconsider black arts' issues regarding theory, aesthetics, and ideology and cultural ownership and cultural production. Accordingly, it is our hope that, as readers, you find that this collection both makes a meaningful contribution to the growing body of criticism that examines August Wilson's plays and his politics and that it offers new ways to think and to talk about black arts and black aesthetics.

NOTES

1. August Wilson, "The Ground on Which I Stand," *American Theatre* 13.7 (September 1996), p. 16.
2. In the interview with Wilson appended in this collection, he admits that there were no significant gains made from the speech, excepting the birth of the African Grove Institute for the Arts (AGIA). But in terms of securing funding for black theaters, the speech had little impact. The one black LORT theater that was open has since, in fact, closed.
3. See Brustein's response to Wilson in "Subsidized Separatism," *New Republic* July 19–26, 1996. Rpt. in *American Theatre* (October 1996).
4. Elmo Terry-Morgan, "Call and Response: The Making of the African Grove Institute for the Arts," *Black Theatre's Unprecedented Times* (A Special Publication of *BTNews*), ed. Hely Manuel Perez, Gainesville, FL: Black Theatre Network, 1999, p. 52.
5. Wilson, *Ground*, p. 73.
6. Ibid., p. 73.
7. Ibid., p. 16.
8. Ibid., p. 16.
9. Ibid., p. 72.
10. Eugene Nesmith, "The Brustein/Wilson Debate at Town Hall: What Happened and Why it Matters," *Black Theatre Network News* 7 (Spring 1997): 13–15.
11. Wilson, *Ground*, p. 72.
12. Ibid., p. 74.

I

BLACK AESTHETICS AS THEORY, ART, AND IDEOLOGY

2

The Development of African American Dramatic Theory: W.E.B. DuBois to August Wilson—Hand to Hand!

Mikell Pinkney

In the fall of 1996, following the June 1996 delivery of playwright August Wilson's now famous speech "The Ground on Which I Stand" at the eleventh biennial Theatre Communications Group (TCG) National Conference at Princeton University, the news publication of the Black Theatre Network organization, *BTNews*, began a series of reports and articles designed to investigate and stir discussion on the issues presented in Wilson's speech and the resulting effects of his message.[1] The question presented or posed in the title of the initial *BTNews* article asked: "Thirty Years After the 'Revolutionary' 60s, Is There Still a Need to Justify Black Theatre?" The introduction to this article went on to state: "It is still necessary to educate the general public about black art's unique spiritual nature. How do we hope to achieve this?"[2] One of the aims of this present essay is to address the question by illustrating a history of theoretical development that predates the 1960s revolutionary era.

One way of achieving this goal is to take a close look at patterns of development in the theoretical and philosophical history of black theater in the United States. African American theater, or black theater in the United States, is a unique American sociocultural phenomenon that has served both public and private functions within the larger American society; an institution born of historical conflict and constantly propelled by a continuous quest for spiritual purpose and self-definition. By mapping a chronological history of theoretical writings concerning African American theater through the end of the twentieth century it is possible to see a clearly evolved history of social ideas and philosophical connections to spiritual awareness, spiritual sensibility, and spiritual purpose inherent within the institution of black theater in the United States. Theoretical analysis of this particular institution reveals five basic aspects or fundamentals of African American dramatic philosophy. These aspects are *protest, revolt, assertion, music,* and *spirituality.* These five aspects may be seen as essential elements, fundamentals, and/or aesthetic principles. A list of seven periods or developmental eras is also definable. They are: the *Plantation* or *Slave* era, the *American Minstrel* era, the *New Negro Renaissance* era, the *Assimilationist* era, the *Black Revolutionary* era, the *Afrocentric* era, and a currently evolving *New Age Post-Revolutionary Movement.*

This essay briefly explains the major precepts of each of these periods, giving special focus to the New Negro Renaissance era, The Black Revolutionary era, and the New Age Post-Revolutionary Movement; all the while illustrating a connective thread of insightful potential and developmental awareness—from the philosophical founding of an African American theater aesthetic in the United States by W.E.B. DuBois at the beginning of the twentieth century, to the revolutionary charge and challenge of Imamu Amiri Baraka (LeRoi Jones) in the 1960s, to the contemporary dramatist and theorist August Wilson.

A major point to be addressed here is how Wilson's 1996 speech rearticulates the theories of DuBois, Baraka, and others. Wilson's "The Ground on Which I Stand"[3] makes many salient points in direct relation to both DuBois and Baraka, as well as a full historical array of African American dramatic theorists, essayists, and philosophers. This present essay argues that Wilson's 1996 speech helps to define him as a leading figure in a New Age Post-Revolutionary developmental epoch for African American theater at the dawn of the twenty-first century. Wilson's remarks in "The Ground on Which I Stand" reinforce much of the past while inciting and inspiring new ways of thinking and illuminating new frontiers to be pioneered. The continuous through-line that connects all things past and present is a constant focus on potential and spiritual awareness, or "blood memory." This survey of African American dramatic theory also responds to the question: "How do we hope to educate the general public about black art's unique spiritual nature?" The answer lies in the acknowledgment and exposure of information regarding the historical development of black theater in the United States. This historical overview of the development of African American dramatic theory concludes with specific comparative insights between Wilson's 1996 speech with DuBois's 1926 speech and Baraka's 1964–66 essay, illustrating the "hand-to-hand" developmental heritage of black art and Wilson's role in that struggle.

We begin with the premise that African American theater emerged without a written philosophical doctrine as far back as the Middle Passage, when slaves were forced to dance and to drum on the decks of slave ships. Slaves were forced to continue these practices on southern plantations.[4] Thus, the first period, epoch, or era of recognizable African American theatrical development is the Plantation or Slave period, where Africans essentially provided the stimulus and motifs for what would become America's first original and indigenous theatrical form.[5] Through careful reading of this unique phenomenon of American slavery it may be understood that the "entertainments" and coded performances by slaves were actually disguised versions of African rit-ual acts infused with spiritual meaning and new purpose.

The appropriation of these slave acts by whites led to the second period of African American theatrical development. This was the American Minstrel era, which had a profound psycho-sociological impact on the entire American nation: white, black, and the shades in-between. The minstrel tradition was the institutional frame that produced and promoted negative images and stereotypes of African Americans through what cultural studies theorist John Fiske calls *Axis of Division*,[6] whereby the dominant social class attempts to "naturalize" meanings that serve their interests into the "common sense" of the larger society. These stereotypes have lingered in the national conscious-ness of the United States for more years than can now be accurately counted.

The minstrel tradition itself is one of the greatest paradoxes in American history for several reasons. Chief among those reasons is the fact that it pro-vided the first opportunity for blacks to take jobs legally on the legitimate stage. But following emancipation, black men took the stage in guises of white men who had imitated black slaves in low comic forms, thereby, rein-forcing long-standing stereotypes of black clowns, buffoons, sambos, and coons. Thus, the entree of true African Americans onto American theater stages also initiated an immediate and warranted need to *protest* against a prevailing form and to *assert* different modes of presentation and new images of themselves as human beings deserving of serious respect and acknowledgment of their artistic talents.

The need to *assert* a "new Negro" image brought on the third distinctive era of African American theater. This was the New Negro Renaissance, or the *Harlem Renaissance* as it was also known. This period began ca. 1917 and spanned the decade of the 1920s. It is quite literally the philosophical and theoretical founding era for African American theater aesthetics. This intel-lectual movement was led by DuBois, who wrote prolifically about the Negro's potential for serious theatrical artistry, both as performers and subjects worthy of serious dramatic treatment.

DuBois became the editor of *Crisis*, an important news journal of the National Association for the Advancement of Colored People (NAACP). The *Crisis* sponsored literary contests to stimulate the writing of plays by Negroes on themes of African American life. During this time an ideological concern for plays of *social protest* and the *assertion* of a new identity of ele-vated style and intellectual recognition fueled the artistic energies of a new generation of post-emancipation African Americans. DuBois was aided in his endeavor by other notable theoretical writers. Three such dramatic theoreti-cians include Alain Locke,[7] editor of the major cultural and literary collec-tion of this era titled *The New Negro*; Montgomery Gregory,[8] critic, scholar, and teacher at the Negro theater training institution at Howard University; and Jessie Fauset,[9] essayist, critic, and literary editor for *Crisis*.

During the New Negro era, there was widespread recognition of African American creative artists of all types: painters, sculptors, concert performers, and writers of literature, drama, literary criticism, essays, and manifestoes on dramatic theory. The essays and manifestoes published during this time on Negro dramatic and theatrical achievements and potentials were the beginnings of a formal written tradition of African American creative aesthetics. They have a particular focus in the realization of the need for African American artists to define and *assert* themselves by their own standards and in their own words. One principal task was to *protest* and *revolt* against a constructed image of Negro character and persona as established by a white hegemonic theatrical structure and to *assert* a "New Negro" image of creative beings with spiritual depth and prophetic potential. The New Negro Renaissance era was then, among other things, the beginning of African America's intellectual search for self-expressive identity in the arts and humanities.

While "Negro folk life" was addressed primarily by white American playwrights throughout the 1920s, the focus on Negro social experience was led by DuBois. As early as the spring of 1903, the tone and dilemma of attempts by African Americans to project their own images in a universe that had been hostile toward such an endeavor was established when DuBois published *The Souls of Black Folk*.[10] In this important first step toward a theoretical foundation and focus for self-expressive Negro stage image, DuBois proclaimed:

> After the Egyptian and Indian, the Greek and Roman, the Teuton and Mongolian, the Negro is sort of seventh son [*sic*], born with a veil, and gifted with second-sight in this American world,—a world which yields him no true self-consciousness, but only lets him see himself through the revelation of the other world. It is a peculiar sensation, this double-consciousness, this sense of always looking at one's soul by the tape of a world that looks on in amused contempt and pity. One ever feels his twoness,—an American, a Negro; two souls, two thoughts, two unreconciled strivings; two warring ideals in one dark body, whose dogged strength alone keeps it from being torn asunder.[11]

The anguish that DuBois expressed in this early work is surpassed by the acknowledgment of a special duality inherent in the very idea of the African as American. This duality combines elements of ancient African notions of intuitive power and spiritual destiny with "new world" ideas of progressive materialism in the dialectical manifestation of the African as an American, or African American. These elements would later become the basis of Kuntu and Nommo aesthetics, which concern cosmic spiritual connection to an African ancestral past and the power of the spoken word as often manifested in passionate vocal expressions associated with black oral traditions. Kuntu and Nommo are concepts that are discussed later with regard to Afrocentric philosophy.

DuBois's 1903 concept of the dual nature of the African American makes it possible to view the complexities of the world, and especially the United States, through unique eyes. With this dual vision, the curse of material degradation is overshadowed by a clairvoyant gift for "second-sight" or intuition. In this view, the physical and psychological oppressiveness of an American hegemony is eclipsed by the African's "dogged strength" and will to survive. The Americanization of the African motivates a new "creolized" or "gestalt" spirit that aspires not merely to survive, but to live freely in the pursuit of happiness and beauty. The later development of these initial ideas would signal inherent pluralism and multicultural aspects within each striving African American spirit.

According to DuBois, living within the dual consciousness of an African American, or a "Black-figure on a White-ground,"[12] does not totally reject all other ideas, but allows for the enrichment of those ideas with the insightful spirit of subconscious understanding. The challenge of DuBois's statements is to expose such a potential that dwells within the dual spirit of Africans as Americans: to acknowledge the complex realities of being black in the United States and to *assert* the positive potentials of such a reality.

The high point of the search for a defining aesthetic aphorism toward the development of an African American theater is DuBois's "Criteria of Negro Art,"[13] an address given at the June 1926 Chicago NAACP third National Conference, in which DuBois announced his view that "all art is propaganda." One finds that this adage referred principally to DuBois's deeply held belief in the ethical and political responsibility of art and literature as a developmental tool for the Negro race. What DuBois presents in this address is essentially a manifesto of Negro/black/African American art and theater for all times. It can arguably be called "DuBois's Poetics." It is primarily concerned with the aesthetics or concepts of beauty as related to a Negro/black/African American worldview. Yet it is profoundly pragmatic as both a foundation for the development of such an artistic view and a sustaining guide for future growth and development.

DuBois suggested that the potential of Negro art would be to express the beauty of an African American *cosmic spirituality*. He associated truth with beauty and called for the masses to trust the beauty of spiritual truth to sustain a forward movement and reign justice in American society. He understood that arts, and especially the theater, were a device by which white America had constructed an image of the Negro to its liking and purpose. In "Criteria of Negro Art," DuBois proposed a reversal of image and ideology through the urging of the (re)construction of Negro image from within the race. He outlined a procedure for this purpose in the following statement:

> [...]it is the bounden duty of black America to begin this great work of the creation of Beauty, and we must use in this work all the methods that men have used before [....]. First of all, he has used the Truth [...] Again artists have used Goodness—goodness in all its aspects of justice, honor and right.[14]

DuBois pointed out that the artistic means that had been used as a propaganda device against a race, primarily in the American Minstrel era, should now be used to uplift that same race. This was his urging. His 1926 speech gave to black American artists of all kinds a ground on which to stand and a light to illuminate their creative spirits. His manifesto remains a statement of profound aestheticism that provides four important points about the needs and purpose of Negro art: (1) An understandable devotion to the pursuit of the beautiful and sensitivity to artistic beauty and refined taste. (2) A doctrine that beauty is the basic principle from which all other principles, especially moral ones, are derived. (3) The belief that art and artists have no obligation other than to strive for beauty. (4) An understanding or acceptance of a philosophy that beauty of the spirit is the means to truth and righteousness and the foundation for just living.

This declaration represented a more fully realized development of DuBois's earlier ideas as presented in his 1903 *The Souls of Black Folk*. His perspectives grew in relation to the theatrical presentations of Negro life he witnessed between 1903 and 1926. His "Criteria" acknowledged both what had been done and what was left to be done toward the full realization of his vision to utilize the arts as a means of uplifting the Negro race. The impact of this historical formation and foundation for African American dramatic theory would be rearticulated in the resounding radical voices that would emerge during the 1960s and early 1970s.

Also in 1926, DuBois called for a new movement that began in Harlem and established four fundamental principles for African American theater companies in cities with large Negro populations such as New York, Chicago, Cleveland, Philadelphia, and elsewhere. His intent was to inspire the creation of "Little Negro Theatre Groups" throughout the country. These fundamentals were a means to establishing a unified purpose for such an endeavor. The four fundamentals are still held as hallmarks of dramaturgical criteria for "serious" African American theater. The rules dictate that in order to qualify as "true" or "serious" the philosophies behind Negro American theaters and dramas must be:

> 1. About us. That is, they must have plots which reveal Negro life as it is. 2. By us. This is, they must be written by Negro authors who understand from birth and continual association just what it means to be a Negro today. 3. For us. That is, the theatre must cater primarily to Negro audiences and be supported and sustained by their entertainment and approval. 4. Near us. The theatre must be in a Negro neighborhood near the mass of ordinary Negro people.[15]

DuBois felt that adherence to these rules was the only way in which serious and authentic dramas of African American experience could be developed. Using the four fundamentals as required criteria, literary contests conducted by the *Crisis*, under the editorship of DuBois and the literary management of Jessie Fauset, mined a substantial number of serious plays about African American life for publication and performance. Throughout the era, prevailing theoretical themes attempted to focus Negro artistic aspirations on creating a new image of black life. Potential was seen as possible only if Negroes could tap into their inherent spiritual power and expose positive and realistic images of themselves in situations unplagued by the dominating influences of white society. But one example of the problematic associated with development of a Negro American theater was expressed in a 1927 unsigned article, "On the Need for Better Plays,"[16] in *Opportunity*, published by the National Urban League under the editorship of Charles S. Johnson.

Like *Crisis, Opportunity* also operated and supported a literary contest as a means of developing the writing talents of the New Negro community. But in "On the Need for Better Plays" an alarming reality was revealed. It seemed that Negro writers of poetry, short stories, and novels of fiction, and essays all made great strides while taking advantage of the serious opportunities and prizes presented by *Crisis* and *Opportunity*. This was not the case for playwrights. The point made by this article was all the more serious because of the contrast presented: that plays of Negro life were being written by white writers while Negro playwrights were "limited for the most part to low comedy which has succeeded commercially, and to a few propagandistic efforts of a defensive character." The article further charged that:

> Negro writers have not, until very recently, sensed the possibilities of Negro drama. They have, excusably, used the drama as a field for the development of histrionic talent within the race and have led themselves off into palpably unreal portrayals of the general plays of the stock company repertoire. They have been too ashamed of the material of their own lives to give it artistic portrayal.[17]

This statement indicates that most of the plays presented by Negro writers in this era appeared to be simple imitations of plays from the white commercial stage or throwbacks to the minstrel type characters and images of earlier times. The article's writer strongly encourages new thoughts and interests in writing for the stage, because the stage might provide "...a medium for the forceful interpretation of Negro life itself, a service which the stage undoubtedly can perform with as great, if not greater, directness and power than either fiction or poetry." Then, the author acknowledges a need and potential for "plays suitable for mixed cast, or plays that will offer aid toward softening the harsh points of racial contact." The article ends with an identification of what it contended to be the major problem associated with the lack of plays by Negro playwrights; primarily, insufficient study of technique and a general lack of knowledge of play construction. Thus, the problem of training and training institutions for Negro theater artists was brought to the forefront as an important issue to be dealt with. However, the potential early solutions to this problem would also give rise to future needs for *revolt* and *assertion* in the waning decades of the twentieth century.

The New Negro Renaissance era was brought to a slow demise following the 1929 stock market crash. However, the 1930s saw the creation of the short-lived but very important Federal Theatre Project (FTP), which flourished between 1935 and 1939, and officially launched the fourth period of formal African American theater development: the Assimilationist era. The title given to this epoch must not overshadow the importance or productivity of the four years at its beginning, for it was during the FTP that African American theater artists received their first widespread opportunities for legitimate training in every aspect of theatrical arts.

Previous to the founding of the FTP the majority of Negro artists used their "natural talents" to gain notoriety and respect on the stage. What they were able to learn during the FTP would serve the development of African Americans in theater for many years to come following the congressional closing of the FTP national theater movement in 1939. The era is still considered assimilationist because it was dominated by Negro artist's attempts to gain respect through traditional Eurocentric means. This meant Broadway for performers and the traditional forms of European-inspired "well made" plays for writers, utilizing the structures and concepts of "modern realism" as a stylistic dictate. Many black performers appeared in musical entertainments, mostly devised and suited for the tastes of white audiences, or in all-Negro cast versions of white Broadway fare. Attempts at success by black writers resulted in several one-act plays for community productions and a few notable, full-length, FTP-produced plays such as Theodore Ward's *The Big White Fog*, J. Augustus Smith and Peter Morell's *Turpentine*, Theodore Browne's *Natural Man*, and even Langston Hughes's Broadways hit *Mulatto*. These plays were notable and acclaimed because of their resemblance to European-derived dramatic forms. This period also saw the development of the first fully organized company of trained, resident professional black actors appropriately named the American Negro Theatre (A.N.T.). A.N.T. enjoyed success as a theater company in Harlem, Los Angeles, and on Broadway from 1940 to 1950. But even the A.N.T. is best remembered for its transfers of productions to Broadway stages of *On Striver's Row, Anna Lucasta, Walk Hard*, and *Freight*.[18] The Assimilationist era continued into the 1950s with Negroes in professional performance roles in Hollywood and on Broadway mostly as servants, laborers, and background characters. Playwrights such as Alice Childress, William Branch, Louis Peterson, and Charles Segree all had plays presented in New York's commercial arenas. All their plays were written in the Eurocentric style of modern realism. But the greatest glory and recognition went to Lorraine Hansberry's play *A Raisin in the Sun*, which won critical acclaim and presented a spiritual preamble to the next major developmental moment.

A Raisin in the Sun first appeared in 1958. Some white critics claimed that it was not really a Negro play at all but more about a Jewish or Irish family.[19] Such comments were double-edged, praising the prowess of Hansberry's use of Eurocentric-inspired dramatic form and structure while suggesting that the play may not have been "Black enough" for white expectations. The play presented a dialectical picture of a Negro family, the Younger family. It included a dominant Mother figure representing the "old Negro" ideology, an Americanized and materialistic adult son, and the most radical of all the characters represented by the female college student daughter with new ideas concerning the place of women in society and the place of things African in the consciousness of young Negroes. Hansberry's play had underlying revolutionary tones that were not clearly apparent to the white public, who saw aspects of themselves and their own aspirations in quest of an "American dream." These revolutionary preambles were not fully apparent to the Negro public either, who would soon understand what was being alluded to in this play about modern Negroes. But *A Raisin in the Sun* may now be viewed as a bridge between the double-consciousness associated with black writers in the Assimilationist era and a burgeoning Civil Rights/Black Power/Black Revolutionary Movement that was to flourish fully in the 1960s.

The fifth period of development, the *Black Power/Black Arts & Aesthetics/Black Revolutionary era* beginning in the mid-1960s, remains possibly the most prolific period of black theater development to date. During this era the ideology of black awareness, black nationalism, and black empowerment fostered a huge number of black playwrights and theater groups throughout the nation. Theorist and playwright Imamu Amiri Baraka, then known as LeRoi Jones, wrote an essay in 1964 titled, "In Search of the Revolutionary Theatre,"[20] which became the major manifesto for this period. Baraka also wrote a number of plays and founded theater groups in Harlem and Newark. But it was his prescriptive theory on the nature of black theater as a revolutionary tool and weapon for positive propaganda and consciousness raising that recapitulated and reinforced the New Negro Renaissance ideology of DuBois in a radically political manner.

The concepts of revolution have certain similarities to the concepts of renaissance. Both concepts are concerned with the creation of a new order, with providing new approaches, and with establishing new criteria of aesthetics and operations. One major difference between the two concepts is the element of *revolt* that is inherent in revolutionary philosophy. Moreover, revolution is often associated with radicalism and extremism in its efforts to achieve newness. The primary distinction between the two concepts is seen clearest in the radical extremism of revolution, which is contrastable with renaissance aims of rebirth and revival more often associated with revival of classical or essentialist ideals. In this regard, defining an American epoch of the 1960s and early 1970s as the Revolutionary Black Theater era becomes complex. This era is often defined on the basis of its pervasive alliance with the most militant factions of the American Civil Rights and Black Power Movements. But too often the renaissance concepts and aims are overlooked, making it difficult to recognize this era as a developmental outgrowth of the black essentialist New Negro era.

The Revolutionary era brought back the ideas of *protest* and *assertion* introduced during the 1920s with radical power and purpose in the 1960s, redressed in the form of anger and *revolt. Revolutionary Black Theater* ideology also reintroduced *spirituality*, but it was a highly radical and reformed version of *spirituality*. Baraka's aesthetic theory outlined new politically militant criteria for African American drama. In addition to the four fundamentals prescribed earlier by DuBois during the New Negro Renaissance, Baraka stated: "The Revolutionary Theater should force change, it should be change."[21] This change was to be on all levels but focused most directly on the socioeconomic status and conditions of black Americans. Through theatrical means, Baraka wanted to "EXPOSE" the racial ills of Western society and teach whites the ramifications of hatred and denial of what he called "the supremacy of the [black] Spirit." His doctrine states:

> This should be a theatre of World Spirit. Where the spirit can be shown to be the most competent force in the world. Force. Spirit. Feeling. The language will be anybody's, but tightened by the poet's backbone. And even the language must show what the facts are in this consciousness epic, what's happening. We will talk about the world, and the preciseness with which we are able to summon the world, will be our art.[22]

In addressing the notion of the spirit, or the spiritual nature of African American people, Baraka was making a direct connection to DuBois and Locke who both saw potential in the depth of an esoteric metaphysical connection between the souls of black Americans and cosmic universal forces. This spiritual consciousness, Baraka suggests, is developed by listening to ancestral voices that speak to the soul or spirit in silent meditative moments. In those moments the world outside the spiritual connection can only see craziness, because they can only see life and the world on a material plain. They are denied the DuBoisian "second-sight" of the gifted black soul to illuminate the cosmic spiritual teachings.

Baraka was essentially calling for the same *Kuntu* (cosmic connection) focus on African American *spirituality* in the 1960s as the aesthetic theorist and philosophers of the New Negro Renaissance era had called for in the 1920s. In Baraka's view, the loss of African Americans' connection to intuitive spirit and power was due to years of indoctrination and victimization by whites. Baraka saw his theater as a theater of victims. Everyone involved in this theater was to see the world through the eyes of the victimized. His aim was to show African Americans and white Americans what had been created by white Western hegemonic domination of the world, so that the world might change. He wanted to show that the very existence of African Americans as descendants of slaves made them victims of an oppositional reality, his way of denoting double-consciousness. For Baraka and a large number of black Americans in this era, social victimization was the true reality of Western hegemony. Baraka wanted to alter the white-ground reality, and to expose that reality from the perspective of the oppressed and abused as a means toward fulfilling a moral obligation to the spiritual purpose of African American existence.

Baraka expressed an expectation and awareness of the effects of his radical theory when he wrote: "[white] Americans will hate the revolutionary theatre because it will be out to destroy them and whatever they believe is real."[23] The revolutionary theater saw whites and their ancestors as victimizers. The white world, as represented by Western society, was seen as evil, corrupt, and totally consumed by materialistic desires. The revolutionary theater accused and attacked Western society for its preoccupation with the material aspects of existence and its rejection of spiritual (not to be confused with religious) virtue. Again in the words of Baraka: "The Revolutionary Theatre must hate them for hating. For presuming with their technology to deny the supremacy of the Spirit."[24] But it must be remembered that the major catalyst for this revolutionary ideology was the pursuit of liberty and the quest for social and racial equality. With that vision at the forefront, the plays presented in this theater were calls to action. While the primary goal may have been a call to political action, the ultimate goal was to move black Americans into a philosophy of positive personal action. Baraka suggested that plays be used as tactical weapons in the psychological war against white hegemony, as "bullets to be used against the enemy."[25]

The practicality of this philosophy is expressed in the following segment from Baraka's manifesto:

> The Revolutionary Theatre must take dreams and give them a reality. It must isolate the ritual and historical cycles of reality. But it must be food for all these who need food, and daring propaganda for the beauty of the Human Mind. But it is a political theatre, a weapon to help in the slaughter of these dimwitted fat-bellied white guys who somehow believe that the rest of the world is here for them to slobber on.[26]

While this statement speaks about the idealistic notions of a theater that presents black dreams and visions of a better life, it also presents two compelling aspects: (1) the revolutionary theater as a theater of reality; and (2) the revolutionary theater as a theater of assault.

Dramatist and theorist Ed Bullins joined Baraka as another important critical voice of the Revolutionary Black Theater era. In 1966, Bullins published an essay that defined his approach to writing for the revolutionary theater titled "Theatre of Reality."[27] In this essay, Bullins follows Baraka's precepts and rejects white theatrical tradition and dramaturgy in radical fashion with the statement: "Aristotle and his aesthetic dogmas are not of this time and never had been meant for the black artist anyway."[28] Bullins explained that method and technique were not the immediate goals of the Revolutionary Movement. The exploration and creation of new characters, new themes, and new definitions were far more important. He was concerned with exposing the negative realities of humanity by presenting honest, rather than perfectly structured, African American characters and themes. In order to dramatize the radical psychological journey being experienced by black Americans, Bullins thought it was necessary to utilize a variety of theatrical styles and methods. He wrote:

> It is not a call for a return to realism or naturalism that this theater calls for; it is the exposure of illusion through exploding myths and lies that are disguised as reality and truths. These myths, and especially those concerning the black man, clutter the heart of his existence, his humanity.[29]

The theatrical reality that Bullins sought was the *assertion* of a black sense of reality, which is counter and oppositional to what white society may see as truth. This reality is bent on exposing the ills of such a society, especially as it relates to that society's degradation of blacks. The aim of Bullins's "Theatre of Reality" was to create characters with "metaphysical yearnings" and use them as propaganda in the war of mind and spirit. He would later identify his focus on African American characters as part of what he called "Black dialectics" with two branches: "dialectic of change," which he associated with *protest* and the prescriptive purpose of black revolutionary writing, and "dialectic of experience," which was the experience of "being" and expressing the realities of the African American "self" and worldview.[30]

The overall Black Power Movement of the 1960s included protests of every kind, from "sit-ins" and marches, to boycotts and speeches, to all-out riots. *Protest* art and literature became a part of this overall Movement in the form of a total black arts agenda. The general Black Arts Movement of this era included the aesthetics of African American dramatists, poets, choreographers, musicians, novelists, and visual artists. It was essentially a new version of the New Negro Renaissance, now renamed the New Black Renaissance. The distinction between this new era and the criteria established during the 1920s involved the use of the term "radical." The Revolutionary Black Theater era gained prominent focus in this regard because it was such a visible and pervasive part of the larger Arts and Power Movements. An estimated 400 plays were produced by nearly 200 playwrights. The overwhelming majority of these plays were unashamedly propaganda for the larger cause of the Black Arts–Black Power alliance. This was the kind of propaganda that DuBois would have been be proud of.

Like the Black Power Movement, the Black Arts Movement sought to change artistic perspectives by use of drastic measures. Poet and essayist Larry Neal, in a 1968 essay for the umbrella Black Arts Movement titled "The Black Arts Movement,"[31] explained that it was a concept which proposed "a radical reordering of the western cultural aesthetic" including "a separate symbolism, mythology, critique, and iconology." It attempted to create an artistic expression that spoke "directly to the needs and aspirations of Black America," rather than trying to assimilate African Americans into white society. Neal wrote:

> Black Art is the aesthetic and spiritual sister of the Black Power concept [...] radically opposed to any concept of the artist that alienates him from his community [...] The motive behind the Black aesthetic is the destruction of the white thing, the destruction of white ideas, and white ways of looking at the world. The new aesthetic is mostly predicated on an Ethics which asks the question: whose vision of the world is finally more meaningful, ours or the white oppressors'? What is truth? Or more precisely, whose truth shall we express, that of the oppressed or of the oppressors? ... In a context of world upheaval, ethics and aesthetics must interact positively and be consistent with the demands for a more spiritual world. Consequently, the Black Arts Movement is an ethical movement. Ethical, that is, from the viewpoint of the oppressed.[32]

Here, Neal makes clear the very important point concerning black revolutionary aesthetics—that artists must accept the notion of art in service to a communal cause and effort. This was a clear doctrine of artistic power of purpose. He leaves no doubt that revolutionary art owes allegiance to an ethical and spiritual use of the cosmic artistic gifts for enlightenment and empowerment of the oppressed and previously marginalized voices of American culture.

The essays of Baraka, Bullins, and Neal helped to clearly define a theoretical era. In addition, other dramatists of the period including Ron Milner in "Black Theater-Go Home!,"[33] Hoyt Fuller in "Toward a Black Aesthetic,"[34] and the literary anthology of the Movement edited by Addison Gayle, Jr. titled *The Black Aesthetic*,[35] provided important theoretical blueprints that energized and focused the revolutionary Movement. These ideas continue to hold ground in present-day black consciousness.

By the mid-1970s the ideology of Black Nationalism that surfaced during the 1960s gave rise to philosophies of Afrocentrism, the sense of a psychological and philosophical return to Africa and things African. Thus, a sixth era evolved, ranging from the mid-1970s through the end of the 1980s, and is named the Revolutionary Afrocentric era. It retains revolutionary ideology while it is marked by a return to African consciousness in the form of ritual-based aesthetics. It is personified in African American theater by the concepts of "Kuntu," cosmic connection, and "Nommo," power of the voiced or spoken word. These concepts were explained primarily in the writings of dramatist and scholar Paul Carter Harrison.

In 1974 Harrison edited an anthology of plays that expressed a fully Afrocentric consciousness. It was called *Kuntu Drama: Plays of the African Continuum*.[36] The plays and the writings that preceded them presented, or resurrected, African philosophical concepts as a basis for African American theater and drama. The preface to this work was written by Oliver Jackson, who defined Kuntu drama as:

> [...] drama that has, as its ultimate purpose, to reveal and invoke the reality of the particular mode that it has ritualized. This theater style depends on power and power invocation. It is magical in that it attempts to produce modification in behavior through the combined use of word power, dance power, and music power. It is sacred theater in the sense that it seeks to fulfill a spiritual revelation.[37]

In the realm of the Revolutionary Afrocentric era, the play or theater piece is a "ritualized context of reality" with positive spiritual purpose. For black people in the United States, who live perpetually under and within the invisible oppressive strain of American hegemonic domination, Kuntu drama has potential to be both prophetic and pragmatic. It includes the audience in the ritual as part of a community and the invocation of the spirits who help bring forth the enlightened insights of the ritual or play and releases beneficent power to the participants, which includes both the audience and the players. Theater in this sense takes on many of the same characteristics of the black church service. Kuntu drama is essentially more ritual than drama. But it allows for group participation in the same way as in the black church service or popular music concerts, where participation in the call-and-response mode is encouraged. This is in direct opposition to the restrained and voyeuristic mode expected at Eurocentric theatrical and "high art" functions. The Kuntu play is intended to invoke power of the cosmos and the spirit world toward some purposeful good for humanity. The play may employ all the devices and elements of conventional theater and drama. But the actors as characters are participants in the ritual and are the vehicles of this power. Their "attitude, speech, dress, song, and music describe and project the aspect of the force or power needed or eventually revealed within the mode."[38]

In 1989 Harrison produced another anthology, this one titled *Totem Voices: Plays From the Black World Repertory*,[39] which provided more depth of meaning and illustrated larger possibilities of the Kuntu concepts. Harrison's introduction, titled "Black Theatre in the African Continuum: Word/Song as Method," is a theoretical essay that explains the importance of the word, song, or sound, and the meaning of the African concept of Nommo. Harrison further contends that the dramatic depth of the African American aesthetic spirit is best explored through sacred experience, such as we have come to know it practiced in the black church. He makes clear his agreement with DuBois that cosmic awareness, or *spirituality*, is an essential element in the formation of a black-ground and framework for artistic and theoretical existence and evaluation.

Calling on Baraka to explain further a musical connection to this spiritually informed approach, Harrison quotes his contemporary, who acknowledges a Euro-Western oppositional aesthetic viewpoint. He quotes Baraka from a 1987 interview in The Drum:

> You'll find [a] contrast between say, the dionysian mode which is African, a complete emotional outlet, whether it's Black church or Black art [...] as opposed to the apollonian kind of Post-Greek, European approach where it's restraint. Nietzsche goes so far as to say life has to be kept separate from art because you might get too excited, it might stop you from being able to think. We look at them as two extremes, in that sense. I think that what the Afro-American has always been trying to evolve is an art that comes out of the basically dionysian, basic African spirit possession, because the Black church has always been about spirit possession. You know, they say the spirit will not descend without song. So you got to have music to make the spirit come down, and you gotta get the spirit, you gotta actually get the frenzy, you gotta get happy like they say, to actually have participated in that religious experience.[40]

Here Baraka contrasts Eurocentric and Afrocentric approaches to theater and justifies an active and participatory (Dionysian) mode in opposition to Eurocentric-derived notions of refined restraint. Harrison uses Baraka to emphasize the importance of spiritual and emotional release to the development of Afrocentric artistic voice and agency within a black-ground. Baraka also points out the Eurocentric proclivity for conservatism and restraint.

Baraka reminds us of the importance of *music* and dance or "frenzy" to the theatrical experience in the Dionysian mode, or black-ground.

Music and dance have been a major part of African modes of performances and rituals since ancient times, including the African influenced Greek theater. *Music*, song, and dance were definite elements of the origins of the American minstrel tradition. The concepts of Kuntu and Nommo help us to see ever-more clearly the sacredness of original plantation slave acts in contrast to the misappropriation of these acts by whites in the form of minstrel shows.

The connection of *spirituality* to *music* and dance in an African American dramatic context had its theoretical foundation with DuBois, who spoke of the spiritual and musical aspect and relevance to black life as far back as 1903 in *The Souls of Black Folk* where he wrote a great deal about the relation and importance of *music* in the lives of African Americans. Chapters 1 and 14 of the work, which deal most directly with artistic endeavors, are entitled "Of Our Spiritual Strivings" and "Of the Sorrow Songs," respectively. *Spiritual music* was, and is, a unique phenomenon drawn from the emotional and experiential realms of black American slaves. It is a music of sorrowful strivings that expresses profound determination and faith in things hoped for but impossible to see through materialist, positivist eyes. Spiritual *music* would later evolve into blues, jazz, gospel, rhythm and blues (R&B or soul), and rap music, all of which express expectations of, or belief in, a magical mode of escaping physical and psychological oppression and anguish.

The expressiveness presented in all forms of African American *music* and dance is a material manifestation of the unique spiritual nature of Africans as Americans and should be acknowledged and accepted as such. The voicing of such expression would later develop into the African American aesthetic principle of Nommo. These concepts flourished in the Revolutionary Afrocentric era in the dramatic works of Harrison himself, and writers anthologized in his two books of plays such as Lennox Brown. This philosophy was also utilized by theater groups such as Barbara Ann Teer's National Black Theater and seen in the approach and style of those who came to be considered black avant-garde (or Afrocentric) directors such as Glenda Dickerson. The Revolutionary Afrocentric form may have reached its high point with the commercial success of Ntozake Shange's *for colored girls / who have considered suicide when the rainbow is enuf.* This piece exposed a fuller potential of Kuntu and Nommo aesthetics by mixing dance, *music*, and spoken poetry with a *spiritual*, yet powerfully revolutionary message of black female liberation. This form required a new stylistic label, now known as the "choreopoem," and around 1976 it marked the beginnings of a bridging into another era of African American theater development, in the same way *A Raisin in the Sun* had done a few decades earlier as a commercial and community triumph.

Now, at the dawn of the twenty-first century there is a need to project a newer, clearer awareness of *Revolutionary* and *Afrocentric* artistic principles and concepts based on contemporary or present analysis and understanding of past experiences, creating new knowledge. This is in direct relation to late twentieth century "postmodern" thought, which warrants a need to (re)consider African American theater traditions from a newer perspective that goes beyond the specific, yet confining, aims of *Revolutionary* ideology. This brings us to a seventh and most current period or era of African American theater development. It may best be referred to as a New Age Post-Revolutionary era.

The New Age Post-Revolutionary era is a developmental outgrowth of both the Revolutionary and the Revolutionary Afrocentric eras, and includes the present insights of postmodern intellectual spiritualism and "prophetic pragmatism," as explained by black scholar and philosopher, Cornel West.[41] The New Age Post-Revolutionary quest is to move beyond the spiritually and intellectually consuming discourse of the binary polar concerns of anti-Eurocentric revolution into the mind-expanding realm of living the positive and possible aspects of a New Age cosmic self. West helps to explain, that the neo-traditions of a New Age Post-Revolutionary Movement will call for:

> [A] new generation of black intellectuals, self-confident, no longer anxiety-ridden, no longer looking for the kind of approval and legitimacy in the eyes of their white peers, but willing to flex their intellectual muscles and move in whatever directions and trajectories that they choose. It is a very new movement, a very new movement of black intellectual life.[42]

This period is marked by *protest, revolt,* and *assertion* in the form of new intellectualism and the mind-expanding desire and capability to go beyond the psychological and sociological limitations of the past. This ideology and aesthetic allows us to look at the past with learned perspectives of the present, leading the way into a new, different, and better future. It utilizes the concepts of the Kuntu cosmic ancestral connection and the spoken word power of the Nommo force, and, it understands the prophetic and pragmatic usage of the Bokongo Circle of Life "where the spirit is connected to earth in an endless circle with no top or bottom—only an endless continuum of expressive 'otherness' and inherent knowledge."[43] This new age of possibilities is most clearly addressed in the theoretical essays of two female dramatists and theorists, Shange and Suzan-Lori Parks. Their philosophies build on the Revolutionary Afrocentric perspectives of Harrison and go beyond, or "post-," the limitations of a Revolutionary era mandate for communal voice and the Revolutionary Afrocentric era's ritualistic and Euro-oppositional positions.

Shange acknowledges the influences of many black and Latin writers, musicians, and dancers on her work. Notable among these influential figures are DuBois and Baraka. Shange's world of cosmic experience and connection to the African continuum is strong. Her vision of the world and the theater incorporates elements of all the essentials required or recognized within the Kuntu/Nommo philosophy. In a 1981 essay titled, "unrecovered loses/black theater traditions,"[44] Shange outlines major concerns for the development of an independently derived African American dramatic theory. Her personal aesthetic is distinguished from traditional Eurocentric culture by its multidisciplinary approach of mixing African American forms of dance, *music*, and poetic language. Her works are particularized within the traditions of African American theater by the inclusion of all of the aforementioned elements in combination with the [Cornel] West-ian prophetic and prag-matic requirement of intellect. Shange's ultimate goal is the creation of "an independently created afro-american aesthetic"[45] that allows for creative expression based on her personal experiences and perspectives as both a female and an African American. In the following passage she speaks of inherent potentials for African American writers in the new age:

> the fact that we are an interdisciplinary culture/ that we understand more than
> verbal communication/ lays a weight on afro-american writers that few others
> are lucky enough to have been born into. we can use with some skill virtually
> all our physical senses/ as writers committed to bringing the world as we
> remember it/ imagine it/ & know it to be to the stage/ we must use everything
> we've got.[46]

Shange's theory is representative of New Age Post-Revolutionary aes-thetics, in that it identifies what theater is in an African American sense rather than an Indo-European one. It stands on multiple hyphens between the African and the American, the female and the human, intellectualism and common sense; all the while illuminating the uniqueness of that hyphened position—that place of one's own. Her work is based on traditions that express the reasons and needs for a distinctively identifiable individual sensi-bility. Toward this end, she attempts to show life in a highly personal and idiosyncratic manner and often takes on a politically radical temperament. Her personal struggle is one of finding objective means to present subjective ideas while avoiding obvious imitation of existing styles. In working against the constructs and limitations of Eurocentric traditions she is forced to reach deep into her own psyche for a unique form of expression. What emerges is the personification of a fiery, emotional intellect and a heightened *spirituality* that is often beyond the comprehension of traditionalist thinkers from both sides of the racial divide. Thus, for Shange the physical action of writ-ing expresses her identified persona and is a New Age Post-Revolutionary statement in itself.

One of the most exciting examples of the ideology and potential of a New Age Post-Revolutionary aesthetic in practice is seen in the work of the African American dramatist Suzan-Lori Parks. Parks is a Post-Revolutionary artist with a concern for deconstructing "both the mythic history of the black experience and the history of America."[47] She also personifies West's call for "a new generation of black intellectuals [...] willing to flex their intellectual muscles." Her plays have been called "incomprehensible" and "perplexing" by some.[48] This is owed to her devotion to nonlinearity and experimentation with style. While Parks is concerned with both nonlinearity and African American folk mythology, her sense of reality is also unique. She follows the trend started by Shange and goes further, with an imaginative rejection of traditional narrative and naturalistic forms. Parks' concern with form and the politics of form leads her into uncharted territories. She explains:

> I'm getting more interested in form and less interested in what critics love for blacks to write about—"the black experience." [...] I think artists who are not from the dominant culture are the best ones to examine form. The question of form runs parallel to the question of the way the world is set up. If you are questioning form in theatre then you are questioning the form of the world.[49]

This statement is in direct agreement with DuBois's philosophy of "second sight" and the ability to see the world through different eyes. Parks also borrows other traits from Shange in the process of examining new forms, specifically a special interest in language and musicality. Her concerns with language include speech as well as the language of gesture or movement— another Kuntu/Nommo connection. Irony and rhythm are also traits in common with Shange. Irony in the works of both these artists aligns them with the postmodern realm, and poetic rhythm is a common trait that provides them with a sense of bonded purpose.

But Parks's personal philosophies illustrate a broad scope of awareness and potential for artists in the realm of the New Age Post-Revolutionary Movement. The new potential of African American theater lies in the ability of its artist to capitalize on a new expressive freedom. This, then, is the aim and task of New Age Post-Revolutionary theater: to open new vistas to the African American mind and to open the world to the vistas of African American imagination, moving all humanity into new realms of awareness.

In 1995 Parks published her personal aesthetic principles as an introduction to her anthology, *The America Play and Other Works.*[50] These principles appear in the form of three unique essays; "Possession," "From 'Elements of Style,' " and "An Equation for Black People Onstage." In the first brief essay, she begins by defining the word "possession":

> possession. 1. the action or fact of possessing, or the condition of being possessed. 2. the holding or having of something as one's own, or being inhabited and controlled by a demon or spirit.[51]

This definition denotes a new way of looking at bipolarity. It expresses the identification of a situation and the impetus to take action, to do something proactive. The definition and the essay itself express this young dramatist's need to (re)identify and (re)create her art in her own way. Much like Shange, and much like the New Negro era artists of the 1920s and Revolutionary era artists of the 1960s, Parks sets out with a particular task in mind: to use history as ground for her artistic focus.

Here is an author who understands the possibilities of the art of theater. She understands the magical power of being able to (re)create the self and present a new and better way of seeing. She says this very clearly when she writes:

> The bones tell us what was, is, will be; and because their song is a play—something that through a production actually happens—I'm working theatre like an incubator to create "new" historical events. I'm re-membering and staging historical events which, through their happening on stage, are ripe for inclusion in the canon of history. Theatre is an incubator for the cause of artificial insemination, the baby is no less human.[52]

Here is an artist who understands the potential talked about for many years but never fully realized. This is the potential of African American theater to (re)write time and (re)create history by telling it from the perspectives of those who have seen it from the bottom up, from the outside in, from very different perspectives with different eyes. The view and the vision is expressed with new insight and the future that follows this way of being and way of seeing is also open to new possibilities. Parks is taking possession of the self, the past, the present, and helping to lay open a new future.

On June 26, 1996, precisely fifty years after DuBois's declaration to the third annual convention of the NAACP, playwright August Wilson stepped forth at the eleventh biennial Theatre Communication Group (TCG) National Conference to provide testimony to the struggles and travails of a long list of artists, theorists, events, and developmental movements that preceeded his landmark address. In "The Ground on Which I Stand," Wilson boldly brought clarion focus to the historical and contemporary plight of African American art and culture. While one can only draw certain speculations or make declarations concerning aesthetic principles that may best serve the needs and interests of African American theater in the millennium of the twenty-first century, the seriousness of the need to make such speculations and declarations has been identified and initiated by Wilson in what amounts to a manifesto or doctrine of historical relevance, truth, and beauty. In doing so, Wilson becomes a significant catalyst for understanding the purpose and position of a New Age Post-Revolutionary focus on the power and potential for self-recognition, self-identification, self-determination, and self-respect within the realities of pluralistic arts. While Wilson often speaks of himself as a Black Power-Revolutionary in direct opposition to the general concepts of multiculturalism, he is actually a New Age Post-Revolutionary philosopher in "an-other" regard, because he reminds everyone of the need to acknowledge and to identify the philosophical terrain on which one will stand and operate. Wilson says of himself and of his state of mind:

> [T]he Black Power movement of the '60s was a reality; it was the kiln in which I was fired, and has much to do with the person I am today and the ideas and attitudes that I carry as part of my consciousness [. . . .] I mention this because it is difficult to disassociate my concerns with theatre from the concerns of my life as a black man, and it is difficult to disassociate one part of my life from another. I have strived to live it all seamless[. . .] art and life together, inseparable and indistinguishable.[53]

By identifying and clarifying the aesthetic frame that he chooses to operate within, Wilson is acknowledging his personal spiritual Kuntu reality, which he refers to as "blood memory":

> I stand myself and my art squarely on the self-defining ground of the slave quarters, and find the ground to be hallowed and made fertile by the blood and bones of the men and wom[e]n who can be described as warriors on the cultural battlefield that affirmed their self-worth.[54]

The bravery with which he speaks his own Nommo truth provides him power to project a kind of supremacy of spirit as explained by Baraka during the dramatic Revolutionary past. This makes Wilson a Post-Revolutionary because he brings the past with him into the present realm with continued purpose, new insights, and new expectations. He also brings new DuBoisian potentials and possibilities, because he speaks assertively *about* black theatre *by* way of his black consciousness *for* the empowerment of black arts; an ideology that is clearly *near* to his heart and soul.

In this present moment in time, Wilson has artistic and ideological power allocated by the cosmic energy that he commands. Whether by direct intent or by cosmic will, Wilson has ignited an energy that is now stirring within the collective community of African American artists, and that energy is very real and much more powerful than traditional-positivist cultural analysts may realize. "The Ground on Which I Stand," reminds black artists that what "was" is only as powerful and potentially as important as what they make it each day. To become successful in the new age of Post-Revolutionary realities, African American artists will need to utilize *all* the resources of their past and present selves to (re)shape and (re)make African American theater into what "is" for the present and what it "should be, could be and ought to be" for the future. Wilson reminds:

> The ideas I discovered and embraced in my youth when my idealism was full blown I have not abandoned in middle age when idealism is something less then blooming, but wisdom is starting to bud. The ideas of self-determination, self-respect and self-defense that governed my life in the '60s I find just as valid and self-urging in 1996. The need to alter our relation ship to the society and to alter the shared expectations of ourselves as a racial group I find of greater urgency now than it was then.[55]

This statement indicates an openness to the ideological concepts of Post-Revolutionary aesthetics. It indicates an acknowledgment of a need to broaden the scope of self-perception. One positive aspect of such awareness lies in the deepening reality of the diversity inherent within each individual "self." Wilson's awareness of this point might be seen in the statement:

> I believe that race matters—that is the largest, most identifiable and most important part of our personality. It is the largest category of identification because it is the one that most influences your perception of yourself, and it is

the one to which others in the world of men most respond. Race is also an important part of the American landscape, as America is made up of an amalgamation of races from all parts of the globe. Race is also the product of a shared gene pool that allows for group identification, and it is an organizing principle around which cultures are formed. When I say culture I am speaking about the behavior patterns, arts, beliefs, institutions and all other products of human work and thought as expressed in a particular community of people.[56]

To acknowledge that race, as "difference" and "otherness," does indeed matter in the make up of each individual should be a compelling realization for artistic sensibilities. To recognize race, difference, and otherness as an integral part of American-ness has even greater potential. The only shame of such realities would be not to make the most positive and beneficial use of the inherent potential of difference and otherness as creative resources. The specific potentials of Negroid-ness or blackness in this regard is further highlighted in the following statement:

> The term black or African-American not only denotes race, it denotes condition, and carries with it the vestige of slavery and the social segregation and abuse of opportunity so vivid in our memory. That this abuse of opportunity and truncation of possibility is continuing and is so pervasive in our society in 1996 says much about who we are and much about the work that is necessary to alter our perceptions of each other and to effect meaningful prosperity for all.... The problematic nature of the relationship between white and black for too long led us astray from the fulfillment of our possibilities as a society. We stare at each other across a divide of economics and privilege that has become an encumbrance on black Americans' ability to prosper and on the collective will and spirit of our national purpose.[57]

This awareness indicates and supports the *Post-Afrocentric* need for healthy concerns with acceptance and allowance of personal artistic freedom of expression among individual artists and clear potential, yet, understanding of the difficulty in the full development of either a collective African American theatrical identity or a national American theater identity.

The New Negro Renaissance philosophies of DuBois, Locke, Gregory, Fauset, and others seemed to share the positive potential of such pluralistic possibilities. The Black Revolutionary philosophies of Baraka, Bullins, Neal, Milner, and others rejected all such notions based on the historical realities of their artistic epoch. Yet, Wilson's 1996 manifesto makes both compelling and contradictory truths about our present historical moment. Wilson points out:

> [...] we are on the verge of reclaiming and reexamining the purpose and pillars of our art and laying out new directions for its expansion. As such we make a target for cultural imperialists who seek to empower and propagate their ideas about the world as the only valid ideas, and see blacks as woefully deficient not only in arts and letters but in the abundant gifts of humanity.[58]

Yet, it is a true testament to the solid ground on which Wilson is able to
stand at this historical moment, for he is armed and supported by a wealthy
theoretical tradition that allows him to declare:

> We will not be denied our history [....] We have voice and we have temper.
> We are too far along this road from the loss of our political will, we are too far
> along the road of reassembling ourselves, too far along the road to regaining
> spiritual health to allow such transgression of our history to go unchallenged.[59]

The power and strength of this statement is supported by a well-defined
tradition of *protest, revolt, assertion, music,* and *spirituality* as essential
elements that fertilize the ground on which Wilson and other African
American theater artists may now firmly stand. Traversing seven developmental eras over the course of nearly 350 years makes it possible for them to
also bring their own set of values and standards to a common ground of
American theater possibilities. Wilson declares:

> We can meet on the common ground of the American Theatre [...] We can-
> not share a single value system if that value system consists of the values of
> white Americans based on their European ancestors. We reject that as Cultural
> Imperialism. We need a value system that includes our contributions as Africans
> in America. Our agendas are as valid as yours. We may disagree, we may for-
> ever be on opposite sides of aesthetics, but we can only share a value system
> that is inclusive of all Americans and recognizes their unique and valuable con-
> tributions [....] The ground together: We must develop the ground together.
> We reject the idea of equality among equals, but we say rather the equality of
> all men [....] The common values of the American theatre that we can share
> are plot [...] dialogue [...] characterization [...] design. How we both make
> use of them will be determined by who we are—what ground we are standing
> on and what our cultural values are [....] We are unique, and we are specific.[60]

In March of 1998, I was called upon by Wilson and the cosmic forces to
be part of a special group of African Americans connected to the theater
world in odd and different ways. We came together for a national working
summit "to meet each other face to face, to address questions of aesthetics
and ways to defend ourselves from the nay-sayers who would trumpet our
talents as insufficient to warrant the same manner of investigation and exploration as the majority." Our ultimate task was to begin the process of developing "guidelines for the protection of our cultural property, our
contributions and the influence they accrue."[61] The other directors,
performers, playwrights, theater administrators, and scholars I mostly knew.
The bankers and lawyers, managerial experts, and foundation folk I did not
know. But we found common ground and ways of communicating, helping
each other to focus on the purpose and the possibilities inherent in the
moment of our presence in the time and space provided.

The full impact of the experiences produced in the events of that
sequestered week in the New Hampshire woods are now much clearer. As I

draw conclusions from this simple survey of the philosophical writings on the historical development of African American theater, a theater born of historical conflict constantly struggling to find its way, its space, justifying itself over and over again, the reality of self empowerment and the understanding of one's intrinsic and inherent self-worth are almost unexplainable. Yet the power of the Kuntu and Nommo forces work their magic. This moment is real and overflowing with possibilities. That is drama at least seven dimensions thick and seven layers deep.

In *Black Theatre's Unprecedented Times*, the publication that reports the outcomes of Wilson's African American Theatre Summit events of 1998, Wilson writes:

> Art is made up out of the spiritual resources of the people who create it. Out of their experiences, the sacred and the profane, is made a record of their traverse and the many points of epiphany and redemption. It empowers and provokes sense of self that speeds development and progress in all areas of life and endeavor.[62]

This passage helps to remind us all that the task of writing for and about theater, the lived experiences of humanity, is an artistic endeavor with profound purpose because it does spring from the spiritual resources of a collective community of ancestors, who provided the materials for subject matter and evaluation. They are reborn through us to impact the present. They inspire and encourage the work at hand through revelations and insights recorded in earlier years.

The reality here is that none of us struggles alone. Because those in the past made a record of their traverse, their epiphanies, and redemptive moments, we are all empowered as we continue to add to the collective development of progress. Our community of theorists continue to speak clearly as Wilson continues to write:

> We have begun the struggle anew. The moment is already in our hands. It is pregnant with possibilities that ennoble. Our collective muscle is no longer in danger of atrophy. It strengthens in its application of will. In the vast sea of culture it proclaims a society indebted to its own origins, its own willful contracts of duty and faith. It is we who decide whether our efforts bear fruit. It is in our hands [....] We know all too well the consequences of the failure of our vigilance. We have ample proof of the dire circumstance that accompanies the failure of faith. It is we who are at the crossroads. The defining moment that parallels our future. This is the history that we are making. Each and every day.[63]

Now we struggle together to move from the present moment into a vast sea of cultural possibilities. The powers of the past must be allowed to energize and invigorate the present; to strengthen our will as we consider new and different possibilities. With a collective will to (re)consider the full richness of our own origins and heritages, our faith can be renewed and reinforced. Wilson's manifesto is both a reflection of the past and a compelling inspiration for the future as African American theater artists attempt to (re)tell black history with present perspective. As the future unfolds, DuBois's 1926 speech, Baraka's 1964 manifesto, and Wilson's 1996 speech remain as constant reminders of a peoples repetition and revision of perspectives, images, and ideas that ennoble the human spirit and illustrate their powers to endure the strain of tremendous odds.

NOTES

1. See, *Black Theatre Network News*, Vol. 7, No. 1 (Fall 1996): 8–12.
2. Ibid., 8.
3. August Wilson, "The Ground On Which I Stand," *American Theatre*, Vol. 13, No. 7 (September 1996): 14–16, 71–74.
4. See Langston Hughes and Milton Meltzer, *Black Magic: A Pictorial History of the African-American in the Performing Arts* (Englewood Cliffs, NJ: Prentice-Hall, 1967; rpt. New York: Dacapo Press, 1990), 2–5.
5. See Eleanor W. Traylor, "Two Afro-American Contributions to Dramatic Form," *The Theater of Black Americans: Vol. I*, ed. Errol Hill (Englewood Cliffs, NJ: Prentice-Hall, 1980), 47.
6. See John Fiske, "British Cultural Studies and Television," *Channels of Discourse: Television and Contemporary Criticism*, ed. R. C. Allen (Chapel Hill: UNC Press, 1987).
7. Alain Locke, *The New Negro: An Interpretation* (New York: Albert & Charles Boni, 1925; rpt. New York: Atheneum, 1992).
8. Montgomery Gregory, "The Drama of Negro Life," *The New Negro: An Interpretation*, ed. Alain Locke (New York: Atheneum, 1992).
9. Jessie Fauset, "The Gift of Laughter," *The New Negro: An Interpretation*, ed. Alain Locke (New York: Atheneum, 1992).
10. William E. B. DuBois, *The Souls of Black Folk*, in *Three Negro Classics* (New York: Avon, 1965; original pub. 1903).
11. Ibid., 114–115.
12. For concepts of "Black-figure on a White-ground," see Leslie Catherine Sanders, *The Development of Black Theater in America: From Shadows to Selves* (Baton Rouge and London: Lousiana State University Press, 1988).
13. William E. B. DuBois, "Criteria of Negro Art: Address to the Annual Meeting of the NAACP, June 1926, Chicago," *Crisis*, Vol. 32, No.2 (October 1926): 290–297. Reprinted in *W. E. B. DuBois: A Reader*, ed. Meyer Weinberg, (New York: Harper & Row, 1970), 251–260; also in *The Oxford W. E. B. Du Bois Reader*, ed. Erica J Sundquist (New York: Oxford University Press, 1996).
14. Ibid., 304.
15. William E. B. DuBois, "Kwigwa Players Little Negro Theatre: The Story of a Little Theatre Movement," *The Crisis*, 32, No. 2 (February 1926): 134.
16. "On the Need for Better Plays." Unsigned article in *Opportunity: Journal of Negro Life* (January 1927): 5–6. Reprinted in *The Critics and the Harlem Renaissance*, ed. Cary D. Wintz (New York: Garland, 1996), 49–50.
17. Ibid., 50.
18. See Ethel Pitts Walker, "The American Negro Theatre," *The Theater of Black Americans*, ed. Errol Hill (New York: Applause, 1980 and 1987), 247–260.

19. See Lofton Mitchell, *Black Drama: The Story of the American Negro in the Theatre* (New York: Hawthorn Books, 1967), 181–182.

20. LeRoi Jones (Amiri Baraka), "In Search of the Revolutionary Theatre," *Negro Digest*, Vol. 16, No. 6 (1966): 21–24. This essay was originally commissioned by the *New York Times* in December of 1964, but was refused, with the statement that the editors could not understand it. *The Village Voice* also refused to run this essay. It was first published in *Black Dialogue* and later printed in *The Liberator*, Vol. 7 (1965).

21. Ibid., 21.

22. Ibid., 21.

23. Ibid., 23.

24. Ibid., 21.

25. Darwin Turner, Introduction to *Black Drama in America* (Greenwich, CT: Fawcett, 1971), 18.

26. Jones/Baraka, "Revolutionary Theatre," 21.

27. Ed Bullins, "Theatre of Reality," *Negro Digest*, Vol. 16, No. 6 (1966): 60–66.

28. Ibid., 64.

29. Ibid., 65.

30. Ed Bullins, Introduction to *The New Lafayette Theatre Presents* (Garden City, NY: Anchor-Doubleday, 1974), 4.

31. Larry Neal, "The Black Arts Movement," *The Drama Review (T40)*, Vol. 12, No. 4 (1968): 29–39.

32. Ibid., 31.

33. Ronald Milner, "Black Theater—Go Home!" *The Black Aesthetic*, ed. Addison Gayle, Jr. (Garden City, NY: Doubleday, 1971), 306–312.

34. Hoyt W. Fuller, "Toward a Black Aesthetic," *The Black Aesthetic*, ed. Addison Gayle, Jr. (Garden City, NY: Doubleday, 1971), 3–12.

35. Addison Gayle, Jr., *The Black Aesthetic* (Garden City, NY: Doubleday, 1971).

36. Paul Carter Harrison, *Kuntu Drama: Plays of the African Continuum* (New York: Grove Press, 1974).

37. Oliver Jackson, Preface to *Kuntu Drama: Plays of the African Continuum* (New York: Grove Press, 1974), ix.

38. Ibid., xii.

39. Paul Carter Harrison, *Totem Vices: Plays from the Black World Repertory* (New York: Grove Press, 1989).

40. Harrison, "Black Theater in the African Continuum: Word/Song as Method." Introduction to *Totem Vices*, xvi. Harrison quotes Amiri Baraka from an interview in *The Drum*, Vol. 1, No. 2 (1987): 16–17.

41. See Cornel West, *The American Evasion of Philosophy: A Genealogy of Pragmatism* (Macon, Madison, WI: University of Wisconsin Press, 1989). Also Cornel West and bell hooks, *Breaking Bread: Insurgent Black Intellectual Life* (Boston: South End Press, 1991).

42. Cornel West, "Decentering Europe: The Contemporary Crisis in Culture," *Critical Quarterly*, Vol. 33, No. 1 (Spring 1991): 1–19.

43. From the opening fly sheet in *Black Theatre's Unprecedented Times*, ed. Hely M. Perez (Gainesville, FL: Black Theatre Network, 1999).

44. Ntozake Shange, "unrecovered loses/black theater traditions," Introduction in *Three Pieces: Spell #7, a Photograph: Lovers in Motion, Boogie Woogie Landscapes* (New York: St. Martin's, 1981).

45. Ibid., ix.

46. Ibid., x.
47. John Heilpern, quoting Parks in "Voices from the Edge," *Vogue*, Vol. 183, No. 11 (November 1993): 174.
48. Elinor Fuchs, "The Politics of Form," *Village Voice*, Vol. 37, No. 15 (April 14, 1992): 10. Fuchs refers to reviews in *Variety* and the *Hartford Courant* respectively, concerning the Yale Rep production of Parks's play, *The Death of the Last Black Man in the Whole Entire World*.
49. Cathy Madison, "Writing Home: Interviews with Suzan-Lori Parks, Christopher Durang, Eduardo Machado, Ping Chong and Migdalia Cruz," *American Theatre*, Vol. 8, No. 7 (October 1991): 36.
50. Suzan-Lori Parks, *The America Play and Other Works* (New York: Theatre Communications Group, 1995).
51. Ibid., 3.
52. Ibid., 4–5.
53. Wilson, "The Ground On Which I Stand," 14–15.
54. Ibid., 71.
55. Ibid., 15.
56. Ibid., 16.
57. Ibid., 16.
58. Ibid., 71.
59. Ibid., 71.
60. Ibid., 71–72.
61. Ibid., 73.
62. Wilson, "Introduction: In Our Hands," *Black Theatre's Unprecedented Times*, 32.
63. Ibid., 33.

3

RITA DOVE'S *MOTHER LOVE*: REVISING THE BLACK AESTHETIC THROUGH THE LENS OF WESTERN DISCOURSE

Tracey L. Walters

According to August Wilson, "There are and have always been two distinct and parallel traditions in black art that is, art that is conceived and designed to entertain white society, and art that feeds the spirit and celebrates the life of black America by designing its strategies for survival and prosperity." While many critics find merit in Wilson's statement, others find his argument problematic, for in a sense, Wilson limits African American literary production to two narrowly defined categories. It is vital to challenge Wilson's assertion for his statement implies that the black artist who does not subscribe to the prevailing concept of what black art is or should be is selling out to the white establishment, or as Wilson says "crossing over." Unfortunately, writers who have elected to draw upon Western literary traditions, rather than African or African American literary traditions, have been accused of constructing narratives that are directed toward a white readership. Adrienne Kennedy, Robert Hayden, Gwendolyn Brooks, and Rita Dove, for example, have all been ostracized for their decision to couch their narratives in British history and culture and Greek and Roman mythology. Exploring the works of these writers such as these though, reveals that their works are authentically black texts.

Ultimately, Wilson's declaration calls for an interrogation of the black aesthetic ideology. What we must discern is, can black writers draw upon Western literary traditions and culture and still adhere to a black aesthetic? An examination of Rita Dove's sonnet *Mother Love* proves that indeed, black writers are able to garner inspiration from European traditions and yet create art that maintains a black sensibility. This study investigates how Dove appropriates the Greek myth of Persephone and Demeter and represents this tale about the relationship between mothers and daughters, or more specifically, black mothers and daughters, from a black perspective. Moreover, indicators of the texts' "blackness" are evident in the literary themes pursuant to black women's writing, cultural markers, the language, and the narrated experiences of the characters.

Before turning our attention toward Dove's appropriation of Greek myth, let us first reexamine the polemical nature of the black aesthetic. The Black Arts Movement of the 1970s was perhaps one of the most significant periods in African American literary history when black artists and critics attempted consciously to set a criteria for judging black art. Addison Gayle's seminal text *The Black Aesthetic* offers the most extensive review of the black aesthetic ideology. As we briefly revisit the dictums of the Black Arts Movement's definition of what constitutes black art, it is clear that the characterization of black art was so rigid that it marginalized a number of poets and playwrights. In his discussion of the Black Arts Movement, Timothy Seibles notes:

> An unfortunate by-product of the militancy that pervaded this period was the dismissal by most black—poets as well as nonpoets—of virtually all nonmilitant poetry. Not only were white writers shunned because of their attitude, but any black writers whose works explored subjects that were deemed unrelated to the "revolution" was cast away as well (probably the best known African-American writer to fall under attack for this reason was Robert Hayden). (183)

Essentially, the black artist of the 1970s had an obligation to produce art that was by and for the people. The idea was to create art that was the "spiritual sister of the black power concept" (Neale 184). This art was also to be a rejection and denouncement of Western literary traditions and devices that espoused a "white aesthetic." For example, Ethridge Knight wrote: "To accept the white aesthetic is to accept and validate a society that will not allow [blacks] to live. The Black artist must create new forms and new values, [...] create a new history, new symbols, myths and legends (and purify old ones by fire) (qtd. in Seibles 183). Knight's assertion that the black artist should replace Western mythology and history with his/her own mythology reminds us that a writer like Adrienne Kennedy, who incorporates British literary history and culture into plays such as *Funny House of the Negro* (1962) and *The Owl Answers* (1968), stands outside the realms of Knight's definition of the black aesthetic.[1] Novelist Ishmael Reed also supported Knight's view that the black artist was to divorce himself from drawing upon Greek and Roman mythology for the Classics were European constructs. Christa Buschendorf shares that in the introduction to *19 Necromancers From Now*, Reed contends:

> The history of Afro-American literature is abundant with examples of writers using other people's literary machinery and mythology in their work. W. E. B. DuBois, in some of his writing, is almost embarrassing in his use of White classical references [....] Black writers [...] have been neo-classicists, Marxists, existentialists, and infected by every Western disease available. I have a joke to I tell friends about a young Black poet who relies upon other people's systems, and does not use his head. He wears sideburns and has seen every French film in New York. While dining at Schrafft's he chokes to death on nut-covered ice cream and dies. He approaches the river Styx and pleads with Charon to ferry him across. "I don't care how often you've used me as a mythological allusion," Charon says, "You're still a nigger—swim!" (72)

Reed admits unabashedly his embarrassment of DuBois's appropriation of white classical references. We might deduce that this kind of criticism would be leveled also toward a playwright like Kennedy whose adaptation of Euripides's "Orestes" and "Electra"—works commissioned by Julliard in 1980—lack evidence of an effort to capture the black experience. August Wilson charges that "For a black actor [or playwright] to stand on the stage as part of a social milieu that has denied him his gods, his culture, his humanity, his mores, his ideas of himself and the world he lives in, is to be in league with a thousand naysayers who wish to corrupt the vigor and spirit of his heart" (5). Much like Reed, Wilson's assertion concludes that the artist who chooses to work within the realm of the "white world" is compromising his/her integrity. Kennedy is part of a tradition of writers who appropriate classical narratives.[2] Writers including Phillis Wheatley, W. E. B. DuBois, Countee Cullen, Toni Morrison, and Rita Dove have all rewritten classical texts in innovative ways—oftentimes placing "blackness" at the center of their narratives.[3]

One of the most useful critiques of the black artist and her/his adaptation of the classics is presented by Samuel Allen who concludes: "we are not heirs to the Greeks, but willy-nilly we inhabit in part this cultural terrain. The poet must simultaneously discover and create his authentic voice. He must find his way in the selective use of elements from these two bodies of tradition [African and Western] the resolution of which must ultimately be felt as one, which must be cast in his likeness and according to his needs" (qtd. in Siebles 187). Dove's sonnet *Mother Love* and her play *The Darker Face of the Earth* are both telling examples of how an artist can create her own authentic voice by marrying both Western and African American traditions.

The alluring quality of classical mythology transcends race and gender. The themes of death, love, war, and betrayal are as equally appealing to both the black or white writer, male or female. However, according to Jane Campbell, black writers who experiment with myth are unique because the act of rewriting myth is actually "a radical act inviting the audience to subvert the racist mythology that thwarts and defeats Afro-America and replaces it with a new myth rooted in the black perspective" (x). Moreover, in "White Masks: Greek Mythology in Contemporary Black Poetry," Buschendorf notes that black writers blend myths so that the "particular myth is juxtaposed, combined, or merged with other myths, while the importance of the individual myth diminishes" (76). The most significant discussion of mythology that relates to this study though, is Alicia Ostriker's assertion that female poets seek to "deconstruct a prior 'myth' or story and construct a new one which include[s] instead of excludes herself" (212). *Mother Love* is a clear example of how Dove writes black women into a well-known Greek myth about the complexity of the mother/daughter relationship.

The Persephone and Demeter myth appears to be a favorite of African American women writers.[4] In " 'Like Seeing You Buried': Persephone in *The Bluest Eye, Their Eyes Were Watching God*, and *The Color Purple*," Elizabeth T. Hayes contends: "Toni Morrison, Zora Neale Hurston, and Alice Walker in particular have created fascinating reenactments, or images, of the Persephone myth in their fiction, images whose differences from the archetype are as significant as their similarities to it" (171). Hayes goes on to note though, that we should not infer that these women deliberately borrow from this mythical archetype. Rather,

> The archetypes of the Mother and the female rite of passage in the Persephone story embody fundamental human experiences and emotions, part of the collective unconscious of writers and readers alike [....] Furthermore, although archetypes can affect both writer and audience on a purely unconscious level, some, like the Persephone archetype, are deeply embedded as well in Western cultural consciousness. (173)

The traditional Homeric or Ovidian renditions feature the tale of a young girl who is out one day playing with her friends and picking flowers when she is abducted by Hades and then raped. Demeter, goddess of the earth, sinks into despair. Overcome with grief she neglects her duty to nurture the earth's vegetation. The Gods are alarmed by Demeter's failure to tend to life on earth and fear the impending consequences that will destroy the earth. After Demeter pleads with the God Zeus for the return of Persephone her wish is granted. However, just before Demeter is to be reunited with her daughter, Persephone is tricked into eating a pomegranate. Eating this fruit has dire consequences for eating the flesh of the underworld forbids Persephone from living fully in the mortal world. Thus, Persephone must remain part of the year in the underworld as Hades's wife, or queen (fall and winter when Demeter is grieving and the crops die), and the rest of the year she is reunited with Demeter (spring and summer when harvests grow). Dove notes that while this story is ancient, the theme of violation is contemporary for: "there comes a point when a mother can no longer protect her child, when the daughter must go her own way into womanhood" (i). Critics have noted that this story has been retold in a number of ways. Oftentimes the focus is on Persephone as the innocent victim who is violated by powerful Hades. Conversely, Persephone has also been presented as the independent young woman who after her abduction, relishes in her new-found freedom away from the coddling arms of her mother.[5]

Dove's version is both Demeter's and Persephone's story. The story is about Demeter's struggle to cope with the separation from her child and the realization that despite the attempt to shield her daughter from the vices of the world, she could never fully protect her. She had no choice but to allow Persephone to live and learn from her own mistakes. The narrative is also about a young woman who strives for independence and the search for her own identity. Dove's text shifts back and forth between Demeter's grief at her daughter's departure and loss of innocence, to Persephone's newfound freedom trying to discover herself and the world. Ultimately the experiences of both these women allow them to think critically about motherhood and how it bears upon their own lives as both mothers and daughters themselves.[6] We should note though, that while the original Persephone and Demeter myth is kept in view (the lifecycle theme of life, death, and rebirth), Dove reimagines this tale so that it becomes her own rendering about the mother/daughter relationship from her own perspective as a black mother, daughter, poet, and playwright. In fact, Dove's narrative is not about one particular mother, but really about any mother: "[a] middle-class American—[or] at times [an] explicitly African American" (Booth 126) woman who experiences the loss of her child either by literal abduction or by growth and maturity. Moreover, in its contemporary setting, Persephone's voyage to the underworld takes place not in hell, but in Paris, Mexico, and Italy. This quest to define and find "self" is a familiar trope of African American women's writing. Usually though, this journey to find self takes place in one's ancestral home such as Africa or the Caribbean (Paule Marshall's *Brown Girl Brownstones* is one example). More recent works, like Shay Youngblood's *Black Girl in Paris* though illustrate that the search for self can also take place in Europe. If we consider that Dove might be drawing upon her own experience of traveling extensively to Europe, it is not surprising that Persephone's artistic and sexual development takes place in European locations, rather than in Africa or the Caribbean.

Within this retelling of Greek myth, what is most essential for discussion is not the theme, but more significantly how Dove effectively represents this tale. What we can observe is that like other writers, Dove uses myth for form and structure, but she constructs her narrative using African American literary motifs and themes. What on the surface appears to be a story devoid of black experience, upon closer reading exposes a black sensibility in the poem's use of language and culturally specific references rooted in the black experience.

One of the first black markers of the text is a cultural reference to the African diasporian concept of "Good Hair." The notion of "good hair" relates to the distorted concept of African American beauty, which is often equated with long, straight hair and a fair complexion. This European standard of beauty is a familiar discussion within black women's narratives. For example, the protagonist Janie in Zora Neale Hurston's *Their Eyes Were Watching God* is despised first by her classmates and later by the women in her community because of her long, straight, black hair. Moreover, at her husband's request she covers her head so that the men of the town abstain from lusting after her hair:

> This business of the head-rag irked her endlessly. But Jody was set on it. Her hair was not going to show in the store. It didn't seem sensible at all. That was because Joe never told Janie how jealous he was. He never told her how often he had seen the other men figuratively wallowing in it as she went about things in the store. And one night he had caught Walter standing behind Janie and brushing the back of his hand back and forth across the loose end of her braid ever so slightly so as to enjoy the feel of it without Janie knowing what he was doing. (51–52)[7]

Here in Dove's *Mother Love*, this reference to "good hair" is presented in the poem "Protection" when Demeter tells Persephone: "I know I'm not saying this right. / 'Good' hair has no body / in this county; like trained ivy, / it hangs and shines...." (11). What might seem to be a subtle inconsequential passing statement is actually highly significant, for straight or white hair—as opposed to natural, thick, curly hair—has always been problematic for African American women who have struggled to divorce themselves from European notions of beauty. Numerous black female critics have written about the complexity of defining black standards of beauty. hooks writes:

> The first body issue that affects black female identity, even more so than color is hair texture. There is a growing body of literature . . . that discuss our obsession with hair. But I want to start with basics. How is it that little black girls learn (even before we know anything about racism) that our hair is a problem? Negative thinking about our hair is usually conveyed in the home by parents, other caregivers, and siblings. One aspect of white-supremacist thinking that seemed to take hold of the black psyche in the 20th century was the assumption that straight hair was better than blackness, overworked black women often found that it took less effort to daily groom straightened hair than hair in its natural state. (85)

She goes on to note:

> Despite the raised consciousness of black people around the question of internalized racism, most black magazines still favor images of black women with long straight hair. Often, in advertisements the light-skinned woman with straight hair will be depicted as the female who has a partner or who is more sexually appealing. (86–87)[8]

In addition to this reference to good hair another culturally specific event in Dove's poem is featured in "The Search," which explores Demeter's reaction to the separation from Persephone (either by abduction or by her own free will):

> Blown apart by loss, she let herself go—
> wandered the neighborhood hatless, breasts
> swinging under a ratty sweater, crusted
> mascara blackening her gaze. It was a shame,
> the wives whispered, to carry on so.
> To them, wearing foam curlers arraigned
> like piglets to market was almost debonair,
> but an uncombed head? not to be trusted.
> The men watched more closely, tantalized
> by so much indifference. Winter came early and still
> frequented the path by the river until
> one with murmurous eyes pulled her down to size.
> Sniffed Mrs. Franklin, ruling matron, to the rest:
> *Serves her right, the old mare.* (10)

This unforgiving reaction of the female community who stand in judgment of the fallen woman is another perennial motif in African American women's writing. Once again, Hurston's *Their Eyes* serves as a useful example. In *Their Eyes*, Janie leaves her emotionally abusive husband Jody Starks, for a younger lover, teacake, and moves away from the community. When teacake contracts rabies, Janie (in self-defense) kills him. After facing trial, both from the legal system and the community, she returns home under the disapproving gaze of the men and women of Eatonville, Florida, who like Mrs. Frazier in Dove's poem, harbor feelings of ill will toward her:

> They sat in judgment. Seeing the woman as she was made them remember the envy they had stored up from other times. So they chewed up the back parts of their minds and swallowed with relish. They made burning statements with questions, and killing tools out of laughs. It was mass cruelty. A mood come alive. Words walking without masters; walking alone together like harmony in a song [...] The men noticed her firm buttocks like she had grapefruits in her hip pockets; the great rope of black hair swinging to her waist and unraveling in the wind like a plume. (Hurston 2)

In addition, just as we see Mrs. Frazier in Dove's poem cast dispersion toward Demeter, here in *Their Eyes*, LuLu Moss drawls "'She ain't even worth talkin' after, LuLu Moss drawled through her nose. 'She sits high, but she looks low. Dat's what Ah say 'bout dese ole women runnin' after young boys'" (3).

While this example demonstrates how black women writers have captured the black communities' judgment of others, black women writers also reveal that the scorned woman is often rescued by the same community of women who condemn them. In "The Grief Council," after the women accept that Demeter is experiencing an emotional crisis, they take over and help her cope domestically and otherwise:

> I told her: enough is enough.
> Get a hold on yourself, take a lover,
> help some other unfortunate child.
>
> > *to abdicate*
> > *to let the garden go to seed*
>
> Yes, it's a tragedy, a low-down shame,
> but you still got your own life to live. Meanwhile,
> ain't nothing we can do but be discreet
> and wait. She brightened up a bit then.
> I thought of those blurred snapshots framed
> on milk cartons, a new pair each week.
>
> > *soot drifting up from hell*
> > *dusting the kale's*
> > *green tresses, the corn's green sleeve*

It was pathetic. I bet she ain't took in
a word I said except that last, like
a dog with a chicken bone too greedy to care
if it stick in his gullet and choke him sure.

And no design

I say we gotta see her through.
I say she can't be left too long in that
drafty old house alone.

No end of day delight
At the creak of the gate

Sister Jeffries, you could drop in
tomorrow morning, take one
of your Mason jars, something
sweetish, tomatoes or bell peppers.

no tender cheek nor ripening grape
destined for wine

Miz Earl can fetch her later to the movies—
a complicated plot should distract her,
something with a car chase through Manhattan,
loud horns melting to a strings-and-sax ending

the last frail tendril snapped free
(though the roots still strain towards her)

and your basic sunshine pouring through
the clouds. Ain't this crazy weather?
Feels like winter coming on.

at last the earth cleared to the sea
at last composure. (Dove 15–16)

Thus, it is the grief council who rescues Demeter. We should also note that here more than ever the language and the tone of the poem is unmistakably African American. Therese Steffen labels this section a "praise song for the spirit of black sisterhood" and further notes, "This effective Olympian council is strikingly African American in its speech (double negations, colloquialisms) and references to self-help" (67).[9] This communal rescue is also significant because it helps Demeter realizes that although her own child is gone, she can pass on her "mother love" to another.

Who can forget the attitude of mothering
              Toss me a baby and without bothering
to blink I'll catch her, sling him on a hip.
              Any woman knows the remedy for grief
is being needed: duty bugles and we'll
              climb out of exhaustion every time,

bare the nipple or tuck in the sheet,
        heat milk and hum at bedside until
they can dress themselves and rise, primed
        For Love or Glory—those one-way mirrors
girls peer into as their fledgling heroes slip
        through, storming the smoky battlefield.

So when this kind woman approached at the urging
        Of her bouquet of daughters,
(one for each of the world's corners,
        one for each of the winds to scatter!)
and offered up her only male child for nursing
        (a smattering of flesh, noisy and ordinary),
I put aside the lavish trousseau of the mourner
        For the daintier comfort of pity: (Dove 17)

In effect, Demeter becomes what some black critics call an "othermother": "women who assist blood mothers by sharing mothering responsibilities" (Collins 47). Unable to mother her own daughter, she becomes a surrogate mother for another child.

While the poem highlights Demeter's experience as a black mother, we are also introduced to Persephone's experience as "a dark girl in a white world" (Steffen 131). In this underworld of Paris and Italy, Dove sheds light on the experience of cultural exclusivity on the basis of artistic and racial terms. For example, while in Paris, Persephone attends a dinner party, but leaves after finding unfulfilling conversations. She notes, "I decided to let this party swing without me" (27). Persephone is never a victim of racism herself, however, as Steffen contends, the racist attitude of the Parisians is indeed present and most notably displayed by Persephone's lover Hades, who is uncomfortable with the presence of African expatriates: "*Merde,* / too many at once! Africans / spilling up the escalator / like oil from lucky soil" (Dove 30).

Steffen also explains that here, Dove is "commemorating the collective abduction of African victims into American slavery . . . ." (136). Thus, this reference to Hades's reaction to the Africans is noteworthy, for while he seems offended by the presence of the Africans, Persephone (perhaps identifying herself too as an African) is unfazed by the presence of the African vendors whom she watches "fold up their straw mats and wooden beads." In reality, Persephone is not much different from the Africans Hades despises. Consequentially though, while in Sicily, Italy, Persephone is made to ruminate on her "blackness" and "foreignness." While in Sicily, Persephone goes to visit the historic site of Persephone's abduction. The guide that she encounters trembles as he touches her arm. Persephone remarks: "His touch trembles at my arm / hasn't he seen an American black / before? We find a common language: German" (69). This statement presents the supposition that the guide trembles, not because he is old, but because Persephone is black. Furthermore, Persephone senses that her "blackness" makes an impression on the guide. In a tone that is somewhat sardonic she says, "Before we find a common language—German, / laced with tenth-grade Spanish and / residual Latin—we descend / in silence through the parched orchard. / The way he stops to smile at me / and pat my arm, I'm surely his first / Queen of Sheba" (70). Here, Persephone's reference to the Queen of Sheba, heightens her own concept of race and the idea that the guide sees her as an exotic anomaly. Persephone is presumptuous, because it is likely that her race has nothing to do with the guide's decision to touch her arm. What is important though, is the fact that she believes her race accounts for the way in which the guide responds to her.

Essentially then, after having witnessed the evidence of the racial markers present in Dove's *Mother Love*, it is clear from the examples that I have provided that Dove succeeds in retelling a myth that is typically not associated with the black experience, into a story that is indeed very much about African American mothers and daughters. Dove's sonnet challenges critics who readily dismiss artists whose works are influenced by Western mythology to take a closer look at narratives like her own and acknowledge that by rewriting the classics these writers are not rejecting or neglecting their own culture. Rather they are presenting narratives that speak to the African American and human experience. In effect, poems like *Mother Love* negate the idea that black art can be neatly placed within a particular category. Ultimately, black artists should have the freedom to create art that does not necessarily conform to a political agenda or aesthetic sensibility. Those artists who choose to write against the established order are perhaps our most important writers for they challenge the "standard" definition of black art. These artists prove that they are capable of writing both within and beyond existing traditions. Their innovative approaches to literature are significant for they expand the definition of black art and prove to the black artistic community and others that black art is not predictable or easily identifiable, rather it is as original and as enigmatic as the work of others across the globe.

NOTES

1. *Funny House of the Negro* features British historical figures such as Queen Victoria, along with African political figure Patrice Lumumba. *The Owl Answers* has a cast of British literary characters including Shakespeare and Chaucer, and also features William the Conqueror.
2. When I use the term "Classics" I am referring to those works written during Greco-Roman antiquity.
3. Interestingly, Wilson himself recognizes the relevance of the classical tradition: "In one guise, the ground I stand on has been pioneered by the Greek Dramatists— by Euripides, Aeschylus and Sophocles...." (1).
4. White women such as H. D. Adrienne Rich and Meridel Le Sueur have also worked with this myth.
5. In *The Long Journey Home: Revisioning the Myth of Demeter and Persephone for Our Time*, Christine Downing notes: "Many concentrating on the myth's account of Demeter's love of Persephone, have seen it primarily in terms of how it valorizes

the beauty and power of the mother-daughter bond. Others have focused on Hades' abduction of Persephone and read the myth as primarily a story about paternal violation; about rape, incest, abuse; about male intrusion into women's mysteries; about the rise of patriarchy and the suppression of goddess religion" (2–3).

6. As Lotta Lofgren notes, "Just as Demeter has been a Persephone, Persephone is an incipient Demeter, watching her unborn child move inside her in "History" (138).

7. The character Maureen Peal in Toni Morrison's *The Bluest Eye* offers another example of the adoration that African Americans hold toward those with light skin and straight hair.

8. Dorothea Smartt's poem "five strands of hair takes an amusing look at how black women endure horrific procedures to transform their hair from its African/natural state to a European or straighter texture.

9. A similar occurrence of communal rescue is featured in Morrison's *Beloved* when the women of the community save Sethe from the destruction of herself and the spite of her supernatural daughter. When Sethe's dead daughter returns to reunite with her mother and destroy her, the women who had snubbed her form a protective bond to assist her: "Some brought what they could and what they believed would work. Stuffed in apron pockets, strung around their necks, lying in the space between their breasts. Others brought Christian faith—as shield and sword. Most brought a little of both. They had no idea what they would do once they got there. They just started out, walked down Bluestone Road and came together at the agreed-upon time" (257).

WORKS CITED

Booth, Alison. "Abduction and Other Severe Pleasures: Rita Dove's *Mother Love*." *Callaloo* 19:1 (1996): 125–130.

Buschendorf, Christa. "White Masks: Greek Mythology in Contemporary Black Poetry." *Crossing Borders: Inner and Intercultural Exchanges in a Multicultural Society*. Ed. Heinz Ickstadt. Germany: Peter Lang, 1997. 64–82.

Campbell, Jane. Introduction. *Mythic Black Fiction: The Transformation of History*. Knoxville: University of Tennessee Press, 1986. i–x.

Collins, Patricia Hill. "The Meaning of Motherhood in Black Culture and Black Mother-Daughter Relationships." *Double Stitch: Black Women Write About Mothers and Daughters*. Ed. Patricia Bell-Scott et al. New York: Harper Perennial, 1991. 42–60.

Downing. Christine. Introduction. *The Long Journey Home: Re-Visioning the Myth of Demeter and Persephone for Our Time*. Ed. Christine Downing. Boston: Shambhala, 1994. 3.

Dove, Rita. *Mother Love*. New York: W. W. Norton & Company, Inc., 1995.

hooks, bell. *Sisters of the Yam: Black Women and Self-Recovery*. Boston: South End Press, 1993.

Hayes, Elizabeth T. " 'Like Seeing You Buried': Persephone in *The Bluest Eye, Their Eyes Were Watching God*, and *The Color Purple*." *Images of Persephone: Feminist Readings in Western Literature*. Ed. Elizabeth T. Hayes. Florida: University Press of Florida, 1994. 171–194.

Hurston, Zora Neale. *Their Eyes Were Watching God*. 1937. New York: Harper and Row Publishers, Inc., 1990.

Lofgren, Lotta. "Partial Horror: Fragmentation and Healing in Rita Dove's *Mother Love*." *Callaloo* 19:1 (1996): 135–142.

Morrison, Toni. *Beloved*. New York: Plume, 1988.

Neale, Larry. "The Black Arts Movement." *Within the Circle: An Anthology of African American Literary Criticism From the Harlem Renaissance to the Present*. Ed. Angelyn Mitchell. Durham: Duke University Press, 1994.184–198.

Ostriker, Alicia. "The Thieves of Language: Women Poets and Revisionist Mythmaking." *The New Feminist Criticism: Essays on Women, Literature, and Theory*. Ed. Elaine Showalter. New York: Pantheon Books, 1985. 314–338.

Seibles, Timothy. "A Quilt in Shades of Black: The Black Aesthetic in Twentieth Century African American Poetry." *A Profile of Twentieth Century American Poetry*. Ed. Jack Myers and David Wojahn. Carbondale: Southern Illinois Press, 1991. 158–189.

Smartt, Dorothea. *Connecting Medium*. London: Peepal Tree, 2001.

Steffen, Therese. *Crossing Color. Transcultural Space and Place in Rita Dove's Poetry, Fiction, and Drama*. New York: Oxford University Press, 2001.

Wilson, August. "The Ground on Which I Stand." *American Theatre* 13:7 (1996): 1–14.

4

The Ifa Paradigm: Reading the Spirit in Tina McElroy Ansa's *Baby of the Family*

Georgene Bess Montgomery

After being introduced to Ifa, an ancient African spiritual system, during a Yoruba language course, I immersed myself into learning more about the religion. The more knowledgeable I became about the religion, the more aware I became of how prevalent the tenets of the religion really are in systems of thought and how they permeate the lives of African peoples. I realized that part of what attracted me to the religion was its practicality and, more significantly, how it was so similar to notions, practices, and attitudes that existed in my community that had been passed down for generations. I also began to see references to Ifa throughout the literature of African American and Caribbean writers when I read or reread texts. This knowledge of Ifa provided me with a whole new interpretation of the literary texts. Upon rereading several texts—Ishmael Reed's *Yellow Radio Broke Down* and *Mumbo Jumbo*, Ntozake Shange's *Sassafrass, Cypress, and Indigo*, Gloria Naylor's *Mama Day*, Paule Marshall's *Praisesong for the Widow*, Charles Johnson's *Middle Passage*, Toni Morrison's *Song of Solomon*, and Elizabeth Nunez's *When Rocks Dance* to name only a few—my knowledge and understanding of Ifa provided for me a significantly different and substantively more meaningful way of interpreting the symbols and ideas embedded in the texts, whose meanings had until that time remained locked.

As I explored the various paradigms for literary criticism, I discovered that missing from those paradigms was a method that could be applied to African American and Caribbean literary texts, which would facilitate and thus validate my particular readings of those texts. I searched for a particular paradigm that would serve to elucidate the many images, symbols, numbers, and colors employed in various African American and Caribbean literary texts. I realized that perhaps there is a lack of literary criticism because many scholars pay little attention to the spirituality embedded in those texts because their approach to, definition of, and paradigm for spirituality is Western oriented. Thus I decided to heed Henry Louis Gates's directive that

African American critics "must redefine theory itself with our own black cultures" and seek to construct a new theory derived "from the black tradition itself [...] [including] the language of [spirituality] [...] which makes the black tradition our very own" (qtd. in Bressler 269). Like Gates, playwright August Wilson issues a call for African diasporic literary criticism grounded in African culture, philosophy, and worldview. For Wilson, this is an essential undertaking because "black American are Africans, and there are many histories and many cultures on the African continent" (Wilson 494). Wilson charges that as writers grow and develop, the critics, then, need to "develop guidelines for the protection of our cultural property, our contributions and the influence they accrue. It is time we took the responsibility for our own talents in our own hands" (500). In taking responsibility for our talents, we must then establish appropriate modes of criticism with which to insightfully analyze and critique our literature, our music, our dance, our culture. These modes must be centered in a deepened understanding and awareness of African diasporic culture. Wilson acknowledges the significant cultural impact of growing up in his mother's house:

> Growing up in my mother's house [...] I learned the language, the eating habits, the religious beliefs, the gestures, the notions of common sense [...] concepts of beauty and justice [...] that my mother learned from her mother, and which you could trace back to the first African who set foot on the continent. It is this culture that stands solidly on these shores today as a testament to the resiliency of the African-American spirit. (494–495)

Thus, for any literary critique to be complete, it must include some analysis of and explanation for cultural specificities embedded in and referenced within the text itself. The Ifa Paradigm can then, in fact, be thought of as informing other models of criticism because it allows for an investigation of cultural specificities that may inform a literary text.

With both Gates's and Wilson's directive in mind, I constructed a paradigm for the interpretation of Caribbean and African American literature, utilizing a method informed by the ideas and worldview of Ifa to unlock deeper levels of meaning in the writing of African peoples. I argue that this methodology, which I name the Ifa Paradigm,[1] can create "a new source of intellectual fermentation [...] [involving] magic, precognition, imagination," which "the experts of facts do not know or recognize" (Smith 140), and will permit us to read African American and Caribbean texts in an entirely new way.

This paradigm investigates how some literary use of colors, signs, symbols, numbers, images, myths, legends, and landscapes reference African culture. It further outlines the particular areas of knowledge that would assist with such a critique. These—Orisha, ancestors, ritual, colors, numbers, symbols, initiation, conjuring, magic, divination—are what will frame the method and be brought to bear on the critique of specific works with a view to enrich understanding of them. According to the Ifa Paradigm, the color red, fire, thunder, lightning, drums, heat, refer to Shango, African deity of truth and justice, who has as his symbols thunder, lightning, fire, and the double-edged axe. The wind, storms, and death refer to Oya, deity of sudden change, guardian of the cemetery, while snakes refer to the Ancestors. Additionally, the ocean, fish, and waves are associated with Yemonja, African deity of motherhood.

The Ifa Paradigm, then, serves to elucidate alternative readings of African American and Caribbean literary texts. It provides a methodology with which to not only examine African American and Caribbean literary texts but also to decipher and decode signs and symbols deeply embedded in those texts. In assigning meaning to the various symbols, colors, numbers, for example, the Ifa Paradigm provides an alternative and more in-depth interpretation of the texts. Significantly, an application of the Ifa Paradigm permits a more culture-based interpretation of an African American and Caribbean literary text.

The Ifa Paradigm stresses the importance of exploring cultural specificities, separate and apart from the dominant culture as well as the understanding that although many Caribbean and African American texts examine and critique the influences and consequences of the dominant culture, those texts may very well have a different point of departure and references. Therefore, while various forms of literary theory and criticism are appropriate in the analysis of Caribbean and African American literary texts, those theories often fall short of offering a complete analysis and understanding of the texts critiqued. For deeper understanding of these cultures that exist as the center to themselves and as a periphery to others, there must be critical models that foreground the specificity of the cultural experience.

Why Ifa? I am not attempting here to suggest the importance of one particular religion in the construction of a literary model. Rather, I am interested in a notion of Ifa that predates division into particular religious groups and suggests the incorporation into all religions of the cultural attitudes of African people. Because of the constant and many similarities between the various traditional African religions and the reality that the African, African American, and Caribbean ancestors came from various parts of Africa, I define Ifa as the *Indigenized Faith Systems of Africa*.[2] While there are differences between the various traditional religions, these differences are based upon differing languages, perceptions of Spirit, and realities. For example, the thunder deity, known as Shango in Yoruba, is identified in Dahomey as Hevioso, whose colors are red and blue and whose number is 7, whereas for Shango the colors are red and white, and the number is 6. I have chosen to use the Yoruba terminology because it is the most familiar, not to assign a preference or primacy.

The incorporation of many aspects of the oral tradition—storytelling, storytelling techniques, call and response, myths, folktales, legends, passed-down truths and superstitions, circumlocution, improvisation, signifying, stories within stories, allusion, polymetrics, polyrhythms, syncopation—a significant component of the African worldview, evidences the far-reaching and profound influence that the Ifa paradigm will help explain. Additionally, there is often the inclusion of and reference to aspects of Ifa—deities, ancestors, ritual, conjuring, divination, dreams, colors, numbers. Colors, for example, often shape dominant images in African American and Caribbean writers' texts. The properties of these colors as interpreted by traditional African religion are utilized because notions about them are prevalent in the society. It must be noted that in Ifa cosmology, one might, for example, refer to Shango through the colors of red and white. Numbers also are of special significance literature. In many religions there is some association, for example, with the numbers 3 and 7. Like other spiritual systems, Ifa has particular roles for numbers. That writers utilize, for example, numbers 3 and 7 in their texts to suggest particular ideas in a symbolic way, may suggest a reference to Eshu and Shango. Like colors and numbers, particular symbols play a major role in the progression of theme and plot. In African diasporic texts, we see the symbolic use of apples, honey, brass, dogs, drums, water, fire, woods, recipes, spells, dances, mountains, crossroads, birds, cemeteries, iron, steel, herbs, plants, the deceased, spirits, wind, thunder, lightening, snakes, dreams, all of which are representative of various deities and the ancestors. Additionally, in the Indigenized Faith Systems of Africa, deities are usually associated with specific characteristics and personality traits. Characters presented in the texts evince, through choice of color and/or particular attitudes, characteristics of various deities. Shango, for example, is described as fiery-tempered, intensely masculine, strong, arrogant, eloquent, passionate, a warrior, and master strategist. Children of a particular deity, then, exhibit the personality and character traits of that deity. The characteristics of these deities may well have an impact on their use in literature.

An Application of the Ifa Paradigm to Tina McElroy Ansa's *Baby of the Family*

Tina McElroy Ansa's first novel, *Baby of the Family*, tells the story of Lena McPherson, the baby of the family. Born with a caul over her face, Lena, the novel's protagonist, is a special child, intimately connected to the spirit world. When the essential rituals having to do with her caul—she was to drink caul tea and keep her caul—to protect her are broken and not performed, Lena is somewhat disconnected from the spirit world and is sentenced to a lifetime of craziness and aloneness. But because of her innate connection to the spirit world, Lena is sent five guides, some of the physical world and some of the spirit world, to help and sustain her. Of the five, there are three who are most pivotal—the ghost Rachel, Mamie the hairdresser, and Lena's newly deceased grandmother's spirit.

Lena's birth in an all-black hospital in Mulberry, GA, is treated with a spiritual reverence normally absent from a facility dedicated to science. Recognizing the profound significance of such a birth, the usually gruff Dr. Williams foregoes his normal delivery-room procedure and "turned the next two minutes into a ritualized dance that had nothing to do with modern medicine" (Ansa 5). Lena's caul—"a gift from God" (16)—is a sure sign that she has been chosen by "God as a special person on this earth. She can't hardly help but do something great in this life because God has touched her in the womb" (16–17). As Nurse Bloom, the midwife who assisted in the birth, tells Nellie, Lena's mother, " 'That caul she [Lena] was born with over her face' " is a " 'sign that your little girl got a link with all kinds of things, all kinds of powers that the rest of us ordinary folks don't have' " (27).

As a midwife, Nurse Bloom knows just what to do; she begins the necessary rituals to "blind" Lena from seeing all kinds of ghosts, bad spirits that would terrorize her, who will often "look like death itself [...] that don't have any heads or any feet, or their heads [...] turned around on their shoulders" (29). She makes a tea from the caul and dries the caul so that Nellie can save it for Lena until her sixteenth birthday. However, Nellie, the "modern new mother," refuses to give Lena the tea; she pours it out and later burns the caul.

By refusing to complete the ritual, Nellie sentences her "special" daughter to a lifetime of alienation, aloneness, ghost visitations, strange voices, sleepwalking, and truly believing that she is crazy. That such devastating consequences ensue because of the broken ritual evidences the significance Ansa attaches to ritual and the connection of ritual to spirituality and African people's spiritual health. While the broken ritual breaks Lena's connection to the Spirit world, she is still intimately connected with that world by virtue of her birth. She has, however, lost the complete protection the ritual would have afforded her. Because Nellie keeps Lena away from Nurse Bloom, the only person who could illuminate Lena's experiences, Lena doesn't realize that she is always in the presence and protection of Spirit via the guides.

Ansa's text is a testament to a spirituality that often goes unnoted by scholars and literary critics because it is grounded in the ritual of everyday living, of living life, of dancing, of cooking, of singing, of walking, of stories and passed down stories, recipes, traditions, culture, customs, and ways of looking at the world and living in the world the best way black folks know how. With its emphasis on ritual, recognition of deity, and ancestral spirit, Ansa's *Baby of the Family* easily lends itself to an application of the Ifa Paradigm.

Ansa consciously wrote this novel as a way of reconnecting with African cultural traditions. Remembering the ghost stories, whose purpose was to teach lessons about morality, respect for others, and good behavior, told to her by elder family members at night and at family reunions, Ansa includes ghosts in the novel to reclaim a vital part of that cultural tradition from Hollywood's "bug-eyed, feet don't fail me now" portrayal of ghosts (Ansa Interview, March 8, 2002). The novel, however, is not just about ghosts. It is also about ritual, a central component of Ifa and the African diasporic community; ritual is the community's link to the Spirit world. *Baby of the Family* teems with rituals that affirm black life and (wo)man's connection with Spirit. By telling a story about a girl born with a caul, and who is intimately connected to the spirit world, who sees ghosts, who is visited by spirits, including her deceased grandmother, who puts magic on things, and who is born into a family for whom ritual reigns supreme, Ansa reconnects with African cultural traditions; she celebrates those traditions in *Baby of the Family.*

Steeped in the rituals of everyday living, of passed down traditions, beliefs, myths, and customs, in the world of spirits and the ancestors, and Deity, Ansa's semi-autobiographical novel is an intensely spiritual work. The story's use of symbolic language invites consideration of the cultural traditions at work. It is Ansa's descriptive use of language and ritual that suggest African cultural traditions. Although written in "standard" English, the novel embodies many aspects of the African oral tradition—stories, testimonies, song and dance, call and response, and proverbs. Conversation is considered an essential art in the McPherson household. Mamie teaches Lena the art of asking questions and ferreting information without appearing to do so. Rachel shares with Lena her story of enslavement, dreams, and desires, inspiring Lena to share her story as well.

Significant to traditional African culture is ritual, the "most ancient way of binding a community together in a close relationship with Spirit" (Some 141). It is through the various rituals of everyday living—cooking, walking, dancing, communing, communicating, marrying, burying—that one witnesses the fluidity of movement between binary worlds of sacred and secular, profane and spiritual, born and unborn within the African diasporic community. The ritual of everyday living is nurtured and exalted throughout the McPherson household, with the exception being Nellie's complete disregard for ritual concerning the caul. Jonah, head of the McPherson household, stresses the ritual of conversation as an essential art: "'Hell [...] knowing how to make conversation at the dinner table is one of the most important things you'll ever learn to do'" (Ansa 108). The ritual of hearing her family say the magic words "'Hold the baby' spoken just so, made Lena feel safe and warm and looked-after" (53). Lizzie McPherson, Jonah's mother, upholds the rituals of old wives' tales and old folks' ways; to cure Edward's stuttering, she "raised her hand from the bed and hit him square in the mouth with a fat greasy piece of raw meat..." (109) and "stood back looking satisfied" (109), and she believes, prophetically, "'Baby, a bird in the house is a sure sign that there's gonna be a death in the family'" (243). She dies that same evening.

Ritual also abounds in The Place, the McPherson's liquor store, bar, and grill. Each ritual connects the folks in some way to the Spirit world. The ritual of "Fight, fight" (121) would occur at regular intervals and then "like a summer rain shower, it would be over, dwindling like mist [...]. And like a quick rainfall it would leave The Place cleaned and refreshed" (121). The ritual of call and response is performed each time people hear their favorite song. There we witness the fluid blending of sacred and secular as folks spiritually connect with their favorite rhythm and blues song as if they were in church responding to an old hymn or preacher's sermon: "[W]hen your record, the one that came closest to saying what you felt came on the jukebox [...] it was customary for you to stop in your tracks, bow your head, close your eyes, raise your right hand in the air above your head, stomp your foot, and command the entire place, 'Be quiet, will you. That's my *song*. Lord. Lord. Lord' " (125).

The novel's central characters can be read as manifestations of deity and ancestral presence. Rachel is child of Yemonja and Yemonja incarnate. As Lena's hairdresser, Mamie represents Lena's personal Eshu-Legba, and Miss Lizzie, Lena's dead grandmother, having transitioned to the other side of life and become an ancestor, learns of the broken rituals and Lena's troubled life and returns to offer Lena encouragement and instructions on what to do to salvage her chaotic life.

Rachel, the ghost of a slave, who visits Lena in a dream and directs Lena to meet with her on the beach, could be analyzed as a representative of Yemonja, the personification of motherhood. As deity of the ocean, the largest environment for life on earth, Yemonja is the "womb for the generation of life. [...] She incubates life in her womb and provides the conditions through which sperm and egg come together and be transformed" (Mason 66). She is also seen as the cradle for life, with her tides representing her motherly effort to rock the cradle of her children who live in her womb (66). It is in this role that Yemonja is personified in Ansa's novel. That both Rachel and Lena have a special connection to the water and are comforted by it suggests Yemonja as their spiritual mother who comforts and provides solace for each, although in different ways. Yemonja embraces Rachel and cradles her in her womb; for Lena, she assumes human form through Rachel's ghost to cradle Lena through her words and lesson.

Lena's birth veil, a thin white membrane, the leftover part of the birthing process, that covers her head when she is born, bears witness to her spiritual connection to Yemonja. Its color is that of the froth that tops the waves. Lena's immediate connection with the beach further evidences a spiritual connection. She loves everything about the beach: "the way the gulls and pelicans squawked and swooped about her, the way the air cooled the closer she got to the water, the salt she tasted on her lips when she licked them, the way the sea oats swayed gently in the ocean breeze, the tiny sanderlings scurrying away from the surf. [...] She felt that she somehow belonged there at the shore, even though it was her first time ever seeing the ocean" (Ansa 152). The way Lena and Rachel connect and commune also evidences their spiritual kinship to Yemonja.

Having long decided that she couldn't wait to grow up, leave home, and finally get the psychological help she knows she desperately needs, Lena earnestly believes that she does not belong in Mulberry: "[Lena] had finally come to the conclusion that she was crazy, truly crazy. [...] She just prayed that she could hold on and not do anything too bizarre—not walk the streets talking and arguing [...]—until she finished college, got a job, and could pay for some professional help" (241). While Lena has had a beautiful childhood—everyone loves her, recognizes her "special"ness, and treats her special; she "could put magic on just about anything: a radio, the television, a stuck door [...]. Her magic was sometimes only temporary, but it nearly always worked for a time" (53)—Lena has also had a tortuous childhood.

She sees evil spirits that torment her, and having seen so many ghosts, Lena never knows if a person is real or is a ghost; strange voices come out of her mouth. The one time Lena tries to tell her family about an almost-fatal ghost encounter, her body is racked by convulsions and thrashes about horribly. She remembers the vomiting, the fits, the sickness and never tells anyone of her many ghost visitations; thus she suffers in silent pain and terror.

These experiences leave Lena feeling alienated, alone, and not belonging anywhere. To provide some comfort to Lena, the Spirit sends Rachel and directs Lena to Rachel:

> Lena was looking for a particular place just a little farther down the beach, where the big rocks that lined part of the coast formed a low overhanging fac-ing the ocean. At that spot, she was sure, there was a curve in the beach that created a protected little cove [...]. She had dreamed about that very spot the night before as she slept with the smell of the sea in her throat. (156)

When Lena sees Rachel, Lena notices "there was something familiar about the way the woman sat there" (157).

Rachel's story serves to give Lena an anchor and teaches her that she belongs anywhere she wants to be. Having been sent by Yemonja or being Yemonja incarnate, Rachel has been waiting on the beach for Lena " 'so [she] can tell [her] all of this, so I can share some of this' " (164), and she tells her not to be scared of her because "[a] child like you [...] gonna see a heap more like me before you dead, too' " (158). It is through her story and her profound connection to the ocean that we identify Rachel as perhaps being a child of Yemonja. Rachel smells like "something out the ocean: salty and wet all the way through, and her skin was scratchy with grains of sand" (158), and that ocean smell—"salty, fishy, alive, green—" (168)—was strong on Rachel.

Seeking to escape the brutal realities of slavery, if only temporarily, Rachel comes to the ocean. She was so connected to the water, repeated whippings couldn't keep Rachel away from it. She recalls,

> They beat me [...] bad too. But I come back. I had to breathe this air. I had to let it play with my skin. Shoo things out of my body. [...] Sitting down chere at the ocean made me feel loved a little. There was something about the ocean that just kept drawing me chere, just tolling me to chere. It asked me questions that just tore my heart. Questions I couldn't answer, but I couldn't stay 'way from chere neither. (161–162)

Like Rachel, Lena can hear the ocean talking; she tells Rachel, " 'Late last night [...] I heard the ocean talking, too' " (162). Spiritual sisters, Rachel recognizes a kindred spirit in Lena: " '[Y]ou the onliest one I ever talked to. You special, Lena' " (167). She knows Lena's thoughts and answers all of Lena's unasked questions. Feeling Lena's pain and desire to not hear this herstory, "Rachel just looked at the child's big brown eyes welling up with tears and slipped inside her thoughts again" (164).

Yemonja, the eternal mother, communes with her children, providing balm and solace for their pains. She " 'sung songs to [Rachel] of what I coulda been if I warn't no slave' " (162). Longing to have serenity, to be one with the ocean always, to always be free to experience the love and nurturing she found in the water, Rachel decides she's not going back to the plantation. And she tells Lena, " 'I just sat there listening to the ocean, to what she had to say to me 'bout what coulda been. [...]' " (166). For Rachel, to be a slave was bad enough, but to be a slave " 'on the ocean, I could not bear it' " (163). So she remains on the beach, ignores the threats of her slave master, and waits for the tide to swallow her up: " '[...] I was glad to be going. I was going to the ocean and couldn't nobody ever stop me from going there again. I been chere ever since [...]' " (167). That Rachel finds so much peace and solace at and in the water evidences her spiritual connection with Yemonja. As Rachel's spiritual mother, Yemonja's motherly embrace brings her back to her womb as her tides gently rock Rachel to an eternal peace.

Rachel shares her slavery experiences with Lena:

> I seen folks—womens, mens—beat till the blood run down they feets and stand in puddles in they brogan boots. [...] Where I was born [...] they beat you through your clothes [...] but down here where I was they strip you mothernaked like you ain't got no decents, then they whips you. (163)

Lena learns of others' pain, pains more horrible than any reality she knows or experiences. Connected to Rachel, Lena now wants to share something with Rachel, and that is Grandmama's belief that "colored folks don't belong on the beach" (167). However, this is also very much Lena's fear—that she, too, does not belong anywhere. But Rachel, or perhaps Yemonja herself, speaks right into "Lena's mouth. 'Don't never believe black folks don't belong nowhere. Don't be afraid, Lena. Claim what is yours. I died to be here on this beach, Lena. [...] You belong anywhere on this earth you want to' " (168). She learns the lesson and tells her brothers emphatically, " 'I belong anywhere on this earth I want to be' " (170).

Rachel and Lena's meeting is mutually beneficial. They each give what the other needs. This give and take is a pivotal concept in Ifa cosmology, which has at its core the principles of balance and reciprocity essential for the maintenance of balance and harmony between and within spiritual and physical planes. Therefore, when one's prayer is answered, an ebo (offering/sacrifice) must be made to replace that which has been given; giving and taking, taking and giving, is the proper order of things. Rachel's story teaches Lena a pivotal lesson. Lena, in turn, gives Rachel some joy and laughter.

After hearing Rachel's heart wrenching story, Lena, sobbing almost hysterically, is overtaken by a wave when she's not looking, "covering her face and head, going up her nose, and putting a salty taste in her throat" (170). This experience makes Rachel's story all the more real for Lena because she now has some idea of how Rachel felt as the waves drowned her: "[Lena] had to fight a panicky feeling that she knew must have been like the one Rachel felt when the tide came in and she was tied underwater to that tree" (170). Scared, spitting, sputtering, with her heart racing and eyes stinging, Lena presents an incredibly funny picture to her brothers, who are laughing at her. Just as she is about to angrily admonish them for their insensitivity, Lena sees a smile on Rachel's "leathery face" (171) as she throws back her head in laughter, "showing her throat and teeth" (170). Not sure of what she feels seeing Rachel laugh, Lena ducks back into the next oncoming wave; under water, Lena hears Rachel's laughter: "The ocean rushing into her ears filled her head with salty water, grains of sand, and what Lena knew had to be the sound of Rachel's laughter" (170). Rachel gives Lena words of comfort to remember and live by; Lena gives Rachel the long-awaited ear and laughter.

Although Lena never sees Rachel again, she remembers her during two critical junctures in her life. After Lena begins sleepwalking, she wakes up in the middle of the night and discovers that she is in the middle of the woods; Lena cries without restraint, distraught, and devastated. She prays to God: "Oh, God, help me, help me" (236). Yemonja hears her pleas and sends to Lena the memory of Rachel to help her "get ovah." Lena finds her way home and upon shifting in bed, her gritty feet rub together, like sandpaper: "The fine grains of sand on her damp feet, [...] put Lena in mind of the watery woman whose skin and clothes felt rough and scratchy when she rubbed against her" (237). Lena remembers Rachel's lesson—she belonged anywhere. However, because "all [Lena's] terrors, the sleepwalking, her childhood memories of ghosts, her skewed premonitions [...] all the things that had frightened and haunted her all her life" (238) were connected to Mulberry, Lena, at that moment, feels she can't trust anybody, not even Rachel.

Lena's lesson not fully complete, Yemonja, with the aid of Oya, deity of wind and guardian of the cemetery, comes back into Lena's life once again to provide solace. When Lena's deceased Grandmama's spirit comes back and takes her to where her caul was burned, Lena was reminded of Rachel again. Oya accompanies Miss Lizzie's spirit back to earth. As Miss Lizzie and Lena stand at the place where Nellie burned her caul, Lena feels as if a storm were brewing in the pit of her stomach and suddenly "gusts of wind set the woods across the stream dancing and swaying in the moonlight" (264). Hand in hand with Yemonja, the wind "seemed to collect itself, whiz over the stream, and whistle around Lena, lifting her gown and robe above her waist. The gust of wind eddied up her body. As it blew past her face, Lena noticed a scent she hadn't smelled in nearly a decade [...] the raw briny smell of the ocean" (264). Yemonja wants Lena to remember Rachel's lesson—she belongs anywhere, and she has to, like Rachel, "claim what is yours"(264). Lena can't run away from her birthright; she has to accept it as a gift, learn how to use it, and make peace with it.

The next guide sent by Spirit to Lena is Mamie, the hairdresser. Mamie could represent Lena's personal Eshu-Legba. As the deity of the crossroads, Eshu has as his domain questions, choices, and decisions. Whenever one questions or has to make decisions and choices, s/he is at a crossroad and should ask Eshu for clarity, that one might make the right decision. Eshu is also considered the messenger for Spirit, and as such Eshu is regarded as the deity of communication. Because Eshu represents the crossroad, Eshu is also associated with travel. Before embarking upon any journey, it is to Eshu that one would pray for a safe and uneventful journey, so as not to take a wrong turn. Mamie provides all of this to Lena. Mamie is, first of all, the messenger for Spirit, recognizable through Lena and Mamie's ritual of communication. In teaching Lena "the private joy of discovering" (188), Mamie teaches Lena how to question, how to ferret information. This lesson is pivotal since ultimately it is Lena's responsibility to learn the significance of her caul. As she travels toward self-discovery, Lena needs Eshu's assistance so that she won't get off track, that she might achieve her spiritual and physical destiny.

Lena feels drawn to Mamie as much as she felt drawn to Rachel. She recognizes something in Mamie's eyes: "with flecks of gold sparkling in them, [they] were alive with something that Lena did not immediately recognize but knew that she admired" (180). Mamie's face, "wide-open [with] radiance [...] pure, clean beauty [...] untouched by any flaw" (183), was one that "beckoned response" (182). As deity of the crossroads, Eshu is intimately connected with earth. To Lena, Mamie smelled like "the dirt outside her home when a sudden thunderstorm hit the dust and the aroma of the earth rose up all over the neighborhood" (183).

Significantly, Mamie does Lena's hair for three years, the number attached to Eshu. Also, Lena's "shoulder-length nappy" (133) hair is red, one of Eshu's colors. As the messenger deity it is appropriate that Eshu be connected to Lena through her hair, for hair serves as a conduit for electrical current. The body operates on electrical current, with the brain sending electrical impulses/commands throughout the body. The tight coil of African hair, also described as kinky and/or knotty, serves as the perfect conduit for electrical current. Lena's "long thick wiry hair" (132) has been a bane to her and Nellie's existence, ever since her birth, "when she had come into the world with a head full of tight bright curls, soft and thick like the wool on a baby lamb" (133). Mamie, as Lena's Eshu, knows how to handle Lena's hair without hurting her. As Mamie washes and straightens Lena's hair, she, unlike all of the previous hairdressers, never hurts Lena's head; instead, "she maneuvered it like a woman washing a big bath towel by hand," (185), not delicately like Nellie, for each time Nellie tried to "wash, comb out, and straighten the girl's long wild hair at the kitchen stove, the attempt had ended in misery" (175). Lena's hair, which became "thicker and more tangled" the older Lena became, symbolizes her growing disconnection from the spirit world because of the broken rituals and her need to communicate with Spirit. With Mamie, however, Lena learns the art of communication, a lesson that will serve Lena well on her journey to self-discovery and Spirit.

Mamie's lesson to Lena is how to ask questions, to learn things about people as well as herself. Mamie explains, " 'What's been important to me is the whys of things. And you can't be learning through no books. No, indeed not. That's the kind of knowledge has to be learned through people, through finding out things about them'" (184). This explanation underscores the lesson Lena learns from ghost Rachel and her personal story of slavery. What Mamie gives to Lena is the "gift of curiosity. [Mamie] let drop the germ in Lena that grew to the desire, the yearning, the obsession to know and understand her world" (183). Mamie teaches Lena how to learn: " 'You just keep asking and asking and digging and searching. When you find out things about folks, you find out things 'bout life, you find out things 'bout yourself' " (184). Significantly, Mamie teaches Lena to think critically and to analyze, a particularly important skill:

> Mamie made Lena think about herself, her family, her schoolmates, her looks, her dislikes, the things that made her sad, angry, joyful, tearful, confused. Mamie showed her how to delve into all these things with a question and come up to the surface with answers that somehow soothed and excited her at the same time. (186)

Each appointment "became a couple hours of instruction in 'questions.' It all began with a question" (182). Lena soon began taking part in "their ritual, [...] repeating an old wives' tale just for the sake of tearing it apart to look for truth" (188). Lena has to learn to discern what is real and unreal, true or untrue. This lesson is pivotal in Lena's journey toward self-acceptance and reconciliation, a journey full of crossroads, choices, and decisions. Mamie's lesson prepares her for a journey she doesn't know she's about to take.

Mamie and Lena are as connected to one another as Lena and Rachel were. They communicate silently and so naturally that no one in the salon notices their conversation; each time they meet, like "two old women on a porch" (184), they slip "comfortably into whatever space the end of the girl's last appointment had led them two weeks earlier" (184).

As the physical manifestation of Lena's Eshu, Mamie is tuned into Lena's thoughts and actions. She sees Lena's aborted gesture to touch her face and winks at Lena with a "conspiratorial grin" (182). Mamie's wink and grin capture the energy of Eshu, which is often characterized as mischievous and playful. So attuned to Lena's emotions, Mamie knows immediately when Lena's scalp tenses, and she "lean[s] forward and look[s] directly into the girl's upside down face [...]" (185). When Lena leaves the shop to "reenter her own life, she took with her a piece of Mamie, the questioning part" (188). Lena instinctively knows that Mamie is a gift from God. Happy with this gift, Lena, with much difficulty, restrains herself from standing up in the beauty salon and testifying, "Yes, Lord, thank you, Jesus. You saw what your child cried for and you answered her prayer. Thank you, Lord Jesus" (189).

The final guide sent to Lena is her newly deceased grandmother's spirit that comes back as an ancestral spirit to remind Lena of Rachel's lesson—she has to claim what is hers. Having transitioned to the other side of life, Miss Lizzie learns of the broken ritual and of all the pain and suffering Lena has endured in silence: " 'Oh, baby, baby, Grandma so sorry,' the spirit said over and over.[...] 'I shoulda known better. If I'da been any kind of grandmama, I would of known something was wrong' " (260).

After Grandmama's funeral, Lena waits for her spirit to come: "Whether she was crazy or not, she knew that she did see things, real or otherwise. And if she could see all these other dead people—a slave on the beach, her infant aunt in the picture—then she damn well ought to be able to see her beloved grandmama" (258). Lena just wants her Grandmama back, "dead or alive" (260). When Lena is jostled awake by her Grandmama's spirit, she immediately recognizes her frantic desire to tell her something.

Grandmama's spirit hastens to reassure Lena that she has never been alone, that there has " 'always been somebody, dead or alive, trying to help you' " (260). She recalls for Lena the various guides sent to Lena by Spirit: " '[...] your friends Sarah and Gwen[.] Didn't you have Mamie all to yourself for more than three years? What would you have done without [...] Frank Petersen? Baby, you wasn't never really alone. And you shore ain't alone now' " (260).

In taking Lena to the spot where Nellie burned Lena's caul, Grandmama's spirit provides the background information that Lena needed to prove that she wasn't crazy. Grandmama's spirit reveals to Lena,

[Nellie] disrupted two rituals, Lena, that you were lucky to even be connected with. They would have helped you in living the kind of life a child like you should have lived. If you had drunk that tea, baby, it would have weakened those scary spirits. Instead, you been scared of what you should have understood. (262)

But most importantly, Grandmama's spirit tells Lena that she has the " 'power to do something with [her] craziness' " (263). She chastises Lena for wanting to rid herself of her gift from God, reminding her of what her gift is and its possibilities: " 'What if your powers can heal people? Don't you remember how you could put the magic on stuff? Or, baby, what if your craziness can just bring some succor to some tortured soul [in much the way sharing her story with Lena brings Rachel]?' " (263). To prove her point, she reminds Lena of all the "roustabouts" at the Place who "seek you out to tell you some little ole thing 'bout their lives, just to share it with you. Don't you think that means something?' " (263).

Grandmama's spirit echoes all of the lessons Lena has been taught by each of the previous guides sent to her. Lena "is special" (167) and has much work to do "over on this side. That's what you were made for. That's why you had that veil over your face when you was born. That was a sign of the things you can do, things you can be' " (263). Having shared with Lena the things she's learned once on the other side, Grandmama's spirit's suggestion that Lena seek out Nurse Bloom for help concerning the broken rituals requires Mamie's lesson—how to find out the hows and whys of things. Distraught at the thought that she'll "never be normal" (264), Lena is comforted by her spiritual mother, Yemonja, as she is reminded of Rachel once again when she smells a scent she hasn't smelled in almost a decade, "the raw briny smell of the ocean" (264).

Emphasizing the notion of diaspora, African spirituality, and traditional African culture, the Ifa Paradigm has as its premise the importance of cultural specificities, a position argued so eloquently by many African American scholars, theorists, and writers. To those who apply it to their analysis of African American literary texts it offers an opportunity to extend their examination beyond the traditional theories of literary criticism. This paradigm, then, is a system by which one can evaluate the artistic endeavors of African diasporic people and one that reflects a profound understanding of their cultural specificities.

NOTES

1. I provide a fuller explanation of the Ifa Paradigm in my dissertation. Here I primarily offer an application of the Paradigm.
2. This notion of Ifa comes from Medahochi Zannu, founder and spiritual leader of the Nu Afrikan Vodun, a spiritual community that recognizes all indigenized faith systems of Africa and the diaspora. Because this perspective acknowledges the spiritual traditions and contributions of Africans and their descendents throughout the world, including the United States, this notion is of particular interest to me and crucial for the development of this paradigm. While this does not represent what is generally regarded as the connotation of Ifa, it seems to speak to a notion of religion already popular in the diaspora and one that this essay is certainly interested in promoting. It must be noted that this is a controversial idea and one that is generally opposed by spiritual leaders who hold to the idea of Ifa as belonging specifically to the Yoruba people of Nigeria. I would argue in fact that the notion of Ifa, which I put forward here, is in a sense anti-essentialist, promoting the idea that while the faith systems are influenced by African traditions, they do not have to be based in Africa to be considered authentic.

WORKS CITED

Ansa, Tina McElroy. *Baby of the Family.* New York: Harcourt Brace & Co., 1989.
———. Interview. March 8, 2002.
Bressler, Charles. *Literary Criticism: An Introduction to Theory and Practice.* New Jersey, Prentice Hall, 1994. 127–141.
Mason, John. *Black Gods—Orisha Studies in the New World.* New York: Yoruba Theological Archministry, 1985.
Smith, Theophus H. *Conjuring Culture: Biblical Formations of Black America.* New York: Oxford University Press, 1994.
Some, Malidoma Patrice. *Ritual: Power, Healing, and Community.* Oregon: Swan/'Raven & Co, 1993.
Wilson, August. "The Ground On Which I Stand." *Callaloo* 20 (1998): 493–503.
Zannu, Medahochi Kofi O. Interview. January 24, 1996.

5

Just 'Cause (or Just Cause): On August Wilson's Case for a Black Theater

John Valery White

... it is difficult to disassociate my concerns with theatre from the concerns of my life as a black man ...

August Wilson, American Theatre, *Sept. 1996*

August Wilson is a black playwright. This fact animates his eloquent defense of the black theater and funding, therefore, his "just" cause. He is *not* a playwright who happens to be black. This fact prompts him to expose and attack theater critic Robert Brustein's neoconservative assault on funding of the black theater. That Wilson is a black playwright seems to lead him, curiously, to denying the existence, legitimacy, and authenticity of playwrights who happen to be black. This aspect of Wilson's speech to the Theater Communications Group takes Wilson on a quest for authentic blackness, a pursuit he ironically shares with Brustein. In their ensuing debate, Wilson and Brustein vie for the critical authority to define authentic blackness, both speaking the anachronistic language of separation and assimilation. This language impoverishes the critical debate over the future of the American theater and the role of the black theater in that future. Thus Wilson's speech, perhaps well received as a typical progressive defense against a neoconservative assault on blackness, distorts the very goal of advancing the black theater, as such. Wilson is trapped into arguing with Brustein over whether there should be a black theater rather than whether there can be an American theater without blackness. In anticipating Brustein's questioning of the need for a black theater, could not Wilson have said, "just 'cause"?

August Wilson cries out for a revitalized black theater. However, throughout his speech he can be heard proclaiming and promoting allegiance to an *authentic* blackness to reside at and to be portrayed by those theaters. This authenticity-seeking project, a project that Wilson would undoubtedly disavow, confuses his otherwise biting critique of the state of the black theater. It also frames his anachronistic debate with Brustein, a debate characterized by the road-worn and muddled binary choice posed for black people in the post–Jim Crow world. Should black people assimilate or separate; should integration or nationalism guide black art (and politics, and life); they bicker.

This debate is tired and misplaced. More importantly, it distorts Wilson's critique of the problems facing the black theater. The choice presented by their debate is false blackness in America, a distinct and fully integrated aspect of American life, simply *is*. This fact animates the basis for Wilson's speech and highlights why his approach to the problem is unsatisfying: black artists must contend with the personal and social implications of blackness in America and profit little from the abstract, ideal types of the assimilation/separation frame. In the end, the frame only commits Wilson to an indefensible, if tacit claim, that there exists an authentic blackness to be promoted and defended, even as it prompts Brustein's paternalistic (and also tacit) suggestion that blackness is an aberrant construct created or preserved by black people in order to maintain a sense of Jim Crow–based victim-hood, but which, in the absence of Jim Crow, no longer rightly exists. Thus Wilson voluntarily engages Brustein's trap, arguing with him over whether blackness exists, rather than debating, as he seems to wish, the role of blackness in constructing *an* American theater.

THE PROBLEMATIC OF BLACKNESS

Blackness in America requires neither justification nor preservation. Blackness is not unAmerican (as Brustein implies); it is quintessentially American. At the same time, black particularity, a product of historical *and* continuing segregation, is not a good to be preserved; rather, it is a status that is no more or less justified than the quality of lives lived under segregation. Blackness is an ever-present and urgent dilemma for the black artist. Wilson's speech is properly rooted in and reflects this dilemma. For black artists, blackness is a personal state with which each artist must contend, working out blackness, even defining their version of it in their art. The "transcendence" of blackness is among the choices presented them, but it is not, as Brustein arrogantly suggests, their sole legitimate response. The black artist might exaggerate her blackness, or ascribe it a metaphysical status, or, concentrating blackness into a personal issue alone, nihilistically usurp blackness as her own, to be used, manipulated, and transcended as needed or desired.

But the personal aspect of blackness is not all that confronts the black artist. The black artist must also contend with the social aspects of blackness. One need not recognize the personal as the political to have to work out the political implications of the socially constructed identity that is imposed on one's work. From Morgan Freeman to Tiger Woods to Steven Carter, black artists, athletes, and academics struggle against the rubric of the "best black," even as they seek to exert control over their racial definitions. None wants to be remembered as a good *black* actor, athlete, or neoconservative scholar. They each seek, instead, to be the best actor, athlete, and scholar. Despite their efforts, they remain defined by the socially constructed categories into which they are fit. That is to say, while denial of the social implications of blackness remains a *strategy* for reconciling both the personal and social aspects of blackness, one must nevertheless address both. In art, where self-expression is the means of achieving the end of universal understanding, blackness is a constant shadow, supplying a parallel, alternative meaning to self-definition and projecting an independent social message. In this context, just being an artist is as difficult as just being black.

Focusing on his own influences, Wilson accurately reflects the dilemma of the black artist. While Wilson notes his place in the Western and American traditions, he highlights that he *found* himself in the inspiring Black Protest Tradition. Through the Black Power Movement his quest for "something to which to dedicate [his] life" brought him to an overt, personal struggle with the limitations of blackness. Wilson's struggle was also social, however, as it imposed on him a duty to participate as a descendent of slaves, "to alter [his] relationship to the society in which [his ancestors had] lived." Wilson's speech emphasizes the dual aspect of this existence not as a double-consciousness but as a tension between personal identity and social existence. For Wilson, the two merge: his personal mission was to participate in a movement that was "searching for ways to alter the shared expectations of ... [black people] as a community of people." Wilson thus powerfully voices the challenge of blackness.

In his response to Wilson's speech, theater critic, Robert Brustein, shows contempt for this dilemma of blackness. Like many contemporary neoconservatives, Brustein dismisses this dilemma. He myopically sees assimilation as the only legitimate response to the problematic of blackness. Thus the only personal resolution Brustein contemplates for the black artist is the "transcendence" of blackness; the only social resolution he envisions is to recast black social problems as unrelated to race. Brustein implies that other approaches to race are illegitimate; like those who see the use of the "race card" everywhere, Brustein's approach is inherently suspicious of any role for race in social policy debates. While transcendence of race is among the possible legitimate responses to blackness, insistence on it as the only legitimate response deprives black people of the agency to confront blackness on their own terms.

In his speech Wilson seems to sense this aspect of Brustein's critique of LORT funding. However, his response fails; it revels in nostalgia, stylizes Africanisms to supplement black "culture," and, ultimately, reifies certain personal and social responses to blackness as *the proper* responses to blackness. This is typical of progressive responses to the neoconservative assault on affirmative action and civil rights. In the end it fails as a defense against the neoconservative assault, and its conception of a *true* blackness proves empty, as it must.

Authentic Blackness and the Paradox of the Demise of Jim Crow

The dilemma of blackness that animates Wilson's speech is magnified by the paradox of the end of Jim Crow: the demise of *de jure* segregation and the overwhelming overt discrimination that accompanied it has freed black people (and black artists in particular) to *actualize* their humanity, to *define* their own personal blackness, even as it is Jim Crow's formal system of segregation and terror that defined the basis for black social identity and made possible the always troublesome notion of black authenticity in the first.

Jim Crow denied black Americans a political identity while severely circumscribing black social identity. Magnifying freedmen's recently shorn badges of slavery, Jim Crow *defined* black identity: black people were regarded and treated as though less than human and excluded from the normal political processes available to citizens. Black people thus forged their identities in response to and under the pressure of these limitations. Jim Crow's demise brought an end to *de jure* segregation and overt racial terror, along with an abandonment of the biological claims of black inferiority. But the end of formal segregation, overt terror, and biological theories of black inferiority has not meant an end to segregation, terror, and theories of black inferiority. Persistent segregation, inequality, and racial terror echo their formal antecedents. Blackness thus persists but has become a problematic. As blackness itself cannot be defined apart from the social grounds for its construction, the demise of the formal basis of those social grounds undercuts the authenticity of blackness itself. But blackness is much more than an echo of the Jim Crow past: it continues to constitute genuine lived experience.[1] Blackness is real in this sense, but it is unreal, in that its formal and scientific bases have been abandoned. Authentic blackness, dependent on abandoned formal and (misplaced) scientific bases, is an impossibility in the post–Jim Crow world. But blackness nevertheless exists for black people who must work out its personal and social consequences.

Wilson negotiates this treacherous paradox by emphasizing the very authenticity that is revealed to be impossible in the post–Jim Crow World. Though Wilson claims to speak only for himself, he trots out the tired "house slave/field slave" distinction to frame true blackness. This frame, although attractive in various ways, proves to be without content. First, empirical study of slave records shows that the general notion that there existed a class of slaves given house duties is not characteristic of the actual plantation distribution of labor. (Rather house slave duty was likely an additional assignment or the assignment of a very young slave prior to working in the fields or an infirm slave at the end of a long period of field service; see Fogel and Engerman, 1974, at 220–221.) The house slave/field slave frame, popularized during the Black Power period, is best understood as an attack against the color caste and class dimensions that had come to dominate intrablack relations during the Jim Crow period. Even as a metaphor for a color cast aristocracy, the house slave/field slave frame is troublesome (Fogel and Engerman summarize studies that show some preference in awarding plum jobs to light-skinned slaves in the Caribbean, but this effect is much weaker in studies of Louisiana; and, in any case, the vast majority of skilled slaves were dark-skinned, and the vast majority of light-skinned slaves were field hands; Fogel and Engerman, 1989, at 47–49). The black aristocracy that emerged in Jim Crow laid claim to the "race spokesman" model that took the place of participatory politics (see Reed 18–28). That aristocracy was popularly regarded as a color caste open only to light-skinned black people, although the topic has been subject to little study. (See, however, Graham.) The house slave symbol, associated with self-appointed, light-skinned race spokesman, came to represent race betrayal; the house slave was the "Uncle Tom," sabotaging black liberation in exchange for individual aggrandizement.

The house slave rubric is a trap, however. It defines betrayal in a circular fashion. There is no content to the accusation: a Tom is a Tom; one knows a Tom when he sees a Tom. Apart from the assumed betrayal, it cannot be said what are the characteristics of Tom-ism. Moreover, the notion of a Tom assumes a black authenticity that the Tom betrays. Like other epithets, the accusation of race betrayal is the resort of someone who has little more to say of his subject than to express his disdain. As amply displayed during the Clarence Thomas Supreme Court confirmation hearings, the resort to accusations of race betrayal also has the unsavory effect of obscuring any actual substantive critique.[2] Wilson's use of this frame thus eventually confuses the substantive critique he hopes to advance.

The house slave/field slave distinction also introduces the assimilation/separation distinction that dogs Wilson's critique. The choice is false. What Wilson seems to want to say is that it is important to support the development of black art because it is American art. Assimilation and separation are superfluous to this fact. Blackness is a fact of American life that cannot be transcended by even the collective efforts of extraordinary people. Assimilation (or transcendence) is at best one of several *individual* strategies a black *person* might employ in his confrontation with blackness. A black artist, intent on working out the personal and social dimensions of blackness, might as easily celebrate blackness (as he defines it), use blackness for his own ends, elevate blackness to a metaphysical matter not of this earth, or transcend blackness to find its and his universal self. None of these responses reflects a focus on either assimilation or separation.

The trap that these distinctions present is most clear in Wilson's critique of Brustein. Wilson and Brustein become cohorts, each manifesting a different aspect of the false debate. They both expertly perform their appointed role. When Wilson alleges that black authenticity should be developed and celebrated, Brustein replies that black people are not sufficiently grateful to be Americans. Wilson's is a tacitly paternalistic approach he *implies* black authenticity; Brustein's is overtly so he *tells* black people how they should negotiate blackness to be "true" Americans. Neither is apologetic or embarrassed by his position, because neither realizes what he's doing. Brustein's argument is in accord with the recent neoconservative backlash against black America. Echoing Jim Sleeper's ridiculous claim that black Americans have snubbed America because they watched *Roots* and became obsessed with being African (Sleeper), Brustein feigns to tell black people what it means to be black. But so does Wilson. Invoking 1960s radicalism as his basis, Wilson implies that black Americana is "crossed-over," an anathema, even nonblack, requiring development of true blackness in the form of dedicated support for the development of authentic blackness in the form of theatrical funding.

The climax of Wilson's speech is incisive and compelling (Bravo!). But it is undercut by the calls for an authentic, pure form of blackness that he employs in the buildup to that climax. Wilson's bold apogee can be little improved:

> So much of what makes this country rich in art and all manners of spiritual life is the contributions that we as African Americans have made. We cannot allow others to have authority over our cultural and spiritual products. We reject, without reservation, any attempts by anyone to rewrite our history so as to deny us the rewards of our spiritual labors, and to become the cultural custodians of our art, our literature and our lives. To give expression to the spirit that has been shaped and fashioned by our history is of necessity to give voice and vent to the history itself.

It is as difficult to dispute the force of Wilson's words as to deny the contributions of black Americans to American life, art, and development. But it is as important that black artists be given agency in preserving, writing, and rewriting that history. That is, there can be no American experience that fails both to incorporate the contributions of black Americans *and* to include black Americans in the process of experience building.

All this is lost, however, in the cloud created by Wilson's preceding remarks. Wilson employs his argument for a pure, authentic blackness to attack, in turn, black productions of white plays, colorblind casting, and cultural appropriation via white productions of black works. For Wilson a (black) value system, and therefore black theater, is polluted if European-based values are included, must reflect the "contributions [of] Africans in America," and must be inclusive of all Americans and recogniz[e] their unique and valuable contributions." Not only is the first of these propositions inconsistent with the second and third, the very construct presupposes pure cultural types that limit any joint effort to a collective, nonintegrated project. This sounds like the anti-miscegenation rhetoric of the Jim Crow period. Wilson thus fashions his case for authentic blackness as a pure form and his case for the black theater as a forum for building and preserving that purity. This foreshadows the substantive arguments he then makes.

Wilson asserts, "To mount an all-black production of *Death of a Salesman* or any other play conceived for white actors as an investigation of the human condition through the specifics of white culture is to deny us our own humanity, our own history, and the need to make our own investigations from the cultural ground on which we stand as black Americans." What? While an all black production of *Death of a Salesman* set at the time Miller wrote it would be strange, given that Jim Crow specifically deprived black people the pursuit of the American Dream that Miller's play critiques, such a production set at any of various points in the post–Jim Crow period would give new and unique meaning to the play, would reveal new levels of meaning implicit in Miller's original idea. Of course, Wilson may mean only that black people playing these roles pretending to be the white people Miller's characters must have been at the time would be weird. But such an explanation only raises Wilson's argument against colorblind casting.

Wilson incorrectly equates colorblind casting with assimilation, rejecting it as an attempt to "blot us out, to reinvent history and ignore our presence or to maim our spiritual product." Perhaps Wilson is reacting to the troublesome racial cross-dressing of minstrel shows, for he seems blind to the possibilities of such casting. Why shouldn't a white actor portray a black lynch victim? The role would put tremendous pressure on the actor, director, and everyone else involved to explore the various levels of meaning in the black experience. This is not an "I don't see color" issue, as Wilson alleges. It is a "we all must address color" issue. Wilson seems to confuse subject and object: he is correct that whitewashing black theater is unacceptable, but he ignores the fact that the meaning of the black experience can and should be everyone's project. He means that the subject must be developed but reduces this to the people must be developed.

Wilson builds borders between experience. These borders thus confuse his last application of authentic blackness. Wilson takes offense to the appropriation of black artists' art by white artists who ride black contributions to fame. Wilson is correct to complain about the disproportionate value placed on the artist being white. But Wilson's bordered blackness does not allow him to fashion a means for protecting the rights of black artists and for holding white critics to task for their errors. Rather than viewing the aesthetic represented by Jerry Butler and Joe Cocker as a single one, a popular one governed as much by marketing as critique, Wilson treats it as an organic one, connected to real categories of people. His examples are all popular artists who are largely immune from critique via their massive product sales. But surely someone must sit in judgment. It is not too much to say that Michael Bolton's songs are uninspired and soul-less, that his success is a product of affirmative action for white artists and that Otis Redding was immeasurably better. Another critic may disagree, but a well-reasoned argument would itself give its due to Redding. Wilson does not suggest this because he later argues that "the true critic does not sit in judgment." Wilson seems to expect his pure-type black authenticity to be self evident, eliminating the need to judge art. Perhaps he fears the project he has nevertheless undertaken: he does not desire to argue what is good black art because he anticipates that saying what is black art is so difficult.

All of this misdirected criticism creates a static that completely distorts Wilson's otherwise powerful claims about the role of blackness in the American experience. Thus, even if one is inclined to believe that Wilson has the better argument over Brustein, Wilson's actual case for the black theater is convoluted.

Black Aesthetics and the Confounded Contemporary Discussion of Race

Wilson and his confederate, Brustein, err because, like most everyone in the post–Jim Crow era, they speak of race-infused social problems in the language of aesthetics. That is, in the post–Jim Crow world blackness is

informed by and takes the form of "the Black Aesthetic" that coalesced in
the overlapping worlds of the Black Power and Black Arts movements. As
defined by the Black Aesthetic, *blackness* is a style, a pose. One is black
because she says so; one manifests blackness by behaving black. Blackness
thus becomes an open text onto which most any narrative can be imposed.
Wilson and Brustein, like most everyone else, speak of blackness in the language of aesthetics because it seems to resolve the paradox of blackness in
the wake of Jim Crow: in locating blackness in subjective notions of identity,
the aesthetical definition avoids confronting the absence of formal bases
for the category. The disturbing circularity of this type of definition also
drives Wilson and Brustein (and most everyone else) to assert a substantive
content to blackness that is alleged to be the authentic blackness.

The form of aesthetical thinking that has come to dominate social policy
discussions of race is a general framework for understanding black artistic
and literary contributions during Jim Crow as a means of mediating black
people's relationship with that system. This frame structures the major
anthologies of black literature and provides an attractive way of understanding blackness, racial inequality, and resistance. It is, however, a fatally flawed
means of understanding identity, inequality, and mechanisms for ensuring
social justice in the post–Jim Crow world. Wilson's and Brustein's largely
unknowing use of this aesthetical approach demonstrates these limitations.

The idea of the black aesthetic that emerged in the 1960s gives an attractive rendering of black intellectual history during Jim Crow. That rendering
proceeds in four parts. The story begins, mostly by implication, with the
beginning of Jim Crow. The focus is on the image of the black people crafted
to justify Jim Crow (and the end of Reconstruction). That image has its origins in the slave period. It is symbolized by the minstrel, which captured and
broadcast the disparate characteristics of inferiority that were said to disqual-
ify black people for full membership in humanity and first-class American
citizenship. Though not always clearly stated, discussion of this period is
overwhelmed by the minstrel, by *Birth of a Nation*, and by the widespread
social, political, and personal violence inflicted on black people. Like all of
the black aesthetic, this early period is characterized by a reaction to *blackness as minstrelsy*.

The early days of Jim Crow are presented, however, mostly as a foil for the
Harlem Renaissance. In this story the Harlem Renaissance disproves the
implications of the minstrel. Black writers are engaged in the production of
high art; a genuine black literature is seen as emerging, as prominence is
ascribed to black figures whose existence contrasts with the buffoonery of
the minstrel. The Harlem Renaissance thus represents the *diversity of blackness* in black people's lives, potential, and aspirations.

As the Harlem Renaissance is disrupted by the Great Depression and otherwise fades, a new period emerges in this story, represented by the writing
in the post-Depression and post-War period. Focusing on the psychological
damage experienced by black people, north and south, rich and poor, the
widely popular work of Richard Wright, Ralph Ellison, and James Baldwin

universalizes the horrors of Jim Crow. Through these works the plight of black Americans could be compared with and could draw from the international condemnation of racism and anti-Semitism that underlay reactions to the Holocaust and fascist militarism more generally. In this way the post-War aesthetical phase laid the groundwork for and defines the terms of the Civil Rights Movement by universalizing the black condition and highlighting Jim Crow as an evil to humanity. Throughout, the writing of this period showed the *unity of blackness* in black people's experience of Jim Crow.

The last stage of the aesthetical rendering of black intellectual history emerges within the civil rights movement and finds expression in the Black Power and Black Arts movements. Responding to the momentum gained during the Civil Rights struggle, the project of both the Black Power and the Black Arts movements becomes a quest to define blackness beyond Jim Crow. Like the other periods, the goal remained challenging minstrelsy; however, given the dynamics of the very prominent and growing split between the Southern Christian Leadership Conference (SCLC) and the Congress on Racial Equality (CORE) and, later, the Student Non-Violent Coordinating Committee's (SNCC) split with both groups, the aesthetic of this period is described as self-consciously rebellious. It rejects prior conventions of blackness, in an effort to define a truly independent blackness that is not a reaction to Jim Crow, minstrels, or old, rural blackness. This urban, Africanist vision of blackness defined blackness as completely independent of the American experience of black people. America is cast as a bad dream from which black people had (presumably) awoken. Genuine, *authentic* blackness was to be identified without reference to the years of Jim Crow, slavery, and general servitude.

The modern black aesthetic found a kernel of *unity within diversity*. So even as black people led diverse lives, they were said to share certain cultural and social traits that bound them. This binding force was "race" but an ambiguously defined race that most often looked like ethnicity and was stated in terms of a shared *African* heritage. Jim Crow and slavery are experiences that inform the heritage of black Americans but not necessarily the definition of that heritage. Ironically, these Jim Crow experiences are to be forgotten, even as they are the ties that bind. "Down home" existence in the South may or may not play a prominent role in this heritage. But in either case, vaguely defined Africanist traits do, as does an urbanism.

It is apparent that Wilson's comments are rooted in this modern aesthetical vision of blackness and social policy. The implication of authentic blackness is shared by both he and Brustein. But this is not to imply that the concerns that Wilson expresses are somehow unimportant. Quite the contrary, Wilson's concerns are very important. However, they are obscured by the aesthetical language that informs his presentation. Wilson's speech reverberates with references to an authentic blackness. Even as he seeks to avoid speaking for other artists, even as he struggles to avoid essentialist implications, the spare content of his underlying frame betrays him. Less apparent, but no less crucial, is Brustein's reliance on this aesthetical story of black intellectual history to frame his response to Wilson. His is a view that accepts the story but chooses to emphasize the post-War period. His invocation of Martin Luther King, Jr., widely associated with neoliberalism, reflects this choice. Brustein wishes black people to retain a stylized 1950s vision of race problems, but given the end of *de jure* segregation, he insists on this basis that black people should abandon further talk of race, race problems, or race inequality.

The entire frame is problematic, at least insofar as it structures discussion of social policy. First, the frame distorts the intellectual and social history of black Americans. Not only does it overlook the World Wars, the Great Flood of 1929, The Great Depression, and the Cold War, it engages significant events in black history (like the Great Migration) only indirectly. The frame, thereby, promotes ahistoricism. Second, the frame preferences subjectivist approaches to social policy. Because it is an aesthetical frame, it builds on the particular mediation of personal and social encounters with and definitions of blackness manifest in artistic expression. Employing this frame to discuss social issues thus implies that social problems have very much to do with individuals' negotiation of the personal and social problems of blackness. Third, and as a consequence of its ahistorical subjectivism, the frame is without content. Just what are the problems that black people face cannot be clearly articulated because of the superficial, historical content of the frame. Taken together, there is a superficial unity that is *required* by the frame. The frame suggests that blackness binds black Americans in a deep, rich, and authentic way but never expresses what constitutes the content of that shared experience.

Wilson's speech is especially a victim of this frame. Building on the Black Power/Black Arts aesthetic leaves Wilson without a sufficiently subtle historical narrative to structure his oratory; the subjectivism of the Black Power aesthetics invests his personal views with more general authority than he means to invoke. This is because the subjectivism preferences the notions of blackness of those who speak loudest and most forcefully. This explains the thundering applause reported to greet Wilson's speech. It also explains the ability of buffoons, poverty pimps, and apparent race traitors to capture the attention of the black populous, despite the strong anti-minstrel, anticrime, and anti–Uncle Tom rhetoric that dominates black popular discourse. While Wilson is none of these, the social noise created by a political discourse that relies so heavily on symbol, image, and art at the expense of organization, mobilization, and democratic accountability earns Wilson's muddled critique of the problems of the black theater an uncritical celebration that ultimately does a disservice to the cause of rectifying the problems with which he is concerned. Moreover, it allows Brustein to effectively group him with a naive buffoonery and to unembarrassingly advance (as solely legitimate) a neutered blackness that envisions integration as acceptance of established power structures.

WILSON'S ISSUES

The serious issues that Wilson hopes to raise are muddled by the overlapping, anachronistic, and misplaced frames. Wilson groups together disparate problems that demand quite different remedies. Focusing on colorblind casting as a symbol of Brustein's vision of assimilation, Wilson does effectively emphasize the need of modern theater to address the unique personal and social experience of blackness in America. Incorporation of black people into an existing and unchanged power structure does not create a representative American theater. But Wilson loses his grip on the symbol. Expanding on the house slave/field slave distinction, Wilson asserts that this distinction has always defined parallel traditions in black theater: black art "for whites" and black art "for blacks." Denigrating black art "for whites" as inauthentic, Wilson pushes the dualist division to the point of absurdity: just as he assumes house and field slaves were different people, distinguished by parentage, color, and degrees of racial solidarity, he treats the dual traditions as though they were hermetically sealed singularities, performed by different people, drawing from different experiences, and with different consequences.

It is in this respect that Wilson most overtly draws on the black aesthetical tradition of the Black Power/Black Arts period. Not only does he locate the birth of black theater in a prehistory of slavery, but he ascribes to the Harlem Renaissance the apex of the development of the minstrelsy tradition. While the Renaissance saw the development of high art, Wilson's radical aspirations lead him to dismiss it as an extension of the minstrel tradition of "puttin' on" for white folk. At the same time, the exalted, authentic black tradition of Wilson's speech finds its roots in Africa, ironically remains relatively uninfected by non-African influences (including the nearly 400 years of black American art), and is completely distinct from the former, inauthentic "for whites" tradition. So Wilson's "for blacks" tradition emerges from "the African in the confines of the slave quarters" and is invested "with the strength of his ancestors by conceiving in his art, in his song and dance, a world in which he was the spiritual center[,] and his existence was a manifest act of the creator from whom life flowed." With this spiritual grounding, the African in the slave quarters "then could create art that was functional and furnished him with a spiritualized temperament necessary for his survival as property and the dehumanizing status that was attendant to that." But if the black slaves' existence was the "manifest act of the creator," was slavery such a manifest act? Indeed, on this ground alone we might imagine alternative aesthetics; but Wilson sees only the Black Power aesthetic that has been committed to a definition of blackness that treats black American existence as slaves, peons, and victims of Jim Crow as separate and apart from their existence as Africans. All this distorts the key questions Wilson implies about black people and the American theater.

The position Wilson champions is considerably easier to articulate than his muddled speech suggests, even if devising policy responses to address the position is rather complicated. A truly legitimate theater, like any American social institution, must tell the story of America, a substantial part of which is the tale of the woe and exclusion of black Americans. Artistic institutions possess the additional special obligation of telling how black people and others have experienced that history and its present effects. Moreover, institutions must be made to account for *their* role in the exclusion of black Americans from their institution as well as for the consequences of the wholesale exclusion of generations of black Americans from mainstream American life. The institutions of the American theater must consider how to include black people in the creation of American performance art, in addition to the obligation of the American theater to tell the story of blackness and to revise the canons of American theater from which the story of blackness has been largely excluded.

Both Wilson and Brustein fail to separate and to contend with the multiple obligations at issue in any meaningful analysis of race and the theater. Even a relatively narrow analysis presents at least five separate issues demanding quite different responses. Consider the different implications of (1) the funding of black theater, (2) the production of black playwrights' works, (3) the dearth of meaningful opportunities for black directors, actors, performers, and others to work in the theater, (4) the limitations on black artists' self-actualization as artists, given the limited opportunities to express their particular reconciliation of the personal and social implications of blackness, and (5) the making of a (or many) black aesthetic(s).

Wilson accurately and powerfully makes the case that black theater should be funded. Brustein's arguments on this account seek to imply that government funding somehow distorts the legitimate (market) forces that would (and should) determine the nature and content of theatrical productions. In the first instance, Brustein is inconsistent, as he is quick to bring out the canon as a means of denigrating current funding practices. But his charge that "sociological considerations" color contemporary funding decisions belies that he regards quality as fixed by the status quo. Brustein misses the issue that the market realities of contemporary artistic production already distort both the art produced and the canon that forms around it. It is not a slight to the black theater to suggest that there would be few productions without government and philanthropic funding. Rather than focusing on these deep flaws in Brustein's critique, Wilson gratuitously suggests that race separation is a necessary component of theatrical production because black and white "cannot meet on the common ground of experience." Wilson need not, and perhaps should not, resort to the ambiguous claim of "cultural imperialism" in order to make the simpler and more powerful point that the black experience in America is a significant and important aspect of American-ness, which ought be explored, in substantial part, by those who live even today with its consequences. The production of black playwrights' plays is an important means of ensuring that the black experience in America is given its just due. Seeing that black playwrights' work is produced makes demands that are potentially inconsistent with Wilson's emphasis on support of the black theater (presumably as the place for those works to be staged). Wilson's blunderbuss approach obscures the fine distinction between the need for a black theater, as such, and the related but distinct need to have the work of black playwrights staged. We might assume a correlation between a vibrant black theater and increased opportunities for black playwrights, but this is not necessarily so. Indeed, we might find that even with a plethora of black theater companies black playwrights' plays might go unproduced. Those theaters might be more interested in staging Shakespeare or putting on the popular, if perhaps dubious, black gospel productions that currently provide work for black actors and singers alike. This third aspect of the problem employment opportunities for black directors, actors, and performers thus potentially runs counter to all others. Black actors may seek to be "actors," without the "black" part; or they may wish to develop their craft in multiple contexts; or they may desire to attain mere fame, a pursuit that could ensure them work and financial security into the future but might require them to ignore (their) blackness. The existence of a vibrant black theater may be related to the interests of black directors, actors, and performers, but it is also distinct. However, it remains true that black people's self-expression is at the root of the need for and value of a black theater.

In this sense, it is the development of a black aesthetic that is the core concern. At issue is whether *a* black aesthetic exists and, if not, how are black peoples' experiences to be included in the American aesthetic. Wilson cannot be faulted for confusion on this point, because confusion has reigned on this matter at least since the end of Jim Crow deprived blackness of its unifying experience.

The inherent problem in developing a black aesthetic in the post–Jim Crow world is avoiding essentialism. No definition of blackness ought dictate a unanimity of belief. This problem would seem less difficult in the arts where the individual's expression of her own beliefs is the *sine qua non* of the enterprise. But the arts is where the problem of essentialism is most acute. Art aspires to comment on the human condition, and art criticism seeks to abstract what various works or artists say about that condition and how. When part of that condition is blackness, aesthetic formation necessarily claims that multiple pieces of art or multiple artists say something about, even epitomize blackness. Unlike politics where participatory democracy provides a structural check on the essentializing tendency of collective expression, there is no mechanism for inclusion and dissent in aesthetic formation. The problem cannot be avoided. So when it comes to saying whether a given work expresses the black experience or does so well, there is little that can be done apart from affixing the qualifier that there exist a multiplicity of black experiences.

This problem of essentialism in aesthetic formation reveals why, when the subject is social policy and when the question is whether to fund theaters, produce works, employ actors, or give away tickets, an aesthetical frame is a quite poor basis for analyzing the issues. The subtle, distinct, and consequential questions of policy raised are muddied by the competing definitions of aesthetical worth offered as decisional bases. Consequently, Wilson and Brustein put on a glorious fight, raising the ire of partisans on each side. But neither says much about the funding of the black theater. The problem seems to be the difficult question of how to manage the inherent aesthetic judgments that infect policy questions. No one would suggest using limited funds to promote "bad" art, or produce "awful" plays, or hire "incompetent directors or actors." But what is an awful play requires judgments of an aesthetical nature that complicates social policy questions. The trouble with Wilson's speech and Brustein's response is precisely that they miss this important issue.

Although Wilson and Brustein each have an implicit view of what is blackness, what constitutes a black aesthetic, and, therefore, what black art ought be funded, they mostly debate on whether black art should be funded. It is the aesthetical frame that distorts their focus. The subtle visions of blackness held by Wilson and Brustein are framed by the legacy of the 1960s aesthetic and are inconsistent and competing. After the 1960s the limitations of *the* black aesthetic of that period come to structure the nature of debate over blackness and race policy. That aesthetic's choices of an Africanist over a Jim Crow–related heritage, of a middle-class based but grass roots aspiring constituency over a grass roots based but middle-class aspiring constituency, of an urban rather than rural rhythm define a narrow, stereotyped blackness. In a way this blackness has morphed into a new minstrel: the urban rebel, gangster rapper with afrocentric wallpaper.

Wilson's vision is a celebration of this image; but it is also an attempt to salvage the 1960s vision of blackness from the minstrelsy of the urban criminal symbol of the gangster rapper. Embracing and rejecting the new minstrel, Wilson's vision is garbled, and he must retreat to ever-grander abstractions about blackness. Thus he focuses on Africanisms, the slave quarter, and the rhythms of the plantation.

Brustein's position is also a mixed embrace of the new minstrel. But Brustein's arguments must be understood in light of the neoconservative climate that produced them. American neoconservatism seeks to explain the present social effects of (past and present) racial thinking as evidence of personal defects. Race is, for the neoconservative, a means of avoiding personal responsibility. Thus, the new minstrel colors the neoconservative definition of blackness: she is the welfare mother; he is the drug-dealing brother; he is the political buffoon, shaking down companies on pain of boycott. The new minstrel is also the black playwright trying to extort taxpayer funding for bad art—that is, for black art. Like Wilson, however, Brustein also rejects the new minstrel. As evident in his response to Wilson, his is also a vision of a better blackness. His tacit alternative glorifies blackness, focusing on the poor black families aspiring for middle class status and who embrace rural values learned in the crucible of Jim Crow's inequities.

Ever shifting, Wilson's and Brustein's visions of blackness, their visions of a black aesthetic, their notions of worthy black art, are inaccessible. Wilson, because he does not think he has to, never articulates it apart from the vague platitudes about life in the slave quarter; Brustein, perhaps because he is afraid to, never intimates it either. Consequently, neither ever discusses just what is good black art, what art ought be funded, and what is the role of LORT funding in advancing black art. Lost in their jumble of incomplete and disjointed ideas is the fact that black art must be funded. Unstated and thus undefended is the fundamental notion that American art is incomplete without black art. Had Wilson addressed this point, it would have been apparent that it is unnecessary to define a black aesthetic to address the basic policy question of funding. As such, when asked why LORT theaters should do a better job of funding black theater, perhaps Wilson should have simply said, "Just 'Cause!'"

NOTES

1. Neoconservatives have emphasized the demise of the formal bases for race and insist that blackness no longer exists. Progressives have, on the other hand, struggled with the implications of this change. Seeking to avoid "essentialism," the notion that one's essence is dictated by imposed identity categories, progressives have recognized that blackness has changed.
2. Justice Thomas's underwhelming record was obscured by the "Tom" accusations, as was an analysis of the extreme legal philosophy he advocated. Moreover, Thomas was able to counter the "Tom" imagery with his claim that he was the victim of a "high-tech lynching." (See Swain 224–226.)

WORKS CITED

Fogel, Robert William. *Without Consent or Contract: The Rise and Fall of American Slavery*. New York: Norton, 1989.

Fogel, Robert William and Stanley L. Engerman. *Time On the Cross: The Economics of American Negro Slavery*. Boston: Little Brown, 1974.

Graham, Lawrence Otis. *Our Kind of People: Inside America's Black Upper Class*. New York: Harper Collins, 1999.

Reed, Adolph, Jr. *Stirrings in the Jug: Black Politics in the Post-Segregation Era*. Minneapolis: University of Minnesota Press, 1999.

Sleeper, Jim. *Liberal Racism: How Fixating on Race Subverts the American Dream*. New York: Penguin Books, 1998.

Swain, Carol M. "Double Standard, Double Bind: African-American Leadership After the Thomas Debacle." *Race-ing Justice, En-gendering Power: Essays on Anita Hill, Clarence Thomas, and the Construction of Social Reality*. Ed. Toni Morrison. New York: Pantheon Books, 1992. 215–231.

II

Black Aesthetics and Interdisciplinary Black Arts

6

"Keeping it Real": August Wilson and Hip-Hop

Harry J. Elam, Jr.

Wilson's provocative keynote address to the Theatre Communications Group (TCG) Conference in June 1996 incited national discussions, op-ed pieces, journal articles, conference papers, and a much-ballyhooed public debate between Wilson and his arch nemesis Robert Brustein, Artistic Director of the American Repertory Theater, moderated by Anna Deavere Smith in January 1997. It also provided the impetus for a National Black Theatre Summit, convened in March 1998, in which black theater scholars, artists, and practitioners from around the country joined together to consider the state of black theater in contemporary America. As the spark for this explosion of dialogue, Wilson's TCG Address challenges the material, economic conditions that govern black artistic production. He confronts the status quo and promotes black control of what Stuart Hall terms "the politics of representation,"[1] these politics concern not only understanding the power inherent in the visible representation of African Americans but with controlling the mechanisms of production that dictate the dissemination of these images. In this speech Wilson advocates a black art that is not suppressed by the dominant culture but an active expression of African American experiences, a practice that is historically grounded, socially committed, and culturally specific. Directly and indirectly, Wilson's discourse considers strategies for how the black artist in America confronts the dilemma of achieving commercial success in artistic mainstream while remaining true to the cultural roots of his or her art and the socio-political needs of black people. In so doing, I believe that Wilson, using the vernacular of contemporary rap culture, demands that black artists "keep it real."

Although Wilson's most recent play, *King Hedley II*, features rap music in its sound score, connecting Wilson to rap may seem a stretch at first glance. His artistic orientation is toward the past; he sees the early blues of Bessie Smith and Ma Rainey as the foundation for his art. Rap music on the other hand is truly a postmodern form grounded in the technological machinery of production, operating on the cultural cutting edge ever hurling toward the future. Nonetheless, at closer inspection, Wilson's platforms on the politics of black art, on black cultural ownership, appropriation, and affirmation are particularly apropos for analyzing rap music's politics and its obsession with keeping it real. In fact, analyzing the politics of rap in relation to Wilson's TCG speech and Wilson's TCG speech on and through the politics of rap produces a revealing reading of the power of visibility and the place of history, of cultural production as a site of resistance, of the politics of representation, of the seductive authority of commercialism, and of both the oppositional possibilities and limitations of keeping it real.

The concept of keeping it real in the politics and aesthetics of both Wilson and hip-hop culture is highly complex, ambivalent, and ambiguous. Nicole Fleetwood's discussion of realness in "Documenting the 'Real': Youth, Race and the Discourse of Realness in Visual Culture" is extremely useful in unpacking these diverse meanings. Fleetwood explains:

> realness operates on multiple levels: as a concept alluding to that which is the essence of reality; as an aesthetic style in popular cultural production, particularly music and film, as a longing for that which exists outside of discourse; and as a set of visual tropes that constitute a particular racialized and gendered subjectification.[2]

As an aesthetic style, realness in rap denotes attitude, behavior, and even wardrobe: a certain bagginess of dress, a particular color of headband, or pattern of tattoos. Rappers walk, talk, and hold the microphone in specific manners, all as expressions of their realness. Similarly, Wilson maintains aesthetic authenticity or "keeps it real" in his plays through his attempts to convey what he calls the "truth of black experience."[3] Yet even as Wilson records authentic black dialect and attends to historic detail, patterns of language and rhythm occur in his plays that are particular to him and his dramaturgy. Performing a Wilson play requires actors who have the verbal acumen for Wilson speak and his specific formalism. Paradoxically, as in freeflow rap improvisation, mastering the formal structure of Wilson's dialogue enables its musicality and produces the illusion of a free and spontaneous discourse. Realness, then, in rap and in Wilson is performed and performative, a doing as well as a thing done. Placed in the verb infinitive form, "keeping it real" is an active practice. One must constantly act, even struggle to keep it real. Wilson's TCG speech and rap lyrics construct realness and at the same time they maintain a stance of keeping it real.

As what Fleetwood calls the "essence of reality" realness in rap and Wilson emanates from black expressive cultural traditions of testifying and truth telling. This black expressive oral tradition is found at spiritual and social gatherings in black churches, in verbal signifying games in black barbershops, in the dozens played by young black men on urban street corners, in historic resonances, and in contemporary African American cultural practices. Wilson's attention to the rhythms, logic, and linguistic structure of black speech enables his work to celebrate the poetry within everyday life and the power of the vernacular in the history of black expressive culture. Linguists John and Russell Rickford in *Spoken Soul* credit Wilson with an ability "to re-create and evoke the beauty, poetry and wisdom of everyday black speech" as he "deploys a battery of [black] grammatical vernacular features including completive *done* ('they *done* trumped') and habitual *be* ('he *be* making out')."[4] Rap singers equally reflect the vernacular poetry of black speech with their lyrical virtuosity, their innovative use and creation of current slang. Wilson and rappers in keeping it real strategically turn to the vernacular, to "the folk" as source, as inspiration, and critical authority.

Through the cultural articulation of realness, rap and Wilson maintain borders around black artistic practice that enables black self-determination and subversively opposes white hegemony. Consequently, "keeping it real" for Wilson and rap reinforces a project of cultural nationalism that even as they discover white audiences and crossover appeal, embodies a politics of resistance to white authority. This cultural nationalism of realness asserts black difference, affirms a black way of creating, and articulates separate cultural system and distinct black identity. It reaffirms the ties of the black performer to the black collective and structures boundaries around how that artistic practice relates to the community. Inherent in this resistance, in this cultural nationalism, and in this aesthetic of realness is an assertion of black masculinity, for realness is as Fleetwood notes highly gendered and constitutes what she calls "a reification of an authentic masculine black subjectivity."[5] Rap and Wilson operate in and simultaneously construct a world of men. The masculinist bravado expressed in rap lyrics and in Wilsonian dialogue seeks to not only define a realness but to refute the derogatory imagery of black masculinity perpetuated by the dominant culture. Cultural nationalism and paradigms of black masculinity intersect in rap and Wilson in ways that recall black political strategies of the 1960s and 1970s as they reconsider and reposition contemporary stereotypes of the black male in American society.

Wilson's title for his TCG address, "The Ground on Which I Stand," "grounds" this speech in a particular rhetoric of black cultural nationalism that implicitly and explicitly recalls a past "realness," the black revolutionary platforms of the 1960s and 1970s. After all, central to any claims of nationalism and the affirmation of national identity is the ground, the land, the nation. In the absence of a land base, black cultural nationalism in the 1960s and 1970s claimed cultural territory and used the space of cultural practice to celebrate and define the "black nation." Wilson's discussion of land, the ground on which he stands, is both material and figurative. The land he wants to claim is quite literally a geographic as well as symbolic space within American theater system for black theatrical production, and he points out that at the time of his TCG address only one of the sixty-seven League of Regional Theaters (LORT) in America was devoted to black theater. In making his demand and breaking new ground for black theater, he strategically situates himself within histories and traditions that give him the right and reason to seek such participatory ownership: "I have come here today to make a testimony, to talk about the ground on which I stand and all the many grounds on which I and my ancestors have toiled, and the ground of theatre on which my fellow artists and I have labored to bring forth its fruits, its daring and its sometimes liberating and healing truths."[6] Reimagining then the paradigms of cultural nationalism, Wilson links the ground of the American theater with the ancestral ground of African American labor. It is these past, unrepeated efforts of his black forbearers that foster his current claims and around which he shapes his rhetoric.

The cultural nationalistic politics of authenticity in rap music are equally situated in geography. The ground critical in rap is "the ghetto," the mythical and symbolic place of origin and inspiration. The urban street is the space that rap artists not only reference and revere in their music, but the homeland that they stress within their publicity and promotional materials as their social, cultural, and musical foundation. Experiences in the "'hood" with drugs, criminality, guns and gang activity, a "hardness" learned and earned in these streets become crucial components in the rap milieu and its aesthetic authenticity. Rap artists "keep it real" by pledging their allegiance to the urban hard knocks environment. The late Tupac Shakur in his lyrics praises the thug life and raps about his own experiences within a culture of violence from an early age. Publicity around the also deceased Biggie Smalls, the Notorious B.I.G., noted that he dealt drugs and hustled in the streets before turning to rap. For white rappers as well land figures prominently in establishing authenticity and the "realness" of the music. Vanilla Ice, famous for his one hit, "Ice, Ice Baby," claimed to have grown up around black people in the ghetto. More recent white rappers such as Kid Rock and Eminem emphasize not so much knowledge of a black experience but of lower class, "white trash" backgrounds. The trailer park becomes their "'hood." Consequently locality is inextricably connected to class within rap music. Suburbia and a middle-class, bourgeois background have no legitimacy in rap. The ghettoland, the raw, gritty, edgy texture of the urban slums is primary. Only through lifestyles of turmoil and turbulence can one create the music of rap.

Land also figures in the politics of rap around the symbolic value and physical and social occupation of public space. Tricia Rose writes,

> the politics of rap involves the contestation over public space ... The struggle over context, meaning and access to public space is critical to contemporary cultural politics. Power and resistance are exercised through signs, language and institutions. Consequently, popular pleasure involves a physical, ideological, and territorial struggles.[7]

Rose argues that black youth attendance at rap concerts in large throngs, the usage of the public sphere by rap artists, as well as the media's depiction of these events, can be read as forms of resistance to normative usage of public space. As they assert possession of and over public space, rap artists, and their youthful followers express a certain degree of power and representational authority. At the funeral for Biggie Smalls in New York, throngs of youth lined the sidewalks, watching as the hearse carrying his body moved down the street. Suddenly, his hit song "Hypnotize" from his album ironically titled "Life After Death" began to play and the funeral became a party of sorts with the crowd chanting the lyrics in unison and moving with the beats. The legions of young people took over the streets. Arrests resulted as the police attempted to reclaim their authority over this public space. Historically, the battle for black liberation has always involved struggles over public space, from the efforts of slaves to steal across the Mason Dixon line or the Canadian border to freedom, to the nonviolent protests of Civil Rights workers to desegregate restaurant lunch counters in the 1960s. And then today on urban buses, black youth crowd in the back of the public bus listening to loud rap music, their noise, sounds, and attitudes compelling adults to migrate to the front. Their conduct inverts previous Civil Rights battles over territory, when African Americans walked for miles and staged nationally publicized boycotts in order to challenge their relegation to the back of the bus. Still, as Nicole Fleetwood points out in an unpublished essay this contemporary act on public buses is equally an expression of resistance against authority and the representational dynamics that dictate how youth should behave or where black people should sit. Fleetwood writes:

> I consider much of the activity of the young on mass transportation, which is interpreted expressions of delinquency, as engagement with adults' anxieties and with cultural representations of youth as deviant.
>
> I theorize public transit as a particular site where youth performatively engage with adults' fears of and media representations of youth as a threat to social order and an encroachment upon safe space.[8]

Through this cultural assertion of occupation, these youth declare their subjectivity, they both reinscribe and flaunt the discourse of criminality and threat that surround the culture of rap and the representations of black male bodies, and they resist past designations of the back as an inferior locale and reassert it as a profoundly racialized space with new meanings. Here again, turf is an issue, one that plays out both on the bus and in gangs. While in reality, the gangs have no economic ownership of these streets, the social reality is that gunfire and threats may find those who refuse to obey or disregard the borderlines of gang territory. The murders of both rappers Biggie and Tupac allegedly resulted from land conflicts, a turf war between West Coast rappers and East Coast rappers that became all too real as it escalated from lyrical battles within the certain songs to the actual death of two of rap's larger than life figures.

As much as the land and its meanings are real with life and death consequence, they are equally a phantasm constructed to signify or represent a black authenticity. The ghetto constructed within the dominant culture as a pejorative site of danger and threatening blackness becomes reimagined within rap music and hip-hop culture as a space of black creative possibility, of survival through determination and innovative creativity, the ability as Wilson would suggest to improvise on a theme. Robin D. C. Kelley writes in

Race Rebels that hardcore rap music attracts [white suburban] "listeners for whom the 'ghetto' is a place of adventure, unbridled violence, erotic fantasy, and/or an imaginary alternative to suburban boredom."[9] Accordingly, in his one-man show, *Jails, Hospitals and Hip-Hop and Some People*, white hip-hop performance artist Danny Hoch's character Flip-Dogg, a white suburban kid in Montana, imagines escaping his stultifying Midwestern environment to the urban ghetto:

> But I mean, even though I live in Montana, I still got the ghetto in my heart. I mean, this is just temporary I'm just chillin' here now. I don't really belong here. I'ma move soon though. I'ma move to like...just to some straight up ghetto thug-ass project type shit. Where the people just kick it every day and keep it real. And chillin' their BMWs and rap, and all the girls got on bikinis, and everybody just...parties...and raps.[10]

Flipp aligns home with identity, but his identity is not fixed by his current locale. Despite his Montana address, he has "the ghetto in his heart." He imagines eventually migrating to his romanticized ghetto, the world he sees on MTV, in order to realize fully his "black identity." "Why would I wanna be white for? This shit is stupid."[11] Black becomes an essentialized fictive embodiment of cool. While he relates to the cool of blackness, he has neither knowledge nor actual connection with the realities of black experiences. Hoch critiques Flipp's naïve notions of "keeping it real" and of hip-hop culture. Yet, Hoch, in satirizing the anachronism of Flipp-Dogg and his "Montana Gangsta Blood Thugs," still structures a boundary around cultural expression determined by authentic connections to "land." He parodies this pseudo-gangsta rapper for his distance from and fantasy image of the " 'hood."

The idealization, reification, demarcation of the " 'hood," initiates a binary that divides those included within or tied to the homeland from those who do not belong, who cannot "be down" or "real." This binary of inclusion/exclusion becomes particularly problematic as a means of determining artistic validity and achievement as it places constraints of "realness" on the artist's practice and erects borders of aesthetic legitimacy. During the Black Arts Movement of the 1960s and 1970s proponents of a black aesthetic promoted paradigms of black cultural nationalism that ostracized some black art and certain black practitioners—feminists, gay rights activists, and others who rebelled against the notion of one monolithic black community, who were not black enough—because they did not sufficiently reflect or adhere to the black revolutionary standards for artistic form and content. Eliding the differences between African American identities, revolutionary black artists imagined black America as one homogenous community joined ideologically and culturally. Consequently, the production of black revolutionary art became to some degree prescriptive and limited. Structuring a binary of reactionary and revolutionary black art sets up a potentially dangerous exclusionary/inclusionary dynamic that allows certain black art or black artist to be discounted or demeaned if their work is not seen to sufficiently serve the cause of black advancement.

Wilson in his TCG speech similarly erects a boundary around black art when he writes:

> There are and have always been two distinct and parallel traditions in black art that is, art that is conceived and designed to entertain white society, and art that feeds the sprit and celebrates the life of black America by designing its strategies for survival and prosperity.... This entertainment for whites [on the slave plantation] consisted of whatever the slave imagined or knew that his master wanted to see and hear. This tradition has its present life counterpart in the crossover artists that slant their material for white consumption. (TCG 16)

What Wilson loses in this Manichean division is any accurate reflection of the African American cultural history that he treasures. African American cultural history informs us, for example, that repeatedly in slave cultural practices African Americans created art that could entertain the master but also contained messages about clandestine meetings, escape strategies, or plans for black resistance. The concept of black arts that entertain whites and arts that celebrate the black experience are not necessarily antithetical. These categories of artistic expression are not pure and can bleed into one another. The cross-cultural popularity of all of his plays to date challenges Wilson's own premise. The first six of the plays in his cycle of ten plays on the black experience of the twentieth century opened at predominantly white regional theaters to predominantly white audiences. He has been lauded by white Broadway critics and awarded two Pulitzer Prizes. Yet, certainly Wilson does not feel that his own work is "conceived and designed to entertain whites." Correspondingly, while rap music's roots are in the black inner city, it has gained new popularity in white suburbs, as white suburban youth have responded to the hard edge of rap and increased its commercial saturation. And yet in "keeping it real," hardcore rap devotees and practitioners constrain and disdain those would-be practitioners who have no claims on life and experiences within the 'hood or those who have such as "the Fresh Prince," Will Smith, and MC Hammer, who choose to forsake gangsta posturing and expletive dialogue for lighter lyrical content and the crossover appeal of danceable grooves. Russell Potter observes that, in rap, "there is a strong ethic against 'selling out' which is not a matter of sales figures but of playing too hard for what Gang Starr calls 'mass appeal.' It is fine if a record sells well, and a large white audience *per se* does nothing to de-authenticate a rap record. 'Selling out' is about attitude, about 'hardness,' about a refusal of stasis, predictability, or music that is too easy to listen to."[12] Wilson, equally, does not deny black art the possibility of cross-cultural acceptance, but he argues that the key lies in a different perspective on the artist's realness and grounding, his or her commitment to "art that feeds the spirit and celebrates the life of black America." Wilson expresses the need for black artists to "keep it real" by maintaining their social and cultural integrity despite the pull of commercial riches and to remain oriented toward the particular needs and interests of African American peoples.

For Wilson, black art must be both functional and political. Fusing aesthetics and ethics, Wilson in his TCG Speech roots himself in a tradition of functional black art that rises out of the particular social conditions and struggles of African American life: "I stand myself on the self-defining ground of the slave quarters and find the ground to be hallowed and made fertile by the blood and bones of men and women who can be described as warriors on the cultural battlefield that affirmed self worth" (TCG Speech 16). Significantly then, Wilson historicizes black power in his speech and thus particularizes it. He constantly positions it in time and space. In his plays Wilson revisits and remakes history questioning specific choices blacks have made in the past, while underscoring how they maintained the will to survive. He imaginatively resurrects collective memories and individual histories, reconstructs cultural practices, and enables previously silent and silenced voices to speak. Correspondingly rap music relies on processes of repetition and revision. Implicitly and explicitly rap returns to history critiquing and reimagining the past as it directs the present and future. The process of sampling, taking a beat from another record and looping it endlessly within a rap song, resurrects historic rhythms, bits and pieces from past music, in particular the funky sounds of the 1970s, and puts them within a contemporary context augmenting them with thumping baselines and hip-hop beats. The process then embodies what Henry Louis Gates refers to as "signifyin(g)," as it repeats and revises the previous music with a critical and signal difference. Present within the song is the history, the trace of the past now re-presented with new meanings. Moreover, the rap lyrics draw on the historic continuum of African American oral expression. The verbal banter in rap replays the traditions of the dozens, of masculine bravado and lyrical wordplay that Wilson constantly returns to and seeks to capture in each play of his twentieth-century cycle of plays. Rap extends the conjunction of music and poetry found in such spoken word artists of the 1960s as Gil Scott-Heron and the Last Poets. The use of scratching, turntables, and a microphone to create new sounds further expands on a black cultural expressive continuum of making something out of nothing or using the materials at hand, a tradition of pastiche found in the collage work of Romare Bearden or the plays of August Wilson.

Wilson in his TCG Speech asks African American artists to utilize history as impulse for their art. Noting the attempts by the dominant culture to deny black history, Wilson calls on black artists to serve as cultural purveyors and protectors: "We must defend and protect our spiritual fruits...To give expression to the spirit that has been shaped and fashioned by our history is of necessity to give voice and vent to the history itself" (TCG Speech 72). Consequently, the role that Wilson defines for black playwrights is an activist one. It is functional because of its engagement with history. Recalling the urgency and idealism of the Black Arts Movement in the 1960s, Wilson proclaims, "we can be the spearhead of a movement to reignite and reunite our people's positive energy for a political and social change that is reflective of our spiritual truth rather than our economic fallacies...What we do now becomes history by which our grandchildren will judge us" (TCG Speech 73). Wilson perceives the historic responsibility for black artists rests not simply in the reckoning with the past, but in preparing a way for the future. Such an engagement with history becomes not only a politics of cultural nationalism but also a methodology for "keeping it real."

For Wilson realness must fundamentally involve history. He argues that black artists must not and could not escape their collective history: "We all share a common past, and despite what some of us might think and how it might look, we all share a common present and will share a common future" (TCG Speech 73). This shared legacy and destiny, Wilson maintains, compels the direction and directives of African American theatrical practice. He exhorts black playwrights: "It is time to embrace the political dictates of our history and answer the challenge of our duties" (TCG Speech 73). Such a call replicates the incendiary cultural nationalistic rhetoric of the Black Arts Movement of the 1960s and early 1970s. Wilson's own critically acclaimed practice, not unlike that of early rappers of the 1980s such as Public Enemy or KRS 1, seeks both to delight and to instruct. Social truths are not necessarily antithetical to human truths, but, rather, Wilson argues, are grounded within the specifics of its social and cultural conditions. Wilson advocates a keeping it real through recognizing and promoting the interconnectedness of art, politics, and history.

An integrated practice is equally present with rap music, for as Russell Potter points out, "it is not so much that hip-hop *tells* history, it's that it is history."[13] Through verbal attacks on other rappers, personal stories of urban adventures, and celebratory details of past conquests, rappers write and rewrite history. Their process is analogous to Wilson's employment of long, textured, poetic monologues in his dramaturgy. Characters like Troy in *Fences* or Doaker in *The Piano Lesson* function as African American griots, oral historians, relating family histories and writing their own experience into the historic record. In the case of both the rapper and the Wilsonian character, the history is idiosyncratic and personal and functions as a critique of the metanarratives of American history that too often ignore the lives of African Americans. With rap the process of sampling the past also serves to reinforce or impose a politics of historic resistance. Potter explains:

> Even those tracks that don't contain obvious political references, the recursion of sampled sounds and the linguistic slippage of Signifyin(g) at least *disorient* the listener, forcing her or him to recheck their "bearings," just as the heavy bass and booming drums have the often-underestimated virtue of *irritating* those who don't want to hear the message they carry.[14]

Form informs content. Yet the refashioning of the past through musical samples as well as lyrical revelations reflect not only a historical consciousness but reveal the inherent presence of the past. History is constantly enacted in the now through the performance of rap. While Wilson's history cycle comments on the present by reaching into and recreating the past, rap narratives and samplings situate contemporary struggles within a continuum of African American history. "Keeping it real" in rap depends on and defines a history.

And yet, how rap's realness involves cultural politics and history appears at times contradictory. For paradoxically, rap music operates as a counter-hegemonic form that attacks conventional capital and consumption even as it affirms the primacy of production and consumption. Hip-hop culture and rap aesthetics too often seem caught up in the seduction of the market, the hyper extremes of commercialism, the immediacy of the moment, the lure of the now. "Keeping it real" can become a strategy of immediate gratification, as rap simultaneously subverts and glorifies systems of commodification, commercialization, and global capital. Potentially lost within this present*ist* focus of "keeping it real" is an activist reading of history that Wilson believes should underscore a commitment to oppositional art.

Spike Lee stingingly satirizes this presentist conceit of rap realness in his latest film *Bamboozled*. In this film, a contemporary rap group called the Mau Maus criticizes and eventually murders Mantan, the star of a new age minstrel show for his misrepresentation and degradation of black people while totally unaware of how they themselves replicate stereotypical behaviors and reinscribe the tropes of minstrelsy. Named for the legendary successful Kenyan insurrection against the British in 1953, these contemporary Mau Maus seem totally removed from that history and any awareness of its meanings in relationship to their own self-serving enactment of black-on-black violence. The Mau Maus distort that history in their destructive acts, their public lynching of Mantan as purported revolution. Without a real connection to historical rebellion, the realness of rap can easily be appropriated for self-destructive ends as in *Bamboozled* or when commercialized to sell products from sneakers to hamburgers.

If the politics of rap emphasize representation over substance, then that substance cannot only be bought but re-presented and not to any revolutionary end. Irreverence and nihilism in rap, as demonstrated by Lee's Mau Maus, do not necessarily make for concentrated or focused resistance but rather a diffuse oppositionality, a representation of resistance rather than any movement toward real change. In fact one could argue that the politics of rap are often a "politics of representation" where the focus and concern with "keeping it real" becomes an end in itself rather than a means to an end. The performance of rap creates a social identity and public persona for the rapper. The imaginative and creative names of rappers, Cool Mo Dee, Snoop-doggy dogg, Dr. Dre, Queen Latifah, Scarface, and GURU all reinforce this sense of a performative self. Robin D. G. Kelley cautions, "Whether gangsta rappers step into character of a gang banger, hustler or ordinary working person—that is, products and residents of the 'hood'—the important thing to remember is that they are stepping into character; it is for descriptive purposes rather than advocacy."[15] Rappers assume an identity, a character; they perform gangsta style and construct a black authenticity. The representation of authenticity then constructs and is itself constructed as the end as well as the starting point.

Yet, I must caution that rap is not one simple or single category, nor is a politics of representation in rap necessarily politically bankrupt. Rappers such as Mos Def and Common, hip-hop groups such as the Roots and OutKast—both Mos Def and the Roots appear in *Bamboozled*—all explicitly and progressively address through their musical form and content the inequities present in the United States as they explore the legacy of black expressive culture.[16] Moreover, even the culturally bankrupt, fictional Mau Maus in their sampling both of previous musical codes and 1960s black nationalist rhetoric, in their selection of a historic name of mythical revolutionary import, are engaged in a process of rewriting history, a subversive project that challenges dominant narratives. A politics of representation is not necessarily without substance or meaning, for there certainly is always a power and meaning in visual spectacle. Image matters. Potter intones, "If images of Willie Horton scared middle-class Americans into voting for George Bush, the images and words of Ice Cube, putting his gat in the mouth of Uncle Sam and shooting ' 'til his brains hang out' will scare them more."[17] Potter speaks to the undeniable oppositional potency of the visuality of rap. The threat inherent and explicit in the spectacle of rap has real social consequences. The question then is to what ends is this visual authority utilized.

The Potter quote above also foregrounds how this visuality is explicitly masculine and how this vision of the black man as violent and dangerous to himself and others functions powerfully not only in rap iconography but within the American social order. Some rappers have performed what, borrowing from José Muñoz, one could term a disidentificatory[18] critique of pejorative associations of black masculinity by using the images of violence and criminality that surround the culture of rap music and black masculinity to their advantage. They have employed the negative associations of black man as threat and the nihilism and visual authority of gangsta style and posturing to commercial success, for the representation of anti-authoritarian criminality associated with rap is not only threatening it is also seductive. While the figure of the black male as brute beast is feared, it is also desired and repeatedly commodified. Images of black men have saturated the media changing the processes and subjects of representation itself. White suburban youth dress like urban black rappers. Bald-headed black men sell everything from Fila tennis shoes to Ralph Lauren Polo Shirts. Rap style politics of representation have profoundly impacted global culture and the process of mediatization and the imagery of America throughout the world. And yet, this hypervisibility of black men in contemporary America is ripe with contradictions as such visibility threatens to reinscribe the stereotype of black male criminality rather then revise it. In a vicious cycle, the emblematic status of black man as "all that is dangerous" too often becomes internalized and then egested in self-destructive behaviors that reinforce the pejorative characterization of black male deviance.

August Wilson's purposeful representation of black men in his dramaturgy addresses this historical stigmatization of black masculinity. He seeks to re-present black masculinity so that it becomes a site of self-determination, pride, self-respect, and historical consciousness. "And now the only duty our young men seem ready to imagine is to their maleness with its reckless display of braggadocio, its bright intelligence, its bold and foolish embrace of hate and happenstance."[19] The loss of historical awareness, Wilson believes, has led to a self-destructive image of black masculinity that has resulted in the devaluation of black life and the escalation of black-on-black violence. For Wilson images of black masculinity need to resist rather than embrace the white cultural and commercial system.

Wilson demands a reorganization of the American arts and theater more specifically to enable black self-determination and allow the black performer to sing his or her own song. To this end Wilson in his TCG Speech rails against the system of what he calls "Cultural Imperialism" that promotes and maintains standards he finds antithetical to black self-definition. He asks the American theater to reexamine its critical standards, its economic organization, and its institutionalized separatism. The black voice has been subdued, suppressed, and commodified within this system, and black artists retain little economic control. Rap moguls from Russell Simmons of Def Jam to Suge Knight of Death Row and Master P of No Limit Records have somewhat usurped the arena of the cultural imperialists by garnering and exploiting different avenues for black artists to sing their songs and by opening up different markets previously ignored by the white-controlled record industry. Within the position and presence of these new cultural capitalists there is power, both symbolic and material, even as Suge Knight was behind bars, and Master P tried to transform himself into a pro basketball player and sports agent. Still, these new musical moguls must operate within the market, and thus have the potential to reinforce the status quo instead of forcing it to change.

While Wilson's speech offers a critique of cultural imperialism, the new rap music power system, in its desire to sell records, looks to take advantage of the capitalist system rather than to restructure it. Rap in both its economics and its performances remains capable of critiquing the regimes of power, while at the same time reinscribing those same technologies of power. It exemplifies the conditions Philip Auslander argues are critical to "postmodern arts of resistance": "postmodern political art cannot place itself outside the object of its own critique . . . Because postmodern political art must position itself within postmodern culture, it must use the same representational means as all other cultural expression yet remain permanently suspicious of them."[20] Rap functions with such a suspicion. Correspondingly, I would argue, Wilson is similarly complicit in the system that he wishes to critique and in which he imagines himself only as a visitor.[21] Because Wilson operates within the so-called white regional theater system then moves his plays to the even whiter world of Broadway, he inevitably must conform to and immensely benefits from a hegemonic system that he concurrently decries for its diminution of black art.

By critiquing this system so blatantly in his TCG Speech Wilson bit, and bit voraciously, the hand that feeds him. Perhaps only the voice of the stature of Wilson's, only an insider with the position afforded him, could have generated such resounding discourse and debate. Marion McClinton, the director of *King Hedley II* concurs: "He took a hit for a lot other people. That's what a champion does—a champion fights."[22] After all, Wilson's stature caused the TCG executive board to invite him to be their keynote speaker in the first place and gave him the platform for his manifesto. Wilson then functions not unlike the socially conscious rapper, both inside and outside of the system, using the tools of the TCG—their platform, their microphone—to voice loudly his resistance. In fact, I would argue that the assertive strategies of rap self-promotion align here with Wilson's identity politics and calls for black unity. Within rap the emphasis on the individual and on heterogeneity need not diminish the collective consciousness and agency of the group, the "crew," the "posse." As Michael Quinn suggests, rap music "marks an assertion of individual as well as group identity, becoming a way to deal with the one's disenfranchised status on both a personal and political level."[23] Disaffected youth, conscious of their own lack of access to and rights within the society, could take Tupac Shakur's lyrical cries and claims about the "thug life" both as individual assertion of their own subjectivity and as a collective social cry for youth resistance and a collective disregard for social authority. In this TCG Speech Wilson presents the personal, collective, and political as he calls on black artists to act communally and to see themselves as activists with the firm commitment that art and culture must be a force for social change. In this way he wants black artists to keep it real.

The realness of rap in both form and content has the potential to develop new cultural symbols, a new power of representation that extends the political agenda of Wilson. And yet the realness of rap offers not old style self-determination but a new politics of cultural traffic that recognizes the power of representation. "Keeping it real" and the politics of representation can recontextualize meanings. Gold teeth, for example, can function as a performative display, a sign of authenticity or realness for southern black rappers, that marks their relationship to the hood. Yet, as the *Wall Street Journal* proclaims, the chief profiteer from this realness, the dentist of choice that installs these teeth, the "Rapper Dentist Daddy" is a white Roman Catholic, Ronald Cunning of Montclair, California who has worked on the teeth of such rappers as C-Murder and Master P.[24] The *Wall Street Journal*, however, misses the point. The fact that this white dentist makes money on this symbol of black rapper realness does not negate the power and impact of the symbol. In fact the symbol of gold teeth becomes unmoored from its association with white dentistry by its placement and significance on or this case in the black body. And yet as noted, such a politics of realness with its extensive focus on visibility does not necessarily translate into a politics of social change. Rather, if keeping it real is just a politics of representation, then it does not disrupt the mechanisms of that representation. Wilson, in his TCG address, identifies an urgency—that there is an immediate need for blacks artists to understand how they have been interpolated within the white hegemony of the American artistic system and to resist. Change must occur in order to keep it real, and keeping it real for Wilson always involves historic change. Yet, how other black artists, black rappers in particular, experience this urgency and respond remains complex without one singular, clear, political path. What the future entails for rap and how it engages Wilson's call will continue to unfold on the global cultural arena.

NOTES

I would like to thank Nicole Fleetwood for her thoughtful reading of this paper and for the impact of her work in shaping its argument.

1. Stuart Hall, "New Ethnicities," *The Post-Colonial Studies Reader*, ed. Bill Ashcroft, Gareth Griffiths, and Helen Tiffin (London: Routledge, 1995), 223–228.
2. Nicole Fleetwood, "Documenting the 'Real': Youth, Race and the Discourse of Realness in Visual Culture," Dissertation, June 2001, Stanford University, 105.
3. John Lahr, "Been Here and Gone," *The New Yorker*, April 16, 2001: 64.
4. John Russell Rickford and Russell John Rickford, *Spoken Soul: The History of Black English* (New York: John Wiley and Sons, Inc., 2000), 29, 28.
5. Fleetwood, "Documenting the 'Real,'" 105.
6. August Wilson, "The Ground on Which I Stand," *American Theatre* (September 1996): 14. All other references to this text are made in the text.
7. Tricia Rose, "Hidden Politics: Discursive and Institutional Policing of Rap Music," *Droppin' Science: Critical Essays on Rap Music and Hip Hop Culture*, ed. William Eric Perkins (Philadelphia: Temple University Press, 1996), 236.
8. See Nicole Fleetwood, "'Get on the Bus': An Ethnographic Study of Youth, Performativity, and Public Transit," unpublished essay, June 1999. Forthcoming in *TDR/The Journal of Performance Studies*.
9. Robin D. G. Kelley, *Race Rebels: Culture, Politics, and the Black Working Class* (New York: Free Press, 1994), 191.
10. Danny Hoch, *Jails, Hospitals & Hip Hop and Some People* (New York: Villard Press, 1998), 20.
11. Ibid., 21.
12. Russell Potter, *Spectacular Vernaculars: Hip-Hop and the Politics of Postmodernism* (Albany, NY: State University of New York Press, 1995), 111.
13. Ibid., 117.
14. Ibid., 119.
15. Kelley, *Race Rebels*, 191.
16. I am thankful to Nicole Hickman for bringing this conscious rap to my attention.
17. Potter, *Spectacular Vernaculars*, 123–124.
18. José Muñoz, *Disidentifications: Queers of Color and the Performance of Politics* (Minneapolis: University of Minnesota Press, 1999), 1–34.
19. August Wilson, "Foreword," *Speak My Name: Black Men on Masculinity and the American Dream*, ed. Don Belton (Boston: Beacon Press, 1995), xiii.
20. Philip Auslander, *Presence and Resistance: Postmodernism and Cultural Politics in Contemporary American* (Ann Arbor: University of Michigan Press, 1992), 23.
21. Commenting on his experience at the Huntington Theater in Boston during rehearsals for Seven Guitars, Wilson said, "I am an invited guest. As such, I'm treated with respect and dignity. But I can't move the furniture around. It's not my furniture. And eventually I will have to leave because its' not my home." August Wilson, quoted by Michael Blowen, "Dreaming with Words Wilson's

Plays are a Matter of Thinking, and Re-thinking What is on the Page," *Boston Globe*, October 25, 1998, sec M: 1.

22. Marion McClinton, quoted by John Lahr, "Been Here and Gone," *The New Yorker*, April 16, 2001: 64.

23. Michael Quinn, " 'Never shoulda been let out the penitentiary': Gangsta Rap and the Struggle over Racial Identity," *Cultural Critique* 34 (Fall 1996): 80.

24. Lisa Bannon, "Word of Mouth Helps 'Rapper Dentist Daddy' Corner the Flashy Market," *Wall Street Journal*, July 19, 2001: 1.

7

Giving Voice and Vent to African American Culture: Katherine Dunham's Struggle for Cultural Ownership in *Mambo* (1954)

Dorothea Fischer-Hornung

So much of what makes this country rich in art and all manner of spiritual life is the contributions we as African Americans have made. We cannot allow others to have authority over our cultural and spiritual products. We reject, without reservation, any attempts by anyone to rewrite our history so as to deny us the rewards of our spiritual labors, and to become the cultural custodians of our art, our literature and our lives. To give expression to the spirit that has been shaped and fashioned by our history is of necessity to give voice and vent to the history itself. (78)

With this statement taken from his 1996 speech "The Ground on Which I stand,"[1] August Wilson unequivocally claims the right of African Americans to their cultural property—a challenge that looks both to the struggles and achievements in the past as well as fuelling a debate on the role of African American culture in the present and future. While underlining the "common ground" of the European and African tradition, acknowledging his own debt to the European theater from Euripides to Henrik Ibsen as well as the Euro-American tradition from Eugene O'Neill to Tennessee Williams, Wilson decisively positions himself in the political and cultural national tradition of the shared experience of resistance in the African American diaspora from Nat Turner to the Honorable Elijah Mohammed (14).

The thesis that "race matters" (14) as a foundation for group identification based on shared biological and cultural roots lies at the heart of Wilson's theory of artistic production; its immediate repercussions for performance art is expressed most directly in Wilson's *Ma Rainey's Black Bottom* (1984). Set in the 1920s, the play can be read as a portrayal of prototypical struggles of the African American performer in the twentieth century. Underlining Rainey's experience as expressed in the play is Wilson's own experience in staging this very play as he related it in his 1991 interview with Sandra Shannon in *The Dramatic Vision of August Wilson*. Here, Wilson points out how important it is for artists to gain recognition for their work, both for their artistic merit, and the intellectual and financial rights to their work. Arguably, August Wilson's difficulty in asserting his intellectual property rights to *Ma Rainey's Black Bottom* as well as the play's plot provides a paradigm for analyzing African American intellectual ownership in the context of the conflicted traditions of the African American past. Wilson asserts:

> I stand myself and my art squarely on the self-defining ground of the slave quarters, and find the ground to be hollowed and made fertile by the blood and bones of the men and women who can be described as warriors on the cultural battlefield that affirmed their self-worth. (16)

Josephine Baker, Bill "Bojangles" Robinson, Hattie McDaniel, Zora Neale Hurston, Paul Robeson, and Langston Hughes are but only a few examples of artists who stand on this hollowed ground. The work of Katherine Dunham—a true Renaissance woman as dancer, choreographer, instructor, dance theorist, as well as anthropologist, whose work spans the 1930s to the present day—provides a further salient example of an African American performer rooted solidly in the black cultural tradition. Katherine Dunham's struggle in the 1950s to define and assert her own portrayal of African American diasporic culture in the Italian American Paramount production *Mambo* (1954), as well as her assertion of her commercial rights to the intellectual property used in this film, provides a specific, historical example of resistance to the unacknowledged European–American appropriation of black culture.

Gertrude "Ma" Rainey, the "Mother of the Blues" and the first commercially successful blues recording artist, is portrayed in Wilson's play as caught between the strictures of the control of the economic means of production and her right to her artistic talent. The profitable "race records" market was in the hands of white producers in the 1920s and seriously impacted Rainey's sense of her art and unique style, a style that was based on but also fed into the grassroots group identity of her African American audience. Her troubled relationship with Paramount records provides an object example of the struggle for African American agency in controlling the production and performance of diasporic art forms. The question of what gets produced and in which style is closely linked, especially after the demise of Black Swan Records,[2] to what white producers think the audience wants and will sell. Hence, Wilson's *Ma Rainey's Black Bottom* focuses on the constant tension between legitimate agency reflected in Ma Rainey's self-assured knowledge that hers is the indisputably correct "black bottom" approach, an approach that is true to her audience and to herself, and the social conditions outside the studio that reduce her to her racial identity, to her blackness.

Wilson feels it is essential to consider the larger social, political, and economic context in which African American performance takes place. Race matters, Wilson asserts—yet "blackness not only denotes race; it denotes condition" ("Ground on Which I Stand" 16). As Toni Morrison in *Playing in the Dark* elucidates, "race has become metaphorical—a way of referring to and disguising forces, events, classes, and expressions of social decay and economic division far more threatening to the body politic than biological 'race' ever was" (63).

In the generation following Ma Rainey, Katherine Dunham, early on in her career as a performer as well as anthropologist, recognized these same fundamental "black-bottom" truths. In her life and art, Dunham fought to change the conditions that in the United States defined blackness as a category justifying social, political, and cultural discrimination. When Dunham left the United States to tour Europe in 1948, she had performed as a dancer in the 1941 Broadway production of and the 1943 film version of *Cabin in the Sky* as well as the film *Stormy Weather* (1943), for which she also provided the choreography. In addition, she had successfully established the Katherine Dunham School of Dance in New York. Her first engagement in England was planned as a three weeks' booking in London, but the engagement stretched into three months. Over the next fifteen years, the Katherine Dunham Dance Company toured over fifty countries as the largest nonsubsidized, independent U.S. dance troupe of its day.[3] Her success on the stage is reflected in the fact that box office receipts, not grants or subsidies, provided the seed money for founding the Dunham School of Dance in New York in 1945 and for sustaining it after it became the Katherine Dunham School of Cultural Arts, Inc.[4] Within a few years over 300 students received instruction based on a holistic approach, emphasizing not only dance instruction, but also, for example, courses in languages, anthropology, sociology, and psychology. Butterfly McQueen, Marlon Brando, James Dean, José Ferrar, and Shelley Winters were among the students; José Limon, Lavinia Williams, Lee Strasberg, and Margaret Mead were among the school's instructors (Long 101). In addition to her New York school, Dunham later established more or less successful dance schools in Paris, Stockholm, and Rome.

Dunham successfully staged performances rooted in African diasporic culture in the United States, but her often open protest against racial segregation and violence had serious consequences for her career. Her 1944 public statement to the theater audience in Louisville, Kentucky, after her troupe's performance there remains as a powerful, public indictment of racial segregation:

> It makes me very happy to know that you have liked us, that you have felt some of the beauty and happiness that we feel when we perform. But tonight our hearts are very sad because this is a farewell to Louisville. There comes a time when every human being must protest in order to retain human dignity. I must protest because I have discovered that your management will not allow people like you to sit next to people like us. I hope that time and the unhappiness of this war for tolerance and democracy, which I am sure we will win, will change some of these things—perhaps then we can return.

Until then,
GOD BLESS YOU—
FOR YOU MAY NEED IT! (Qtd. in Clark 88)

In Santiago de Chile in January 1951, Dunham premiered *Southland*, a dance performance about lynching. *Southland* opens against the backdrop of an antebellum plantation in the South, the "Greek chorus of singers" that "represent the fundamental simplicity, the earth-dignity of the Negro" asks: "Is it true what they say about Dixie? Does the sun shine all the time?" The production then openly parodies the falsified, derivative culture of minstrelsy: "one of them sings a standard concept of a Negro's nostalgia for the Swanee River, another with the same ironic touch sings 'Carry me back to old Virginie.' " These two songs from the minstrel tradition are then juxtaposed with a rendition of the politically resonant "Steal Away" sung "with the force of the true Negro spirituals." The chorus is then unified in singing the revival hymn "Dry Bones" (117).

Dunham's juxtaposition of the falsification of folk culture in minstrelsy and authentic African diasporic culture in the opening scene of the performance underlines the distortion of African American culture in European–American theater, but *Southland* goes on to foreground directly the infamy of the lynching of African Americans. At the foot of a magnolia tree in the plantation scene, field hands sing work songs and dance African *Juba*, a traditional ring dance that links African and African diasporic culture. It is this magnolia tree which then bears "Strange Fruit," the lynching that results when, in his attempt to help an unconscious white girl, one of the young black field hands violates the South's ultimate taboo by touching her. "Strange Fruit," the evocative song about lynching recorded by Billie Holiday in 1939,[5] underlines the theme musically. Not only the content of *Southland* is forceful and direct in its indictment of random violence against African Americans, but Dunham's outspoken statement in the program notes also overtly underlines the artistic and political intent of the performance:

> This is the story of no actual lynching in the southern states of America and still it is the story of every one of them.... The ballet "SOUTHLAND" is a comment on violence and its attendant guilt, which often acts in the human individual as the most powerful agent of destruction. In 1952 [*sic*][6] for the first time in the 70 years that such incidents have seemed newsworthy, there was no recorded lynching in the United States. Mob violence, racial hatreds [*sic*] continue there however, as in many other great nations of the world. The ballet is directed, insofar as its intentions surpass purely theatrical and artistic aspirations, toward the conscience not of one nation, but of all human beings who are not yet aware of the destructive dangers of hatred. (Qtd. in Clark 118)

Southland was never performed in the United States, and it is very likely that as a direct result of such open political protest, the State Department refused to support her financially as an overseas cultural ambassador for the United States.[7] Dunham was, therefore, forced to rely on her own ticket sales to support her dance troupe and production crew on her European tour; a constant struggle for solvency was the result. But she was able to perform more successfully in Europe at this point than in the United States, and Dunham clearly acknowledges this fact: "Without Europe we couldn't have survived" (Aschenbrenner 35).

When Dunham toured Europe in the 1950s, European "negrophila"[8] could look back on a long tradition, and the Africanist influence on twentieth-century European art was well established. The monumental effect of Picasso's Africanist aesthetics in *Les Demoiselles d'Avignon* and its influence on subsequent modernism had fundamentally changed European visual arts. Josephine Baker had taken Paris by storm, and post–World-War-I Europe had enthusiastically joined the United States in the craze for dances such as the charleston and the black bottom. The fascination with black "primitivism" became a racially essentialist modernist trope, relegating blacks to "natural" primitivism and Europeans to "learned" culturalism. The mimicry of "blackness" more clearly defined "whiteness" in Europe's search for release from early-twentieth-century ennui. In the period after each of the two world wars, it was in the accepted space of ballroom dancing, in the black bottom dance craze of the 1920s, and the jitterbug and mambo dance crazes of the 1950s, that Europeans and European Americans found the potential for release from the anxieties of war as well as sexual repression. White Europeans and European Americans thought they had discovered a way to escape from want and suffering in a derivative African American pleasure culture—a way to act black without actually being black.

It was in this context in 1953 that Italian film producer Dino De Laurentiis was looking for a vehicle to showcase Silvana Mangano, his wife, and to present her talent as a dancer.[9] At the same time, Robert Rossen was also looking for a way to alleviate his own financial problems after two years on Hollywood's black list.[10] The Italian stars Silvana Mangano and Vittorio Gassman along with the U.S. stars Michael Rennie, Shelly Winters, and, of course, Katherine Dunham were to guarantee financial success on both sides of the Atlantic. The resulting parade of stars were gathered in the Carlo Ponti-Dino De Laurentiis production *Mambo* (1954), a film that remains significant not so much because it is completely artistically successful, but because arguably it marks a significant step in unmistakably recognizing and visualizing African American agency in cultural production.

The body of the film, with strong parallels to Mangano's own biography, consists of a flashback relating how Giovanna Mansetti (Silvana Mangano), a Venetian shopgirl of lower-class background, became the star we see dance in the opening scene. She is in love with Mario Rossi (Vittorio Gassman), a black-market operator and a part-time croupier at the Venice Casino. Giovanna meets the wealthy Count Enrico Marisoni (Michael Rennie), who invites her to a lavish masked carnival ball in a Venetian palazzo. Giovanna, under the influence of a liberal dose of alcohol and the general license of the carnival setting, is carried away by the sexualized performance of the Dunham troupe, spontaneously joining them in an overtly eroticized dance. The Venetian carnival setting enables the suspension of the ethical categories of good and evil as well as the strictures of class, race, and gender—a fundamental characteristic of the carnival tradition. The remainder of the melodramatic Cinderella-esque plot revolves around the poor girl caught in the conflict between two men who want to possess her and her recognition that to be true to herself, she must be true to her art, true to her talent as a dancer.[11]

In addition to its visualization of African American cultural agency, surely the film's most lasting contribution is its preservation of valuable footage of Katherine Dunham teaching Dunham dance technique. Based on her anthropology research in the Caribbean in the 1930s,[12] Dunham developed her instructional technique to teach African diasporic dance forms based on the isolation of various parts of the body by breaking down the elements of traditional dances into individual movements. Another significant contribution to dance theory and especially dance based on African diasporic elements is Dunham's explication of the difference between unlearned, "natural" essentialism and learned culturalism. Dunham insists that all dance culture is learned and not "natural," even if it is acquired in an informal setting and not a studio. Furthermore, Dunham's insistence on the use of diasporic dance tradition based on her own anthropology research in the Caribbean is based on the explication of the changes that are necessary when staging these cultural elements outside their traditional context for a nontraditional audience. It was Dunham's conviction that this diasporic folk cultural heritage is transformed on the way to the stage and is a learned artform based on hard work and dedication that is clearly visualized in *Mambo*'s instructional footage. But Dunham goes one step further and claims her legal rights to this specific part of the film as well as to the songs performed by Mangano, a process that is documented in her correspondence and her application for copyrights to the Italian Musicians' Union.

In her application for the intellectual property rights to the lyrics of the songs as well as to the scores of the traditional music used in the dance instruction segments, Dunham specifies the film footage shot (see "Letters and Lyrics to Dottore Faccena," March 5, 1954). She documents precisely which segments were actually included in the film after final editing since not all segments that were filmed were actually used. For example, the final U.S and Italian versions differ significantly. The U.S. release is reported to have been severely edited, making it a full fifteen minutes shorter than the European version; it was "recut several times after Rossen finished it, and it is said to bear little resemblance to the original" (*Monthly Film Bulletin* 71). Some of the music and many of the lyrics were provided by Katherine Dunham, and her correspondence indicates that she had difficulties in registering her copyrights in Italy.[13] Her application became particularly important after she learned that two of the songs—one a blues Mangano sings and dances to in the last third of the film—had been completed for record production. Considering the star status of Mangano in Italy, this was surely a serious financial consideration (see "Letters, Lyrics and Lists of Titles of Music").

The complexities involved in Dunham's assertion to intellectual property rights and royalties is reflected in a letter dated November 12, 1954, in which Dunham writes from Buenos Aires to Enrico Leonardi in Rome, asking him to obtain information on the record releases, "because it could very easily involve considerable sums of money since the music for *Mambo* has already been released." Dunham maintains that "[a]ll of the music for 'Mambo' was written either by Bernardo Noriega [who Dunham had hired from Buenos Aires specifically for work on the film] or Dave Gilbert. Large sections known as 'rehearsal music' were folkloric in nature to which I personally have a claim for returns … (the lyrics in all cases were mine)" (1). If there are seeming ironies entailed in trying to apply for copyrights to cultural forms based on anthropological research, it is only in the context of the fundamental changes that African Caribbean folk culture must necessarily undergo in its artistic transition from folk culture to stage and film culture that Dunham's application seems justified:

> The concept of each dance is a thoroughly accurate one but the presentation is creative. I don't believe in transplanting purely authentic material to an urban stage in its original form, because I feel that primitive[14] folk material is functional in the community it's a part of. Its use in our theater should be purely derivative and creative. (Dunham [1943] Qtd. in Aschenbrenner 57)

Since Dunham was not a member of the Italian musicians' union, all of the rights were registered under Noriega's name,[15] and the rights that Gilbert held were signed over to Dunham after production (2). Dunham suggests that "in view of the fact that he was under salary to me and had been transported some distance for this particular job, I [should] receive one-third of any monies whatsoever which he receives…." Especially the rehearsal music and a song "which may very well be a hit song entitled NEW LOVE NEW WINE and the BOOGIE Movement from the BIG BALLET MAMBO" (2) should, she stressed, be paid to her in full. One can see the many conflicting interests that were at stake in Dunham's negotiations as well as the pressure she was under to constantly monitor her interests as well as the interests of her dance troupe as a whole under different national legal systems.

Already in the early phases of her work in Italy, after only several weeks into production, Dunham had run into problems over who had the rights to the cultural material used in *Mambo*.[16] Fighting on numerous fronts at the same time, Dunham felt pressed to assert her right to cultural ownership and her intellectual property in Italy during production and simultaneously with her agents in the United States and France. In a letter to Dale Wasserman dated December 18, 1953, she traces a less than friendly, even quite stereotypical, portrait of Italian business relations: "I can only say this much about Italians: they plagiarise [*sic*] without even thinking it is unusual or wrong, they make promises with no intention of keeping them and an untruth represents no breach of moral code whatsover [*sic*]" (2). Shortly thereafter, Albert Travel and Felix Marouani, Dunham's agents for her European tour, were asserting their rights to commissions on any profits earned. On December 9, 1953 Felix Marouani writes:

> In our business we have to attend constantly to deals which are either profitable or unprofitable, according to whether the deal comes through or not...it is therefore quite normal that I should ask you a commission on any deal made by you on the Continent. I admit that I did not have any expenses on the de Laurentis [*sic*] deal. I do feel, however, that if I had not booked you on the Continent, and arranged successive successful tours of your show in Italy, there is a great chance Mr. de Laurentis [*sic*] would not have been in a position to judge your talent and therefore come to a deal with you.... In short, I still feel quite entitled to ask you for 5% on the de Laurentis [*sic*] deal, and 10% on the bookings whenever you get your full salary. (1–2)

At this point in her career, Dunham had certainly learned from painful lessons in her early career. For example, George Balanchine had and Dunham had not been credited for their respective contributions to the choreography of *Cabin in the Sky* during its Broadway run in 1941. According to Brenda Dixon Gottschild:

> Balanchine's early American career included a substantial apprenticeship on Broadway. Between 1936 and 1948 he choreographed or co-choreographed a number of musicals, including "The Zigfield Follies" (1936), "On Your Toes" (1936), "Babes in Arms" (1937), "I married an Angel" (1938), "The Boys from Syracuse" (1938), and, with Katherine Dunham, "Cabin in the Sky" (1940). (69)

In a letter dated May 17, 1941 to her agents Goldie and Gump with reference to the Broadway production of *Cabin in the Sky*, in which, in addition to her contribution as choreographer, she played the role of Sweet Georgia Brown, Dunham wrote:

> I am under the impression that Mr. Schubert saw the choreography, all of which was originated by me, for my concert performances at the Windsor Theatre, as well as that in "Cabin in the Sky" which was done by me almost in its entirety (changed to: "in great measure").
> [Dunham added the following qualifying note dated May 18, 1941 at the bottom of this letter]
> You will note that I did make one change, however, in reference to the choreography in "Cabin in the Sky." It hardly seemed fair, in view of the fact that Mr. Balanchine cooperated so well with me to say "almost in its entirety," so that I have changed this to say "in great measure." I hope that won't change the body of the letter. (2)

One can, of course, read the subtext here—she cannot claim the choreography totally as her own, but she hopes that this will not change the substance of her demands—in other words, she, not Balanchine, should have the intellectual and financial rights to the choreography in the production.

It is significant that Dunham emphasizes Balanchine's cooperation with *her* and not the reverse. Dunham feared, justifiably as the failure to credit her reveals, that a white, male, Russian immigrant choreographer would get more recognition for his contribution to an all-black musical than a black, female, dancer choreographer would.[17] To add insult to injury, in the film version of *Cabin in the Sky* (1943), Lena Horn was given the role of Sweet Georgia Brown and the film credits again fail to mention Dunham for her choreography. This clearly meant not only immediate loss of status, but also the loss of future benefits—financial profit as well as advancement in her own career and that of her dance troupe. But Dunham did not rescind her rights easily but rather personally and legally asserted her right to her contribution to this landmark film. She tried to negotiate the touchy territory of her intellectual property rights to her choreography at a time when Hollywood unashamedly denied them to African American performers.

Conditions relating to African American cultural assertiveness, it seems, had not changed substantially by the 1980s. Dunham's difficulties in asserting her rights to cultural property and her agency in the production of *Cabin in the Sky* are disturbingly similar to Wilson's own experience in the first production of *Ma Rainey's Black Bottom*. Wilson emphasizes how essential credits are to an artist, not only financially but also psychologically. Early in his career during the Broadway production of *Ma Rainey's Black Bottom*, he experienced the painful lack of esteem granted to him and other young dramatists: "It didn't have my name on the marquee . . . But I think any playwright—first play, last play, or whatever—should have their name on the marquee identifying him as the person who wrote this play" (qtd. in Shannon 219). In 1984 he desperately needed money and was offered large sums by the producers of the Drama Guild for the rights to this play. Nevertheless, he decided against the Drama Guild production and decided to have a staged reading by Lloyd Richards at the O'Neill Theater. This staging was followed by a production at the Yale Repertory Theater, and subsequently the play had a Broadway run of eight months: "They [the producers at the Drama Guild] could have ruined my script, turned it into a musical, and I would have been a one-shot playwright" (qtd. in Shannon 218).

A two-page memorandum written in Venice by Dunham to Robert Rossen, dated March 4, 1954, shortly before the Paramount release of *Mambo*, reveals she encountered similar production problems. Her notes concerning the carnival scene indicate that Dunham was very specific as to how her ideas should be staged, including her demand to have a say in the film's final editing. Although this memorandum was written very late in the editing process, it reveals Dunham's strong commitment to shaping the final product. Nevertheless, it also reflects her previously marginal involvement in the overall process: "Miss Dunham feels that this scene [the carnival masked ball scene] needs to be embellished and the atmosphere of elegance and ease to be accentuated" (1). She then goes on to detail the opening palazzo scene, defining everything from the appropriate material for a sari to noting that "no one is smoking [in the scene]; this is not normal" (1) and that the "eastern potentates are not dark enough" (1). Finally, she criticizes the lack of expertise of the designer, who, Dunham regrets "did not know more concerning the details and atmosphere that such a ball scene would show" (2). She concludes: "Miss Dunham feels that character as well as costume is vitally important in these shots and therefore people with character must be spotted" (2). Most assuredly, these are instructions issued by a professional confident of her capability to stage a scene precisely as she envisions it—a professional demanding her right to agency in shaping her art.

In its visualization of the appropriation of African American culture by Europeans, one scene in *Mambo*, however, stands out in particular as a reification of the appropriation of African American culture as well as of Wilson's paradigmatic assertion that African Americans must control their own cultural property rights. Several scenes in *Mambo* shot in a dance studio setting show Dunham actually training Mangano in Dunham technique.[18] We see an African American dance instructor confident in her control not only of a large number of racially diverse dance students, but also of a major European film star—certainly a strong visual documentation and recognition of Dunham's importance as a dancer, choreographer, and instructor.[19] After several short scenes of dance training, the film cuts to a rehearsal room equipped with an upright piano. A Latin-looking guitarist and a piano player are positioned to the fore of the piano. A black male singer is to the piano's left with Dunham in the middle behind the piano. They are teaching Giovanna [Mangano], standing to the right of the piano, how to sing. Dunham, who is clearly frustrated by Giovanna's lack of progress, asserts: "Now look, Giovanna. If you can talk you can sing," which could translate to, "If you can walk you can dance." Giovanna struggles with two lines of a song: "Black night, creep in; come hide my sin." She rebels in frustration: "I can't do it this way." Toni, the manager of the dance troupe, played by Shelley Winters, enters and admonishes her: "Make it your own. Your voice. Your personality." Toni demands that Giovanna go beyond imitation to actually possess the song and sing it in her own style. Visually, the "color-line" moves from the male singer, who has the darkest skin at the far left, to Dunham, who is more light-skinned and positioned in the middle, to Giovanna, who is white-skinned with long dark hair on the right, and, finally, to Toni, entering on the extreme right, who is white-skinned with short blond hair. In the final shot, the viewer sees only Mangano and Winters; Dunham and the black singer have disappeared from our vision.

The primal scene of Euro-American appropriation of African American culture has been staged in this carefully structured visual move from blackness to whiteness. Yet, *Mambo*'s is a primal scene of appropriation with a difference: the European American appropriation of African American performance style, a process that is usually invisible, tabooed, is here explicitly staged and visualized—a reverse minstrelsy scene, if you will—instead of "blacking up," we see diasporic African culture "whiting up."[20] In *Mambo* the whitening of black culture is explicitly staged as a black male singer and a black female dancer/choreographer commissioned by a white U.S.

manager to instruct a white European dancer/singer and to transform her from a talker into a singer, from a walker into a dancer. This fundamentally challenges the Eurocentric perspective, visualizing the "black bottom" African diasporic influence on American and European culture.

For the viewer this is potentially a moment similar to the one Toni Morrison describes in *Playing in the Dark*. Quoting Antonia S. Byatt, Morrison focuses on the moment while reading when our understanding of reality can be fundamentally changed in the recognition of the "always already" knowledge that has been repressed: "a sense that the text has appeared to be wholly new, never before seen, is followed, almost immediately, by the sense that it was *always there*, that we, the readers, knew it was always there, and have *always known* it was there, though we have now for the first time recognized, become fully cognizant of, our knowledge" (xiii–xiv).

Mambo's performance of cultural appropriation clearly foregrounds the African diasporic cultural roots of Giovanna's art in its stubborn refusal to hide Dunham's (and the anonymous black singer's) role in the process of cultural appropriation and transformation from black to white, from African Americans to Europeans. But, as Jane C. Desmond points out, we must be cautious when reading the meaning associated with *Mambo*'s daring reversal of the widely held model of cultural appropriation:

> In cases where a cultural form migrates from a subordinate to a dominant group, the meanings attached to that adoption (and remodeling) are generated within the parameters of the current historical relations between the two groups, and their constitution of each as "other" and as different in particular ways. For example, the linkage in North American white culture of blacks with sexuality, sensuality, and an alternately celebrated or denigrated presumably "natural" propensity for physical ability, expressivity, or bodily excess tinges the adoption of black dances. (37)

Locating the film in the context of the carnival challenges this binary that identifies body with the African and mind with the European. *Mambo*'s carnival setting logically and daringly locates European culture at the interstices of subliminal sexuality and ritualized release, and loss of control. *Mambo* contextualizes European and African diasporic culture in one and the same frame of reference, breaking down the binaries of mind/body, black/white, and African/European. The enabling context is provided by the carnival, where, as Dunham noted in her *Dances of Haiti*, "an entire population is gradually released from moral and civic obligations, and the diverse social, economic, and religious groups become closely united in a single mass activity" (42). According to Umberto Eco, during carnival "the law must be pervasively and profoundly introjected as to be overwhelmingly present at the moment of its violation" (6). But therefore, "every tragic or dramatic text not only tells the story of a violation of a rule, it restates the rule" (4). *Mambo* reflects this dual movement of the carnival's trajectory—a simultaneous breaking of the rules during the ritualized carnival period and the substantiation and reinstatement of these rules in the period following carnival.

There is, therefore, a utopian moment of transcendence inherent in the carnival. "Carnival opened up a space for a free and frank investigation of forms that were otherwise represented as 'natural' or eternally 'given,' and was a site for the invention of improbable collocations and associations" (Cunliffe 50). A crucial aspect of the carnival is its refusal to "acquiesce in the legitimacy of the present social system which, for many theorists, is the hallmark of the oppositional utopia." (35). The carnival can express our "deepest fantasies about the nature of social life, both as we live it now, and as we feel in our bones it ought to be lived" (Jameson qtd. in Gardener 38).

It is exceedingly doubtful if Hollywood actually understood the subversive impulse in this staging, and none of the contemporary reviewers mention the singing instruction scene. One reviewer sees the film as a "sordid and murky story" (*Motion Picture Herald* 387) and another notes that "[c]ollaboration between Italian and American film-makers has produced some eccentric and unhappy results," seeing it as "another of these uneasy hybrid productions" (*Monthly Film Bulletin* 71). And the *Hollywood Reporter* asks why Mangano is given such a central role when Dunham and her dancers are so much more capable:

> When you know that the justly famous Miss Dunham and her company are present, you naturally want to see them really cut loose. It also confuses the story, since it is hard to see why an organization that has so specialized in Negro choreography and music as to place it among the top modern arts should want to spend so much trouble featuring a white performance. (3)

But this is exactly the point: Mangano is the European star, and she appropriates blackness via the Mambo dance craze, making it her own. We see Europeanist culturalism pitted against "the Katherine Dunham troupe at their primitive best" (*Motion Picture Herald* 387). The contemporary viewers were almost certainly caught in the same essentialist trap as the reviewers who are able to see only the stereotypical tropes of "blackness" and "whiteness" without seeing the Africanist roots of much of European American culture. Perhaps these truths can only be recognized in moments of transgression and the resistance to them is so great that, like in the carnival, the "natural" order is reestablished after the "fools" have had their say.

"To cast us in the role of mimics is to deny us our own competence" ("Ground on Which I Stand" 498), Wilson maintains in his assertion of the origins of a black aesthetic. Yet in *Mambo* it is Mangano who is cast as the mimic, making visible the moment when European and European American culture mimics black art, the moment when the African American roots of much of American and European performance disappear, making it invisible, leaving us with Fred Astaire rather than the Nicholas Brothers and Elvis Presley rather than "Big Mama" Thorton as the major, money-making stars (see Dixon Gottschild 23–24). Nevertheless, for generations African Americans have transcended mimicry through subversion, turning mimicry and signifying into an art form. In *Mambo*, however, we see Mangano as the mimic learning to transcend mimicry, making it her own—the flip side of the same appropriative coin—raising the mimicry of black culture to a white art form. Nevertheless, in its visualization of this process, *Mambo* refuses—most remarkably—to make its African American roots disappear.[21]

Dunham's performance in and her insistence on cultural ownership of her contributions to *Mambo* does the tough cultural work of rubbing against the grain of the dominant discourse of essentialism. However, *Mambo*'s visualization of the process of cultural appropriation allows no easy answers in reference to what the viewer actually understands to be the film's intentions. Not only the Africanist roots of much of European and U.S. performance disappear in the racialized context of European American theater and film, but there is a direct loss of esteem for both the performers as well as the authors and choreographers of black art—with all the attendant personal and financial consequences. In his speech at the National Black Theater Festival in 1997 Wilson touches on precisely this point:

> Are we to subjugate ourselves to the European-American version and vision of the world? Or are we gonna demand equal time, equal vision? We need theater to recreate an image of ourselves as positive and industrious life. If you are the spiritual heritage of Africa, what is the context to which you owe your identity, your life, your struggle? Wherein lies your duty? If the theater as art expresses, contains, and is itself a part of that energy which is life, which is fuelled by the blood of Africa and has been kept alive on the continent of North America for 386 years in the faces [*sic*] of those who would deny your manners, your mores, and even your humanity, then it is theater and art whose concerns are different than concerns of European Americans who are distrustful of other sources of vitality…even though our fate is inextricably woven together. (491)

Essential to both August Wilson's and Katherine Dunham's project is the proposition that African American culture is an integral element of European culture, but that the reverse is also true, that European culture is part and parcel of the African American diasporic experience—and this without the loss or rejection of the specificity of either the Africanist tradition or the Europeanist tradition. It is apparent that we are not dealing with the culture of the Other from the European perspective or vice versa, but that the Other is but two sides of the same coin—a rejection of the Africanist elements of European culture is to close our eyes to the context that unfairly skews financial success and recognition of African diasporic art, assigning invisibility and lack of support to the Africanist side of that coin. It is this invisibility that Katherine Dunham and August Wilson have fundamentally and courageously resisted in their struggle to give voice and vent to African American culture.

NOTES

1. Address delivered June 26, 1996 to the Theatre Community Group National Conference at Princeton University.
2. Harry Herbert Pace started Black Swan records after he observed that "white recording companies bought the music and lyrics from Pace and [W.C.] Handy and then recorded them using white artists. When they did employ Blacks they refused to let them sing and play in their own authentic style." Black Swan signed Ethel Waters, but, for example, failed to sign Bessie Smith, who Pace felt was too "nitty gritty." Black Swan's initial substantial financial success was undermined when white recording companies started to bid competitively for black recording artists and Black Swan records had only four short years of recording success. See Weusi <http://www.redhotjazz.com/blackswan.html> February 2, 2002.
3. Please note that "U.S. dance troupe" is not qualified by "African American."
4. The fact that the troupe could even exist without subsidies was already noted in 1949 by the British dance historian Richard Buckle, who points out that to some "[i]t comes as a shock to learn that a Negro should successfully run the largest unsubsidized company of dancers in the United States" (ix).
5. Billie Holiday faced her own problems in trying to get this open protest against lynching recorded:

   > Although Billie Holiday made "Strange Fruit" a permanent part of her repertoire soon after her decision to sing it at Café Society, she was unable to convince Columbia, the recording company with which she was under contract, to let her record it. "They won't buy it in the South" was the company's excuse. "We'll be boycotted.... It's too inflammatory." Holiday persisted and eventually Columbia released her for one recording date on Milt Gambler's Commodore label. (Davis 195)

6. The "Southland Program" reprinted in Clark is dated January 1951.
7. "While the State Department subsidized other less well-known groups, it refused to support the Dunham company (even when entertaining army troops), although it took credit for them as 'unofficial artistic and cultural representatives)' " (Beckford qtd. in Aschenbrenner 84).
8. For a thorough analysis of European "negrophilia" see Petrine Archer-Straw, *Negrophilia: Avant-Garde Paris and Black Culture in the 1920s.*
9. Silvana Mangano was "discovered" while she was a competitor with Gina Lollabrigida in the Miss Italy contest of 1947. Mangano starred in *Bitter Rice* (USA,1950; *Riso Amaro*, Italy, 1948), a film that made her face and legs a legend. In this early film she dances a rhumba with Vittorio Gassman, who is also a part of the later *Mambo* film project.
10. Rossen had refused to name names to the House Committee on Un-American Activities in 1947 when he was among the first to be called before the committee. In 1951 he was again subpoenaed but refused to talk about his past *activities* or those of anyone else. "Two years of forced inactivity and inner-searching followed. In 1953, he testified again and did talk about his own past and did verify names from the lists furnished by the committee" (Casty 20). He left for Europe shortly thereafter.
11. The theme of a performer who has to give up everything to possess her talent as a dancer under the tutelage of an extremely demanding instructor had, of course,

been explored several years earlier in the extremely successful British film *The Red Shoes* (1948, directed by Michael Powell and Emeric Pressburger), based on the fairy tale written by Hans Christian Anderson. Thanks to Susan Jones of Oxford University for pointing this out to me during a discussion of *Mambo* at the National University of Ireland, Galway.

12. After Dunham had finished her Bachelor's degree with Robert Redfield at the University of Chicago, Melville Herskovits of Northwestern University, one of the founders of anthropology research on the Africanist roots of diasporic culture, supported Dunham's training in preparation for her dance anthropology research in the Caribbean. There was interest on the part of both Dunham and Herskovits in her pursuing a doctorate with him but Herskovits demanded she give up her ambitions for the theater if she wanted to pursue her academic career. Dunham made a clear decision for a career as a performer. This is the same period that Zora Neale Hurston, under the guidance of Franz Boas at Columbia University, was pursuing her folklore research in the Caribbean that she would document in *Tell My Horse* (1938). Dunham's research predates Hurston's by several months and they were competitors for the meager funding available during the 1930s.

13. I would like to thank Katherine Drickamer and the staff of the Special Collections, Morris Library, Southern Illinois University, Carbondale, for their support in locating this and the subsequent archive material.

14. Dunham used the term "primitive" throughout her career in a nonpejorative sense to denote unadulterated folk culture as opposed to stage culture.

15. Noriega was obliged to pass an Italian examination in score writing in order to become a member of the Italian Musicians' Union. Gilbert failed the exam "creating an awkward situation" and he therefore agreed to sign over his rights to Dunham ("Letter to Enrico Leonardi" 1). The task of trying to negotiate copyrights in the context of very different legal systems was surely daunting.

16. Immediate financial concerns undoubtedly moved Dunham to such elaborate efforts to secure her royalties. Dunham had a large troupe of dancers and a production company to support. In addition, she was in the process of buying "Habitation Le Clerc," a plantation in Haiti, which she intended to turn into "a really serious living center of culture and learning and as a monument to Haiti" ("Letter to Dr. René Piquion" 1). Dunham desperately needed funds to implement her vision of supporting, interpreting, and elucidating African diasporic culture to a larger national and international audience.

17. In the PBS production *Free to Dance* (PBS 2000) several sections are devoted to Dunham's work. In the context of Dunham's own experience with the failure to credit her for her work, it seems ironic that film footage shot by Maya Deren, a Ukranian immigrant born Eleanora Derenkowsky, taken from *The Divine Horseman: The Living Gods of Haiti* (1951) are incorporated in the PBS production in such a way that by implication the footage is attributed to Dunham and not Deren. Here, the contemporary Deren/Dunham relationship mirrors the earlier Dunham/Balanchine relationship in that a Ukrainian immigrant, dance anthropologist, and avant-garde film maker is not credited in the voiceover. For the viewer it seems that the footage of Vaudun ceremonies in Haiti that are shown are Dunham's work.

18. According to Roy Thomas in "Focal Rites: New Dance Dominions," Dunham shot over 10,000 feet of black and white film in Haiti alone (113). The

cinematography in the dance studio scenes were a source of contemporary critical controversy with most critics seeing the material as confusing and substan-
dard. Cinematically, these are the scenes that are most interesting to us today.
Unfortunately, I have not been able to find material documenting the extent of
Dunham's influence on the cinematography in these dance instruction scenes.
Thomas maintains that "the best dance films will be made when the cinematog-
rapher is also a dancer" (115) and perhaps Dunham did have an (uncredited) say
in the shooting of these scenes. For a detailed discussion of the cinematography
and the subversive staging of a Vaudun possession in the *Mambo* dance studio
scenes see my "The Body Possessed: Katherine Dunham Dance Technique in
Mambo."

19. The racially integrated dance and instruction scenes in the film are certainly remarkable for the early 1950s. But perhaps even more remarkable in
their unpretentious racial integration are scenes of free, racially integrated interaction amongst equals in *Mambo*'s nightclub scenes and shots of boat rides
on Venice's Grand Canal. In the Italian neorealist tradition, the ideological
focus of this film is more on class than race. In an early club scene, Giovanna,
the ingénue, is clearly rejected by a group of upper-class Venetian snobs and
is later considered free for sexual exploitation by wealthy men in the carnival
ball scene. In a 1978 interview, Dunham relates her shock at returning to
the United States in terms of unchanged or even regressive negative race
relations: "we thought that we had really conquered everything that had to
do with racial division. Going away to Europe in 1947 and coming back to
stay in 1967, in effect, was quite a shock to me. I couldn't believe that everything
we had done had not progressed but regressed" (qtd. in *Kaiso!* 37).

20. A well-known example of a black performer who coached white performers
is Buddy Bradley. He trained stars such as Mae West, Ruby Keeler, as well
as Adele and Fred Astaire, developing routines for their performances. "Bradley's
name was rarely mentioned . . . there is little doubt that the use of Afro-American
performers and materials without recognition was widely practiced"
(Aschenbrenner 31).

21. The origins of Latin dances such as the samba, rhumba, and mambo are all based
on African rhythms brought by the slaves to South America, marking cultural
appropriation from the African by the European communities as well as simultaneously cultural assertion among the African diaspora:

> *Samba* was originally a synonym for *batuque* (beat), which is also a word
> from Angola and the Congo. It designated neither a type of music nor a
> particular rhythm, but the act of dancing the *samba*. . . . The *batuque* is
> known to be danced in the rites of procreation, and the navel-to-navel
> bump movements—the dance's characteristic—are considered a represen-
> tation of the sexual. Therefore, in spite of the fact that the *batuque* was the
> negroes' favorite dance after their arrival in Brazil, that beat was prohib-
> ited by the authorities. . . . Among the six to eight million negroes who
> came to Brazil, corporal expression manifested itself through the tribal
> dance without any preestablished rules. *The rhythm was so catchy that it was
> gradually absorbed by all negroes and later by white people.* So the samba is
> not merely a musical expression of a marginal social groups, but *an effec-
> tive instrument in the struggle for negro ethnic affirmation in Brazilian
> urban life* [my emphasis] (Sondre qtd. in Rector 65).

WORKS CITED

Archer-Straw, Petrine. *Negrophilia: Avant-Garde Paris and Black Culture in the 1920s.* London: Thames and Hudson, 2000.

Aschenbrenner, Joyce. *Katherine Durham: Reflections on the Social: Political Contest of Afro American Dance.* Dance Research annual XII. NY: CORD, 1981.

Buckle, Richard, ed. *Katherine Dunham: Her Dancers, Singers, Musicians.* London: Ballet Publications, 1949.

Casty, Alan. "Robert Rossen: A Retrospective Study of His Films." *Cinema (US)* IV.3 (Fall 1968): 18–22.

Clark, VèVè A. and Margaret B. Wilkerson, eds. *Kaiso! Katherine Dunham: An Anthology of Writings.* Berkeley: University of California Institute for the Study of Social Change, 1978.

Cunliffe, Robert. "Charmed Snakes and Little Oedipuses; the Architectonics of Carnival and Drama in Bakhtin, Artaud, and Brecht." *Bakhtin, Carnival and Other Subjects.* Ed. David Shepherd. Amsterdam: Rodopi, 1993. 48–69.

Davis, Angela Y. *Blues Legacies and Black Feminism: Gertrude "Ma" Rainey, Bessie Smith and Billie Holiday.* New York: Random House, 1998.

Desmond, Jane C. *Meaning in Motion: New Cultural Studies in Dance.* Durham: Duke University Press, 1997.

Dixon Gottschild, Brenda. *Digging the Africanist Presence in American Performance: Dance and Other Contexts.* Westport: Greenwood, 1996.

Dunham, Katherine. The Dances of Haiti. Los Angeles: University of California at Los Angeles Press, 1983. Revision of "Las Danzas di Haiti." *Acta Anthropolgica* II.4 (Mexico; in Spanish and English, 1947) and "Les Danses de Haiti (Paris: Fasquel Press, 1957).

———. "Letter to Goldie and Gumm," May 17, 1941 with correction dated May 18, 1941 (2 pages). Special Collections, Morris Library, Southern Illinois University, Carbondale.

———. "Letter and Song Lyrics to Dottore Faccena," March 5, 1954 (8 pages). Special Collections, Morris Library, Southern Illinois University, Carbondale.

———. "Letters, Lyrics and Lists of Titles of Music submitted to Societa Italiana [*sic*] degli Autori ed Editori," November 11, 1954 (2 pages). Special Collections, Morris Library, Southern Illinois University, Carbondale.

———. "Letters, Lyrics and Lists of Titles of Music to Datt. Enrico Lonardi," November 12, 1954 (12 pages). Special Collections, Morris Library, Southern Illinois University, Carbondale.

———. "Letter to René Piquion," December 18, 1953 (2 pages). Special Collections, Morris Library, Southern Illinois University, Carbondale.

———. "Memorandum to Robert Rossen" of March 4, 1954 (2 pages). Special Collections, Morris Library, Southern Illinois University, Carbondale.

———. "Southland Program." Rpt. in *Kaiso! Katherine Dunham: An Anthology of Writings.* Ed. VèVè A. Clark and Margaret B. Wilkerson. Berkeley: University of California Institute for the Study of Social Change, 1978. 117–118.

———. "Statement." Rpt. in *Kaiso! Katherine Dunham: An Anthology of Writings.* Ed. VèVè A. Clark and Margaret B. Wilkerson. Berkeley: University of California Institute for the Study of Social Change, 1978. 88.

Eco, Umberto. "The Frames of Comic 'Freedom.' " *Carnival!: Umberto Eco, V.V. Ivanov, Monica Rector.* Ed. Thomas Seboek. Berlin: Mouton, 1984. 48–69.

Gardiner, Michael. "Bakhtin's Carnival: Utopia as Critique." *Carnival!: Umberto Eco, V.V. Ivanov, Monica Rector.* Ed. Thomas Seboek. Berlin: Mouton, 1984. 20–47.

Hurston, Zora Neale. *Tell My Horse: Voodoo and Life in Haiti and Jamaica. 1938.* Ed. Henry Louis Gates, Jr. New York: Harper and Row, 1990.

"Italian-Made Film is Too Depressing." Rev. of *Mambo. Hollywood Reporter* March 29, 1955: 3.

Long, Richard. *The Black Tradition in American Dance.* London: Prion, 1989.

Mambo. Dir. Robert Rossen. Prod. Carlo Ponti, Dino De Laurentiis. Screen Play. Guido Piovene, Ivo Perilli, Ennio de Concini, Robert Rossen. Perf. Silvana Mangano, Michael Rennie, Vittorio Gassman, Shelly Winters and Katherine Dunham. Paramount Pictures, 1954. B&W, 94 minutes. VHS Dist. Hen's Tooth Video, 1991.

Mambo. Rev. *Monthly Film Bulletin.* January 1955: 70–71.

Mambo. Rev. *Motion Picture Herald.* April 2, 1955: 387.

Morrison, Toni. *Playing in the Dark: Whiteness and the Literary Imagination.* London: Picador, 1993.

Rector, Monica: "The Code and Message of Carnival: 'Escolas-de-Samba.'" *Carnival!: Umberto Eco, V.V. Ivanov, Monica Rector.* Ed. Thomas Seboek. Berlin: Mouton, 1984. 37–165.

Seboek, Thomas, ed. *Carnival!: Umberto Eco, V.V. Ivanov, Monica Rector.* Berlin: Mouton, 1984.

Shannon, Sandra. *The Dramatic Vision of August Wilson.* Washington, D.C.: Howard University Press, 1995.

David, ed. *Bakhtin: Carnival and Other Subjects.* Amsterdam: Rodopi, 1993.

Thomas, Roy. "Focal Rites: New Dance Dominions." *Kaiso! Katherine Dunham: An Anthology of Writings.* Ed. VèVè A. Clark and Margaret B. Wilkerson. Berkeley: University of California Institute for the Study of Social Change, 1978. 112–116.

Wasserman, Dale. "Letter to Katherine Dunham," December 31, 1953 (2 pages). Special Collections, Morris Library, Southern Illinois University, Carbondale.

Weusi, Jitu K. "The Rise and Fall of Black Swan Records." <http://www.rehot-jazz.com/blackswan.html> February 2, 2002.

Wilson, August. "Speech at the National Black Theater Festival, 1997." Rpt. *Callaloo* 20.3 (1998): 483–491. November 24, 2000. <http://muse.jhu.edu/journals/callaloo/v020/20.3wilson02.html>.

———. "The Ground on Which We Stand." *American Theatre* (September 1996): 14–19, 77–80.

———. "Ma Rainey's Black Bottom." *Three Plays.* Pittsburgh: University of Pittsburgh Press, 1991. 9–93.

8

THE MUMIA PROJECT: THEATER ACTIVISM AT HOWARD UNIVERSITY

Sybil J. Roberts

In the wake of August Wilson's challenge to American theater practitioners in his speech "The Ground on Which I Stand"; and his specific charge to African American theater artists at the Black Theater Summit at Dartmouth University it would seem imperative that the fundamental reasons that African American people first began to create art on these shores be revisited. In essence Wilson has issued a call to arms for African American performance artists to create works to intervene in the face of renewed attacks on our social, political, and economic rights. The very act of creating art itself, apart from expressing beauty, is to speak to some cause, person, or idea either positively or negatively. As John Edgar Wideman says in *Hoop Roots*, "Art is someone speaking, making a case for survival" (230). Art by its very nature is never neutral. Hence, Dubois's assertion that all art is propaganda is indeed true. African American performance art, particularly theater, has taken an active role in shaping, rejecting, or clarifying an issue, or point of view. For example, in 1821, the first African American professional theater company, the African Grove Theater, founded by William Henry Brown and James Hewlett, emerged in New York City's lower Manhattan amidst a hostile political and social climate of hotly debated issues of suffrage, segregation, and censorship. The idea of a company of actors of African descent performing Shakespeare was initially a curiosity for some white theater patrons, but it quickly became a target for those who would continue to promote the idea of African American inferiority.

Clearly any performance displaying our ability to adapt, even transform, a staple, no a hallmark, of European culture would give the lie to any notion of intellectual, emotional, or social inferiority being forced on nineteenth-century New York society. It may not have been James Brown's intention to refute society's prevailing arguments for racism and segregation, but his theater certainly did function in that interventionist mode. Thus, beginning with Brown's defiant statement in building the African Grove Theater challenging any attempts to consign African American artists, and by larger implication, African Americans in general, to inferior social, political, and spiritual status, the mission of African American theater artists was established. These hands are the ground on which I stand. From this place of vision and purpose I "image" the path of African American theater and my place in it. African American theater is a secular, albeit spiritual, ritual that allows us to define, refine, and codify certain cultural practices that reflect either consciously or unconsciously our African heritage in both form and content, even when adapting or borrowing theatrical modes from other cultures. Further, it addresses ideas and issues relevant to the African American community in a distinctive African American "voice" that when functioning at its best challenges status quo. My role as a playwright is to create such works.

I am not alone on this journey. I am challenged, buoyed, and awed by those who've walked this path before me, with me, and beside me. I pay homage to them by calling their names and acknowledging their work. There is Barbara Ann Teer who, according to Barbara Lewis in *A Sourcebook of African-American Performance*, even as late as 1998 was still asserting:

> It is now time for us as cultural leaders to fuse spirit with materialism and come with a totally different paradigm which I think is the vision of the artists ... we are in the business of human transformation, lifting the thought patterns of our people out of that victim culture and putting them into a heroic liberated victorious culture ... (69)

In Teer, we have a theater practitioner who understands the power of ritual not only as a healing tool, but as a means of giving people a specific spiritual and cultural vocabulary to speak to their own needs. While this is understood to be the standard practice of ritual, the potency of the act lies in the fact that it allows participants to identify that part of themselves—their society, history, religion/spiritual beliefs that may have been previously unknown. In short, ritual is a self-defining practice. It creates what Richard Schechner, Eleanor Traylor, and others have defined as a "temenos," a magic circle of language that lends a vital exclusivity to certain cultural practices and ideas. Theater is a secular ritual that allows us to make manifest parts of ourselves that are not readily accessible, at the point in which we can see ourselves on stage we are made whole. The effect of ritual then is recognition; an understood "oneness" with a "self" or part of a "self" discarded or simply previously unknown. In essence, ritual creates a "knowing" that extends beyond our physical (empirical) experience. I'm not simply describing the result of vicarious experience but the clarity, razor-sharp clarity, that comes with gaining insight into the overall condition of being human through one's total physical, emotion, and intellectual being. Because of its physical immediacy and intimacy, theater, like ritual, is the most efficient means of purveying this "wholistic" knowledge. The work of Barbara Ann Teer laid the foundation for theater to devote itself to the work of deep transformation of African people.

Then there is Robbie McCauley who affirms the role of activism in African American theater:

> [Amiri Baraka's] work is based in the idea that the aesthetic is the activism itself, the involvement in the struggle. . . . I am not struggling to get a piece done. I am struggling to get us through to a more equitable society. (Patraka 237)

Her work, her words, return us to the African tradition of creating/making art that is functional in a practical, tangible way. There is also Ntozake Shange whose groundbreaking "choreopoems" made the stage more accommodating for the African American woman's voice. She freed us from Aristotle and let us speak in circles, layers, color, and line to create images of ourselves that we wanted to share with the world. Shange explains her aesthetic in "unrecovered losses/black theater traditions" in her collection of plays *Three Pieces*:

> i am interested solely in the poetry of the moment/
> the emotional & aesthetic impact of a character or
> a line. for too long now afro-americans in theater
> have been duped by the same artificial aesthetics that
> our white counterparts/. . . . if the lives of our geniuses
> arent artfully rendered/ & the lives of our regular &
> precious are ignored/ we have a double loss to reckon
> with . . . . we must move theater into the drama of our
> lives/. . . . (ix–x)

Finally there is Abena Joan Brown, cofounder, president, and producer of ETA Creative Arts Foundation, a theater and cultural arts complex in Chicago. As president and producer of a theater that has successfully produced plays for, by, and about African people in southside Chicago for nearly thirty-two years she is nothing less than a national treasure. She's taken a critical step in the development of African American theater by creating the Playwright Discovery/Development Initiative (PDI), which develops playwrights using aesthetic principles that best reflect the culmination of the ideas of Dubois, Locke, and Larry Neal. Quietly this program has been nurturing and supporting playwrights, some of whom now enjoy quite a national reputation. Long before August Wilson issued his challenge to American theater in 1996, Abena Joan Brown had implemented the very remedy he prescribed.

Each of these four women—Brown, McCauley, Shange, and Teer—have helped me define and articulate my own aesthetic. As a theater practitioner, my work is to create simple interdisciplinary performance rituals that address international issues of justice, peace, and sustainable lifeways on the planet that extend/blur the boundaries of theater and life, thus removing theater from the confines of the stage and its conventions to the street platforms of protest rallies and marches in the tradition of street/protest theater in South America and South Africa, as well as theater-for-development throughout

Southern and East Africa. In this style of theater, members of the audience are not reduced to mere voyeurs, but are agents working to achieve political/ social change using the power of ritual. Both the performers and the audience are committing themselves to struggle without any degree of separation. When faced with injustice such as the harassment of outspoken, uncompromising political activists; the wrongful conviction and imprisonment of social activists; and the murders of innocent men, women, and children resistance is survival, and such resistance is always made evident by struggle. Struggle is the presence of grace in everyday life coming always to provide us with the opportunity to rise above ourselves. As a result, my art, my work, at its best, functions in an interventionist mode, which has long been our tradition in American theater.

In the stillness, in the quiet intensity of the moment just after the second reading of *A Liberating Prayer: A Love Song For Mumia*, in a singular moment of clarity, I finally knew what I wanted from myself, from the brave students who had undertaken the journey of developing this play with me and from the play itself. I acknowledge that I was perhaps being a bit ambitious, but I wanted us to discover the principle of justice in ourselves. Not simply to discover it but to actualize it. The words of John Africa from *25 Years on the MOVE* rang in my ear: "Revolution starts with the individual. It starts with a person making personal commitment to do what's right... To understand revolution you must be sound. Revolution is not imposed on another, it is kindled within them" (69). They were followed by the voice of Che Guevara in his classic text *Guerilla Warfare*: "When the forces of oppression come to maintain themselves in power against established law, peace is always broken" (8). These were followed still by the voice of Dr. Martin Luther King, Jr. in his *Strength to Love*: "The hope of secure and livable world lies with disciplined nonconformists, who dedicated to justice, peace and brotherhood" (26). This chorus of voices further clarified what I wanted not only for those of us involved in the creative process but the audience/seers as well. (I must say that when I talk about those involved in this work, both as audience/seers and performers, I'm primarily talking about students since this project was designed with them in mind.) I wanted nothing short of a revolutionary commitment to do what's right for themselves as individuals, for their communities, and, by extension, humanity; and an understanding that revolutionary commitment begins with the actions that we take in our most intimate relationships—the kind of relationships where we are willing to risk losing ourselves to love, love defined as the ability to tap into the largesse of the human spirit made evident by struggle, the kind of love that Mumia Abu-Jamal has consistently demonstrated from his youthful days as a Panther, through his determination to give MOVE (MOVE is a revolutionary religious organization committed to the preservation and principle of LIFE as maintained by John Africa its Founder and Coordinator) and others a platform to speak and to be heard, thus becoming the voice of the voiceless, and in his perseverance and courage to continue telling truth even while in disciplinary custody under an active death warrant on death row. His love is like a prayer, and we have all been blessed by it. Such a tenacious fearless love demands reciprocity.

My decision to engage the struggle to save Mumia's life as an artist is rooted in many experiences, each birthing a new self to face a very old world. Yet, in a singular moment of clarity, to quote a dear friend, I can recall three distinct experiences that set me on this path. It is the mission that defines my life at this moment. The first experience I actually detail in the play itself, that is the murder of eleven MOVE members by bombing (which resulted in the fiery deaths of five children and six adults), air-bombing, sanctioned by another African American man, Wilson Goode, then mayor of Philadelphia. As Sage recalls in the play, I recall sitting up watching my father watch Osage Avenue burn until 3:00 o'clock in the morning. "Look at this!" My father stood transfixed by the image of night and flame. "They bombing Black people!" I ease up beside him, drawn into what first seemed like awe in the original sense of the word. But that wasn't it, not at all. The images crackled and flame-danced on the screen in front of us. Long arms of orange flame stretched through what was once doors, walls, and windows of the seemingly tiny rowhouse on 6221 Osage Avenue cupped its hands and reached up to heaven offering up the lives of its occupants. "Now, if that bunker is full of weapons why they gonna drop something on it that explodes?" My father's voice interrupting the silence of my prayer, "It's some extremist group...call themselves MOVE...still that makes absolutely no sense. Said they shooting at the firemen trying to get at the blaze. Said they got tunnels dug all under that house." Together we are sitting now my father and I. Pondering what kind of death awaited the men, women and children inside. I'm thinking this fire, maybe it's all a diversion, a trick, sleight of hand. Maybe there are tunnels under the house, an ark of earth, a womb, transporting them back across the Middle Passage to home. It would take almost fifteen years before I would understand the meaning of this vigil, one that would give birth to a promise—a promise rising phoenix-like from the destruction of the lives of these wild-haired, joy-filled, rage-wearing, curious-smelling, too-loud, too-black, too-close-to-the-earth men, women, and children; a promise never to forget. Never to forget what this country will do to those it can't buy, pacify, or discredit. Not vicariously, by listening in horror to stories of innocent young boys stolen from their mothers, their helpless grandfathers, and being beaten and tortured to death. By listening in horror to stories of innocent young adults set upon by ferocious southern sheriffs with their equally ferocious dogs. By listening in horror to stories of young adults shot down in Orangeburg, Ohio, and Chicago by overzealous soldiers who for some reason were not loosed on southeast Asia. No, that night with my father I saw my America in my own time, with my own eyes, and the experience was mine. All mine. MOVE's only crime was simply that they wanted no part of America or anything she had to offer. They insisted on what they understood to be LIFE, the right to their own "beingness" without question or interference. And for that they would pay dearly.

Another moment, a step along the way, was turning thirty-five in Africa. I'd traveled to Tanzania to learn the process of "theatre-for-development," to make theater in Mlongonzilla to illuminate serious issues affecting their community, and to create a forum to discuss those issues. But what I encountered was an incredible family of women flourishing beautifully. In spite of near nonexistent healthcare, education, skill-training, or economic resources. Women like Sijuii. Sijuii which translates loosely into something like "I don't know." Her name is certainly fitting. She is full of energy and audacity; and she has a wicked sense of humor. She is small like me, with arresting eyes that speak long before she does, even though one of them is sightless. Only Sijuii can tell the story of a mother who travels miles away to the next town to the hospital with a sick child only to be told by rude nurses to go home and bathe; then when she returned a second time to produce proof of residency; and when she returned a third time to produce a means of payment, with such uproarious laughter that it brings you hope, faith in the future of these women that holds tears at bay. In learning to love Sijuii I discovered the most challenging issue facing us in this theater process was the fact that generations of women would live and die in Mlongonzilla never having had a forum to discuss their issues in their own language. To para-phrase bell hooks: "they needed a vocabulary to move from silence to speech." This is precisely the work of theater. Suddenly, I had a radically dif-ferent understanding of the term "development."

A third step along the way, crystallizing my resolve, was meeting Carlos Africa. We had come together to save Mumia's life, activists from all over the Metropolitan area. In the cool oak sanctuary of the church our collective energy was a prayer. A prayer to save the "voice of the voiceless." A prayer to save our belief in justice. Carlos Africa sat with his arm thrown carelessly across the back of the pew. A casual olive-drab smile. Humbling itself as it acknowledges me. Soft. He takes my hand. Soft. Saying, "yes, Sister we'll all come out on the other side." In Carlos, I saw the beauty of life made mani-fest in the power of truth. I saw Carlos and I understood strength and patience. Mumia Abu-Jamal represents uncompromising resistance, and the heroism, the simple heroism that comes from attempting to live by your word. Mumia's life is an example of the "deep soul-work" that marks my life.

The Mumia Project is a series of performance works that serve as an exam-ple of the kind of theater activism that, in my opinion, Howard University's Theater Arts Department should be involved in more consistently. It started over a year ago during spring semester 2001 as a means of having Dance and Theater Arts students explore arts activism by engaging a specific social or political issue to bring about a desired transformation/resolution of that .issue—in this case, the freedom of Mumia Abu-Jamal. For well over four years now, my colleague, a choreographer, Sherill Berryman-Johnson and I have been exploring the use of spoken and literary text as well as the language of the body moving through space to create a sinuous, continuous dialogue. Sometimes this dialogue is call and response. Sometimes it is a plaintive cry. Sometimes it is a point of departure from which we journey into a place that defies the language of both of our respective disciplines. In this place dia-logue becomes prayer, a leap of faith. This first work titled "Hearing the

Voice: Mumia Abu-Jamal" gave me the opportunity to meld my own activist aesthetic with our ongoing collaborations. The piece was choreographed to the words of Mumia himself as recorded on *All Things Censored*, which then blended seamlessly into a series of monologues by Cornel West, Helen Prejean, Martin Sheen, and others also recorded on *All Things Censored*. The monologues slowly fade to Arrested Development's "United Minds," and a lone dancer begins to circle the other performers in a movement that symbolized both hope and defiance, her movement extending the words of Mumia culminating in prayer for Mumia's safe return to us, and for justice. A single candle is lit center stage, and all the performers kneel in prayer:

> hear our voices
> raised in the round-melody
> of a prayer circle
> Mumia, our brother, elder, seer
> may the wisdom and compassion of all creation
> bring you health and long life
> so that we may know the reward of faith and
> the power of struggle
>
> may the deft hands of the ancestors
> protect and free you
> revolutionary spirit
> so that we may know your legacy
> is ours to own
> may these words
> given life by our breath
> be sweet music to yours ears
> knowing that you are loved (Hearing the Voices April 20, 2001)

As their voices soften to a whisper the performers fade into darkness. Leaving the audience in complete silence.

The process by which this performance work was developed is more important that the culminating product that was staged. It was in the process of conceptualizing (creating) and rehearsing the work that my aesthetic is clearly illustrated. To begin our working process Dr. Johnson and I "invited" a group of students to participate in this project on the basis of their demonstrated commitment to artistic development, a personal commitment to a particular political/social/spiritual ethic or movement, and the willingness to accept the challenge of experimentation in performance. Once the selection process was complete, we began to have a series of meetings/rehearsals with the students. During our initial meeting, I explained my own belief in Mumia, and my commitment to save his life.

I told them who Mumia Abu-Jamal is and why he matters to all of us. I also told them about the MOVE Organization, their history, and the subsequent bombing of their headquarters as it is relevant to their understanding of Mumia's work and spiritual beliefs. The students were given readings from *Live From Death Row* and *Death Blossoms*. During our second session, they were assigned an essay to address their understanding of justice and why the fight against injustice is important. The students wrote about their personal struggles in fighting against homophobia; racism; sexual violence; and domestic abuse all within the context of Mumia's struggle. We then listened to Mumia's own voice, which startled many students. They were startled not only by his eloquence but by his articulateness. Their reactions both shocked and disappointed me. A clear stereotype revealed itself, the stereotype of the average prisoner, particularly a death-row prisoner, as someone who is ignorant, uneducated, and unable to communicate a sense of his own beingness and self-worth, not to mention their intimate knowledge of the criminal justice system. Moreover, there was a general opinion that Mumia sounded "white."

Though no one openly said so, the comments tended to be "he doesn't sound like I thought he would . . ." My response to their comments, and my own shock and disappointment, was to point out the possibility that their responses were appropriate only in proportion to the media and judicial system's cooperative effort to criminalize the African American male. This campaign of criminalization is bolstered, if not made altogether possible, by the steady diet of negative images served up in all aspects of mass media on a daily basis. Thus our perceptions of our men, particularly those involved in the criminal justice system, are often not our own. My challenge to them is a result of my knowledge that too many African Americans know, personally, if not intimately, someone who is or has been incarcerated or is under some kind of judicial supervision. This is a terrible "fact" to acknowledge in an alleged democratic society. Of those individuals that we may know casually or intimately, are they ignorant and unable to speak to their situation? More often than not, just the opposite is true. In fact, we may be bearing witness to a horrible truth, that Mumia is not the exception, but closer to the rule.

Next, we assigned each student a "monologue" from the *All Things Censored* (c.d.). Dr. Johnson and I listened to these short, censored, NPR radio commentaries to determine which ones would create the narrative that would have the impact we sought for the performance. As we listened, we realized that in order to provide students with an understanding of the historical, social, and political significance of Mumia's case we would need not only Mumia's voice, but the voices of so many others who've enlisted in the fight against injustice on his behalf, hence, our use of the voices of Cornel West, Helen Prejean, Ramona Africa, and others. The students were not simply called upon to "act," to present these "voices" as characters. But they were asked to "embody" the words. To allow someone else's words to tell their own stories, raise their own questions, speak their own affirmations. They were required to do the same with the choreography. Following the performance, the students were not only inspired by the audience's response, but by the changes in themselves. The first phase of Mumia Project had been successfully completed.

The second phase of the Mumia Project began when Professor Denise Saunders approached me about the possibility of directing one of my plays.

I explained to Prof. Saunders that I was interested in a great deal more than the act of producing a play, but I was more interested in seeing what theater was capable of doing as we move into a new millenium. Moreover, I'm more interested in working in an interdisciplinary mode, than a collaborative one, which requires a unique relationship among a number of skilled artists. In addition, for me, aesthetically, theater must be a functional communal event, galvanizing and energizing the community to complete some task, to address some crisis, to challenge or reinforce current ideas or trends that shape our culture. So we completed a proposal to create a new work for the department that would satisfy all the demands of my aesthetic. I was commissioned to write *A Liberating Prayer: A Love Song For Mumia*, a multimedia, interdisciplinary ensemble performance work that uses video, music (specifically early traditional African American music such as shouts, field hollers, work songs, spirituals, and blues), movement, and poetry to "actualize" its audience in the fight to save the life of Mumia Abu-Jamal.

It is an unlikely love story that tells of the fateful meeting of a freedom fighter/dreamer/literary artist, Sage, and a merchant, Odysseus, who undertake a spiritual journey to find the wisdom and courage to fight to win the freedom of political prisoner Mumia Abu-Jamal. The action takes place on the morning Sage decides to attend her first "Save Mumia" rally after being given a flyer by a group of "Save Mumia" activists while passing First Congregational Church, the site of the rally. Odysseus is given a flyer too, but decides to forego the rally to continue plying his trade, selling African cloth. While erecting his stall in front of the church, he catches sight of Sage and presents her with a gift of cloth. Further, for reasons unbeknownst to him, he offers to wrap her hair with the fabric. After Sage accepts his invitation they journey through storytelling to heal each other of past wounds and to dedicate themselves to this struggle. As they journey, they are joined by the "Save Mumia" activists, who turn out not to be activists at all, but a chorus of ancestors who whisper, sing, and praise-speak their history while encouraging them to fight. Even the featured speakers at the rally (Pam Africa, Ramona Africa et al.) stop to engage the young lovers. They are also joined by the spirit of Mumia, "the voice of the voiceless" giving them the strength to reach beyond themselves.

The first reading of the script was held in July 2001 in the Environmental Space Theater at Howard University. It featured recordings of Mumia Abu-Jamal himself and sometimes simply his words to provide a constant exhortation to protest, to take action, to make revolution. As with all the performances of this work, it was followed by a question and answer session where the audience could not only critique the work, but share their concerns about Mumia and the state of justice in America. In the next stage of development, each performance of this work featured a "guest activist" making a cameo appearance as him/herself. This allowed for a great amount of improvisation/flexibility to include those currently working diligently in the struggle to free Mumia. As part of its development, a second reading was held in November, featuring Ramona Africa as "guest" activist. The run of the performance, which was a series of staged readings using sets, blocking, props, music, dance, and video, occurred in the last week in January through the first week of February. Each evening a different activist was featured including: Pam Africa; The Seeds of Wisdom (youth MOVE members); Sam Jordan (one of Mumia's attorneys); Ms. Sabrina Green (DC. Chapter of Friends of MOVE); et al. *A Liberating Prayer* played to sold-out houses most nights. The work also involved audience participation through the affirmation of prayer and struggle; as well as direct challenges made by featured activists asking them to commit to saving our brother's life. An overwhelming number of audience members being community activists excited that Howard University in keeping with its legacy engaged this significant struggle. Equally impressive were the scores of students who came every night to learn about the Mumia case.

The cast of students was put through the same process as they were with the initial Mumia work. They attended rallies in Philadelphia; met with Pam and Ramona, wrote essays; and we spent a great deal of time talking, talking, talking. However, because we worked for approximately a year together, and as the process is continuous it is not possible to fully describe it, certainly not in this brief essay. This fall a new revised Liberating Prayer script was performed at Howard University with Pam Africa and Attorney Sam Jordan as our guest artist. We are still growing with this script and this project, and we will continue until our work, freeing Mumia and ourselves, is done. Yet, it is fitting to close with a journal entry from Roxi Trapp-Dukes who created the role of Sage; and a note that I found under my door one morning from "a student":

2/4/02

I haven't written in a while. I needed to take some time to reasses[s] my thoughts. This production has been quit an experience. We have defined & redefined our existence as a cast, an ensemble, and as a body of people praying to manifest a work to free a political prisoner. We have had ups, downs, set backs, set forwards, inspirations, epiphanies, etc, etc, etc . . .

We've had feelings [ac]cepted, feelings rejected, feelings misunderstood, feelings hurt and so on. I guess I write or am writing to release, to understand *my* process, *my* growth, *my* experience. It's so interesting, we've done so much as a group for sooo long that the time I have had to myself to assess, to process, i really haven't wanted to spend on Mumia @all. In all honesty just trying to keep up w/ the progression of the piece textually has been *hectic!* But all of that being said, what have we learned? I have learned that this particular play was bigger than us when we started. The quest to collectively pray to save Mumia is one that must be actively considered in all its seriousness every time we gather to manifest the work. *WE NEGLECTED TO DO THAT.* We eventually came back to it, but as a whole we became caught up in overwhelming aspects of the production that in all honesty had nothing to do with simple task of praying to Mumia . . . . All I can do [is] listen & learn from my listening . . . . A man's life is at stake . . . [the] system must be challenged . . . .

—Roxi Trapp-Dukes

Professor Roberts:

> Profound is the symbolism behind hands being trained
> to silence the history that they were born with, like
> muting the music scored on the lines of our palms.
> "I gave my hands a ritual" not knowing that [the] ritual
> itself caused the song to be sung. Was the memory
> that Odysseus had that summer when everything changed
> to mute his song? Was the choice to touch & connect
> with Sage the reading of the score that was engraved
> in his hands from the beginning? Thank you Professor
> Roberts for being a vessel for God & allowing some
> of us to remember the score in our hands.

—A Student

The Howard University Department of Theater Arts is ONAMOVE; reborn in the spirit of resistance and experimentation that has marked our presence in theater since the beginning.

WORKS CITED

Guevara, Che. *Guerilla Warfare*. Lincoln: University of Nebraska Press, 1998.

King, Martin Luther, Jr. *Strength to Love*. Philadelphia: Fortress, 1981.

Lewis, Barbara. "Ritual Reformations: Barbara Ann Teer and the National Black Theater of Harlem." *A Sourcebook of African-American Performance*. Ed. Annemarie Bean. London and New York: Routledge, 1999. 68–82.

Patraka, Vicki. "Obsessing in Public: An Interview with Robbie McCauley." *A Sourcebook of African-American Performance*. Ed. Annemarie Bean. London and New York: Routledge, 1999. 219–245.

Roberts, Sybil. "Hearing the Voice: Mumia Abu-Jamal." *Speaking The Voices of Our People*. Dr. Sherrill Berryman-Johnson, Artistic Director/ Choreographer. Live Performance. April 20, 2001.

Shange, Ntozake. "Unrecovered Losses/Black Theater Traditions." *Three Pieces: Spell #7, a Photograph: Lovers in Motion, Boogie Woogie Landscapes*. New York: St. Martin's, 1981. ix–xi.

Wideman, John Edgar. *Hoop Roots*. New York: Houghton Mifflin, 2001.

25 Years On The MOVE. 1996.

III

AUGUST WILSON'S PLAYS AND
BLACK AESTHETICS

9

PHANTOM LIMBS DANCING
JUBA RITES IN AUGUST WILSON'S *JOE TURNER'S COME AND GONE* AND *THE PIANO LESSON*

Reggie Young

In *Signifying Monkey*, Henry Louis Gates claims "If 'the Dixie Pike,' as Jean Toomer put the matter in *Cane*, 'has grown from a goat path in Africa,' then the black vernacular tradition stands as its signpost, at the liminal cross-roads of culture contact and ensuing difference at which Africa meets Afro-America" (4). If this figurative path can be looked upon as a cultural corridor that connects African and African American cultures, it has had transported upon it much more than a vernacular tradition of language usage—it is also the thoroughfare used by the people of African descent to transport their spiritual beliefs and ritual practices for use in their everyday American lives. August Wilson, throughout his ever-evolving canon of plays, but more specifically in *Joe Turner's Come and Gone* and *The Piano Lesson*, explores what critic and playwright Paul Carter Harrison calls the "bedrock of racial memory and particularity of expression," one that transcends the Middle Passage. In his plays, Wilson reveals the interrelationship between physical and metaphysical reality in black diasporic culture, a relationship that has been surveyed increasingly by African American expressive artists in various genres over the last several decades and one in which the reconciling of the slave past is an important factor in personal redemption.

A number of critics have cited Wilson for his departures from conventional theatrical fare, especially in *Joe Turner's Come and Gone*. His allegiance to a *particular* tradition, one rooted on the fringes of, if not totally outside of that of the American theater, is possibly the main factor that has limited appreciation of his plays from certain mainstream theater critics. As Harrison acknowledges in the introduction to his anthology, *Totem Voices*, Wilson's plays are representative of dramatic works written by black playwrights throughout the diaspora as part of a black world repertory. They are clearly ensconced in the tradition of New World African expressive writing and are much more akin to fictional narratives such as Henry Dumas's "Ark of Bones," Toni Morrison's *Beloved*, Paule Marshall's *Praise Song for the Widow*, and cinematic works such as Julie Dash's *Daughters of the Dust* and Charles Burnett's *To Sleep With Anger*, than any body of works found in the mainstream of the American theatrical tradition. It is interesting to consider that most of these works have been discussed as possessing elements of magical realism by scholars in their attempt to explicate certain attributes that cannot be explained in Western humanistic terms, but the expression magical realism in the context of these and other African American works that use similar modes of representation is at best misapplied. Spiritual realism is a much more effective way to understand these works, especially Wilson's. Although works of spiritual realism might, at times, *seem like* magical realism, these expressions are unique because they are firmly rooted in the culture of juba, ring-shouts, spirituals, and the blues, and share a cultural connection to Africa and not Latin America or Western Europe, except in incidental ways.

Magical realism was originally conceived as "marvelous realism" by Alejo Carpentier in an attempt "to ground otherness in New World space" (Dash 88). According to Michael J. Dash, "Carpentier's conception of the marvelous nature of New World reality is yet another permutation of the need to establish a separate and unique American identity" (88). But in New World African spiritual realism, expressive artists realize the need to do more than to establish American identities—*the* goal is to seek wholeness and self and community redemption through the realization of an Africanized past. Magical realism, as it evolved and distinguished itself from Carpentier's marvelous realism, is a method of fictional representation most successfully employed by Latin American writers to relate the complexities of life, history, and culture in New World societies in their various regions and is best illustrated in the works of Gabriel Garcia Marquez. In magical realism, strange images and occurrences are often rendered in a deadpan manner, while normal occurrences are described as bizarre or with a sense of wonder as writers attempt to distinguish their narrative representations of life from those that were passed down to them from Europe. But even in seeking autonomy from Europe, these writers and their works are largely grounded in continental European culture and its cultural aesthetics. This form of representation is subversive in many ways, but the writers never truly break away from the worldview of their European motherland; basically, they warp this Eurocentric reality through their works, deforming it through the use of a surrealistic gaze at the physical world. African American writers, however, who have produced what, in essence, appear to be similar modes of narrative expression, are not merely trying to subvert Eurocentric influences through their narrative representations; instead, they are trying to *re*locate the aesthetic reality constructed in their works away from those espoused by Western culture and the values inherent in modern Western technological societies. In doing this, they attempt to deemphasize the Westernized humanistic values generally embraced by Eurocentric Americans.

Spiritual realism attempts to negotiate through artistic expression the demands faced by black people in the Americas who must cope with living in a secular, individualistic, material-based society while trying to preserve and maintain the essence of a sacred, communal past, based on folk values and spiritual beliefs. In such works, there are significant *moments* where acts or events are realized outside of the context of a Eurocentric or Western frame of reference. In magical realism, these moments surface most often when two or more cultures are superimposed (for example, the cultural beliefs of Vatican Catholicism with those of South American Catholic peasants), but most often in New World African spiritual realism just the opposite takes place: such moments occur as a result of characters disconnecting themselves from their American experience and the values imposed on them through that experience. This allows them to disengage themselves from the debilitating paradigm of American cultural reality and seek a redemption that is only possible in the context of a different value system. Instead of African American and American cultures being superimposed, what occurs is a process of differentiating and delineating uniquely African cultural values and beliefs from American ones. In African American literature, spiritual realism often functions as an opportunity for characters to renew or redeem themselves through a process of rituals that allow them to reconnect their values and beliefs with sacred elements of the culture.

In this essay, I would like to examine some of the elements in two of Wilson's earlier efforts in his cycle of twentieth-century plays, *Joe Turner's Come and Gone* and *The Piano Lesson*, especially those that make them important to the ongoing process of rediscovery of an African American past. Wilson's process of exploration and [re]discovery is one that focuses on black people as subjects and not objects of their own story in recalling a history that is not limited to or confined by the worldview of America and Western culture. The plays, in the framework of a New World African aesthetic, seek to overcome a fragmented African American past under a Western religion of forced submission and enslavement with an art that offers the hope of personal redemption through ritual renewal.

Joe Turner's Come and Gone is set during the early years of the twentieth century when the great migration of African Americans from the rural South to the developing urban areas of the North was still in a relatively early stage. It is during this time that Herald Loomis arrives at Seth Holly's boardinghouse in Pittsburgh in the midst of a seemingly never-ending sojourn. The boardinghouse is, in essence, a liminal way-station where lost souls often stop in their pursuit of a true sense of self-fulfillment, something Bynum, a resident conjure- or hoodoo-man calls "their song." Seth, the son of free black parents, and one who never suffered the direct consequences of slavery and the betrayal of post-Reconstruction due to his family's history of living in the North, attempts to reconcile his own dilemma of double consciousness through economic and material means. As a result of his own limited perspective and narrow mindedness concerning the hoards of African Americans he sees leaving the South and moving about through the North, he holds little esteem for those who check in for short periods of time as they search, according to Bynum, "up and down them roads" to find a place for themselves *in the world* and a sense of their own nature and being. Loomis, in particular, arrives at Holly's as only a piece of a man. He believes his completeness can only be attained by locating his estranged wife and reuniting both himself and his traveling-companion daughter with her. As he puts it: "I just wanna see her face so I can have me a starting place in the world."

A former servant to the Christian faith, Loomis had been kidnapped ten years earlier by the nefarious Joe Turner while preaching a message of repentance to a group of roadside gamblers near Memphis and found himself forced to work as a virtual slave on a chain-gang. After being released seven years later, Loomis was now a man without a life. His wife, Martha, assumed he was dead after waiting years for his return and not knowing what had happened. In order to reconstruct her own life, she decided to leave their daughter behind with her family, marry herself over to her northward bound evangelistic church, and change her last name to Pentecost, thus marking her new bond with the Holy Ghost. When Loomis and Martha finally meet up with each other, for we discover she has been looking for him, too, it is obvious that finding her is not the real solution for Loomis to satisfy his quest of finding himself. He tells her, "Now that I can see your face I can say my goodbye and make my own world" (Wilson, *Joe Turner* 90).

In making his own world, Loomis must be able to lay to rest his past on Joe Turner's farm and find resurrection as a man who has been cleansed of the sins perpetrated against him and his ancestors through slavery. In redeeming himself, he must overcome his own blind submission to a biased God who exists to promote the interests of the system of slavery, even fifty years after manumission, a God who not only condoned the enslavement of Africans but one who also has given justification to its past and present practice through interpretation of His word by the slave-holding class. Loomis must come to the awareness possessed by Father John in "Kabnis," Toomer's concluding psycho-drama in *Cane*, and realize the truth concerning the sin white folks committed when "they made th [*sic*] Bible lie" (Toomer 115). Only in doing so will Loomis emerge out of the darkness of his past blind faith to an enslaving savior to walk in the light of his own true self as a fully realized human being. By regaining his song of self-fulfillment, he can become what Bynum calls his "Shiny Man."

In Loomis's mind, there is little difference between Joe Turner and Jesus Christ: the two might well be one and the same. He was apprehended by the legendary Turner, whose fame of state-sanctioned thievery of black male bodies has spread by word of mouth through a popular blues song whose lyrics inform women whose husbands have disappeared that "Joe Turner got your man and gone." In spending seven years in captivity, Loomis never saw Joe Turner in the flesh, which denied him a chance to question the captor who lorded over him during the time of his incarceration about the reason for his abduction, something that has continually haunted him while eating at his soul. When Martha appeals to him after their reunion "to look to Jesus" and begins reciting the twenty-third Psalm, Loomis objects to hearing anything about the hills and valleys mentioned in this scripture passage.

Instead, he says "I done been all across the valleys and the hills and the mountains and the oceans" (Wilson, *Joe Turner* 92). He tells Martha of what he witnessed during his trek:

> Great big old white man . . . your Mr. Jesus Christ. Standing there with a whip in one hand and tote board in another, and them niggers swimming in a sea of cotton. And he counting. He tallying up the cotton. "Well, Jeremiah . . . what's the matter, you ain't picked but two hundred pounds of cotton today? Got to put you on half rations." And Jeremiah go back and lay up there on his half rations and talk about what a nice man Mr. Jesus Christ is 'cause he give him salvation after he die. Something wrong here. Something don't fit right! (92–93)

Clearly, Loomis sees this "Mr." Jesus Christ as a symbol for Joe Turner and discovers that he must reject the continued domination of this figure over him to ensure his own sense of self and to affirm his own humanity, which is a necessary factor if he is to ever realize the light of a true, self-sustaining salvation experience. In essence, he realizes that he must be born again, but not in the typical sense of New Testament Christianity. His rebirth is one that must take place out of the womb; the rebirth Loomis must undergo, however, is not just of water and spirit, but also of blood and flesh. His rebirth must entail a reclaiming of both his spiritual and physical being. During his time of incarceration, Loomis was aware that he was being robbed of something, and that when Joe Turner tried, as Bynum put it, to steal his song, Joe Turner was trying to appropriate the very essence of his personhood. To Seth Holly, from his highly pragmatic and overtly cynical perspective, all Turner wanted of Loomis was his free labor, but Bynum sees it differently:

> What he wanted was your song. He wanted to have that song to be his. He thought by catching you he could learn that song . . . Now he's got you bound up to where you can't sing your own song. (72)

Even though Joe Turner failed to appropriate Loomis's song, he was successful in making Loomis lose it; thus, the ordeal reduced him to a seemingly less than human condition. However, Joe Turner's efforts to devalue Loomis actually gives him some insight into his own self-value. He tells Bynum:

> He told me I was worthless. Worthless is something you throw away. Something you don't bother with. I ain't seen him throw me away. Wouldn't even let me stay away when I was by my lonesome. I ain't tried to catch him when he was going down the road. So I must got something he want. (72)

Loomis's realization of his own self-worth, in knowing that Joe Turner would not have kept him in captivity but would have instead thrown him away, means all that remains for him to "reconnect" himself to his past life is seeing his wife again to tell her "good-bye." According to Douglass

Anderson, in relinquishing the past, Loomis

> reclaims it as his own, in a sense, nullifying Joe Turner's expropriation. Loomis's declaration, "Well, Joe Turner's come and gone and Herald Loomis ain't for no binding," transforms the meaning of the words sung by women whose men had been taken away. The words no longer communicate present loss but consign Joe Turner to a history of which Loomis is the subject. Repossessed of the past, Loomis is no longer its victim but the measure of its meaning, free to judge it and reject what seems false, including the Christian faith that Martha tries to lead him back to. (457)

If Loomis's self-sufficiency is found in his rejection of Martha's Christian faith, a derivative of Joe Turner's own religion, it is necessary to discuss just what is Christian faith in the context of the play.

In *The Dramatic Vision of August Wilson*, Sandra G. Shannon asserts "the Shiny Man that Loomis becomes at the play's end is the African alternative of what August Wilson calls 'the white man's God'" (137). Wilson, himself, has said:

> when you look in the mirror you should see your God. If you don't, you have somebody else's God. So, in fact, what you do worship is an image of God which is white, which is the image of the very same people who have oppressed you, who have put you on slave ships, who have beaten you, and who have forced you to work. (Qtd. in Shannon 137)

The conceptual god who is the desired object of worship by the characters in this play is neither totally black nor white, but a figurative combination of a deity possessing elements derived from West African and biblical sources. It is not a god of a socially constructed, racialized hue, but a god defined by the dual African and American cultural backgrounds of the characters. Since the God of the Bible is one who professes to be a spirit and who implores His followers to worship him in spirit and *in truth*, African slaves and their descendants found Him to be a rather familiar and comfortable deity, nothing like the enslaving figure of god forced upon them by a nation of Joe Turners. Kim Pereira has noted that Loomis and other Wilson characters "discover their real identities to be African, not Christian, though this 'African-ness' is transfigured with multiple images drawn from a Christianity in which they may find truth and affirmation of their deepest beliefs" (83). Therefore, Bynum, the son of an African healer, and one who practices the African art of binding souls himself, nevertheless has witnessed a vision when he saw his first shiny man not unlike the one Paul of Tarsus experienced on the road to Damascus. This shiny man, whom Bynum describes as "One Who Goes Before and Shows the Way" (Wilson, *Joe Turner* 10), was a precursor to Loomis, just as John the Baptist was a vanguard figure for Jesus. Although Seth is appalled at Bynum's African-based "heebie-geebie stuff," he implores his wife and all of his tenants to participate in a regular Sunday evening juba, a virtual African ring-shout ceremony of ritualistic trance and spirit possession, even though many of his tenants attend Christian church services earlier in the day. Even the devotedly pious Martha Pentecost, despite her symbolic union with the Holy Ghost, places her faith in Bynum's charms and not in Christian prayer to bind her and her daughter together. Loomis, although he rejects "Mr. Jesus Christ" because he cannot differentiate him from Joe Turner, nevertheless has his own Old Testament–like vision and at the play's conclusion cuts himself and cleanses his being in his own blood. Through this ritualistic act he finds himself a resurrected African man, as opposed to a man who has achieved a separate American identity, one who is able to stand on his own two feet. He has rediscovered his song and now shines in the light of his own true self-fulfillment.

The connection Wilson makes between the descendants of African slaves and the ritual practices of their ancestors is an important one. In works of spiritual realism, an individual or a small group of community members are often instrumental in the process of ritual renewal that the central character must undergo, and this is a role that Bynum plays in helping Herald Loomis to eventually "shine." (It is important to note, that the relationship between the two is reciprocal, since by helping Loomis regain the song of his personhood Bynum receives confirmation of his ministry as a binder.) In the earlier scene when the tenants of the Holly boardinghouse participate in the juba ritual and several evoke the name of the Holy Ghost, Loomis, who overhears the call, offers a vehement response that leads him into a trance-like state. In this previously mentioned vision, he recalls memories of the Middle Passage and begins to talk in tongues, dance in the spirit, and describe in a call and response exchange with Bynum an experience not too dissimilar to what Ezekiel witnessed in the Valley of Dry Bones and figuratively close in context to the encounter of Headeye and Fish-Hound in the bone collecting soul ship in Henry Dumas's "Ark of Bones." Loomis describes the fragmented bones of his ancestors coming together to walk on the waters and then standing with their flesh restored on dry land. Through this symbolic action, the ancestral spirits of former slaves urge Loomis to stand and walk like a renewed man. Both Trudier Harris and Dana A. Williams have examined how Dumas's work as mythmaker sets the stage for Wilson's use of myth in his plays, especially *Joe Turner's Come and Gone*. Like Dumas, Wilson challenges those who experience his works to accept the various possibilities that transcendent encounters with an external world might offer.

The importance of the rhythmic musical incantations performed by the participants in the ceremonial dance help to establish the climate necessary to call forth the presence of the ancestors in Seth Holly's boardinghouse and are crucial elements that should not be overlooked. According to Leopold Senghor, the Senegalese poet, statesman, and leading figure of Negritude, "rhythm turns all these concrete things towards the light of the spirit. In the degree to which rhythm is sensuously embodied, it illuminates the spirit" (Qtd. in Harrison, "Mother/Word" xxv). Music has the ability to transcend the limits of material reality to connect the world of the spirit with the world of the flesh in what Wilson Harris has described as a "phantom limb"

(Mackey 32). According to Nathaniel Mackey, "Music as a phantom limb arises from a capacity for feeling which holds itself apart from numb contingency. The phantom limb haunts or critiques a condition in which feeling, consciousness itself, would seem to have been cut off" (32–33). The sublime qualities of music give it the power to bring to the surface previously submerged intense feelings and help induce radical changes in the essence of a person's being. In *The Piano Lesson*, Wilson uses this musical "phantom limb" to invoke the external forces that aid in the resolution of the play's central conflict. Music as a spiritual conduit is of even greater importance in this play because it is the phantom limb extended through the efforts of one of the characters that helps the work achieve its resolution.

Whereas *Joe Turner's Come and Gone* deals with the plight of fragmented individuals in their quest for the reconciliation of self, *The Piano Lesson* focuses on an entire family whose lives are haunted by the ghost of a slave past. Centered around a piano, the play, which is also set in Pittsburgh, but two-and-a-half decades after *Joe Turner's Come and Gone*, explores the ordeal faced by a pair of siblings whose different readings of their family's history lead them to pursue conflicting remedies to overcome that past and help them stand with firm footing in the present. *The Piano Lesson* might not seem like a revolutionary play on the surface, but like so many of the most enduring and influential works in the African American literary tradition one of the play's principal themes involves the quest for personal and group liberation. In this case, it is the liberation of the Charles family, past and present, from slavery and its lingering effects. The play is set in Pittsburgh during the Depression in 1936, a time that was challenging enough for most but especially so for African Americans who had found it difficult to find legitimate work even during more robust economic times. It also takes place during the continued shift in the African American population from the rural South to the urban North, as those with southern rearing packed their down home ways, boarded trains, and moved to the big city. The various passages delivered by characters in blues narratives provide both theatrical audiences and individuals reading the work insights into the lives of African Americans who fled the South during the Great Migration. But weighing down the baggage of those who left were the shared pieces of their past identities, aspects of their being shaped by the various psychological and spiritual wounds that continued to infect their present-day realities with the pain and suffering of past subjugation and bondage. Just as the Dixie Pike represents a metaphorical goat path in Africa, it can also be seen as a migratory pathway running through the heart of the developing black enclaves of the North.

Wilson's use of storytelling serves as a counter to what Toni Morrison has described as the dominant "Master Narrative." According to Morrison in a PBS interview with Bill Moyers, the Master Narrative is "whatever ideological script that is being imposed by the people in authority on everybody else." She further describes it as "the master fiction" and asserts "it has a certain point of view." Master Narratives represent the interests of the descendants of those who profited from slavery and not the enslaved, no matter how they are rendered, and Wilson is conscious of that in his process of writing. As Jay Plum notes: "Rather than writing history in the traditional sense, Wilson 'rights' American history, altering our perception of reality to give status to what American history has denied the status of 'real'" (562). Challenging the Charles siblings for ownership of the piano, which has carved into its body the story of the family's slave legacy, including a depiction of how two of their ancestors were bartered in exchange for the instrument, is the ghost of the recently deceased Sutter, a surviving member of the family that once owned them. He is intent on retrieving the piano as a way of symbolically regaining ownership of the Charles family even in the realm of the dead. Throughout the play characters use narrative devices, especially ghost lore, not only to introduce the plot and to progress the action, but also to reveal the family's background and how their past and present struggles for freedom are tied to the instrument, which represents a sacred shrine.

It is important to note that slaves often believed that they were not safe from their masters even after their masters' deaths (Olson 287). One of the factors that led to former slaves moving far away from the places where they were held in bondage was to put as much distance as possible between them and their masters' ghosts. In this sense, the Great Migration could be seen as an attempt by African Americans to put distance between them and the ghosts of slavery's past, but in *The Piano Lesson*, not even the 1,000 miles from Sunflower, Mississippi, to Pittsburgh is enough distance between the Charles's family legacy and the embodiment of their past subjection. The telling of ghost lore and other stories of the supernatural by several characters, such as the tale of the Ghosts of the Yellow Dog, is not a distortion of the play's realistic depiction of early twentieth-century African American life. As Lawrence Levine notes, to slaves and their descendants "ghosts were familiar phenomena," and in the oral narratives constructed from the perspective of black folk beliefs, the supernatural was often used "as a means of controlling the supernatural itself" (78). Very often these narratives depicted the actions of deceased blacks "who returned to demand justice from the whites who abused or killed them," but also included tales about "the spirits of masters who returned after death to continue the torment of their black bondsmen" (79). Wilson's play contains both kinds of narratives. Although all of the adult members contribute bits of narrative information about the family's past from their own biased perspectives, it is Doaker, the uncle who shares a house with Bernice in Pittsburgh, who is the play's most important storyteller.

The first story he relates is one concerning the goings and comings of trains, which is of particular relevance to his character since he is employed as a railroad cook. He is an especially adept storyteller, one whom Shannon describes as "steeped in the rich folklore that evolved among this exclusive class of railroad men" (158). The story that is central to the action of the play is Doaker's telling of how his grandmother and the young boy who would become his father were traded away from the rest of the family in Mississippi to a new owner in Georgia in exchange for a piano that their former owner's wife coveted. According to Doaker, Robert Sutter, the slaves' owner, offered one and one-half slaves to a fellow named Joel Nolander as trade for the wooden object. Soon after, Miss Ophelia, his wife, began to miss the two slaves and wanted them back, but the new owner refused to rescind the trade. Her husband ordered one of his remaining slaves, Doaker's grandfather, the original Boy Willie, an expert wood sculptor and the great-grandfather to the present day Boy Willie and Bernice, to carve the image of the two traded slaves—Papa Boy Walter and Mama Bernice—on the body of the piano as a means of pacifying his wife. Instead of merely carving simple cameo images in the instrument's wood, Papa Boy Willie sculpted life-like depictions of not only the woman and the boy as they looked at the time of the trade, but also pictures of Papa Boy Willie's mother, Mama Esther, and his father, the first Boy Charles. Then, according to Doaker,

> he put on the side here all kinds of things. See that? That's when him and Mama Bernice got married. They called that jumping the broom. That's how you got married in them days. Then he got here when my daddy was born… and here he got Mama Esther's funeral…and down here he got Mr. Nolander taking Mama Bernice and my daddy away down to his place in Georgia. He got all kind of things what happened with my family. When Mr. Sutter seen the piano with all them carvings on it he got mad. He didn't ask for all that. But see…there wasn't nothing he could do about it. When Miss Ophelia seen it…she got excited. Now she had her piano and her niggers too. (Wilson, *Piano* 44)

As Devon Boan argues, *The Piano Lesson* is a multilayered slave narrative (264), although the relationship I see with it in terms of the slave narrative tradition is a bit different than his. I would suggest that the play contains elements of the three forms of slave narrative expressions that span the entire gamut of the African American literary tradition. First of all, the inscribed narrative, conveyed to us through the performance of Doaker's oral narrative, the one Papa Boy Willie scripted on the body of the piano with his carvings, represent a classic, antebellum slave narrative. The piano itself serves as a key nonspoken narrative device, since the figures carved on it tell the story of past captivity and a struggle for freedom. The text of Doaker's narrative, one that looks back on the slave past from his own twentieth-century perspective, possesses elements of what Bernard W. Bell, Deborah E. McDowell, and others have defined as the neo-slave narrative. Wilson's play, however, is a contemporary slave narrative: a "liberation tale" set in our contemporary times but that deals with the plight of African Americans who are left to cope with the ramifications of past bondage—with the figurative ghosts of their slave pasts. The two former categories of liberation tales explore the area of the past that many African Americans regard as the holy ground of their history, and the narrative expressions of such works are often lyrically informed by the spirituals, field hollers, and other kinds of traditional expressions.

Contemporary slave narratives, however, are steeped in the blues and other more recent forms of musical expression. The stories expressed in *The Piano Lesson* are blues narratives of the kind that blacks transported with them on their northern sojourns up the Dixie Pike in their efforts to find refuge and respite from their former masters.

Doaker's narrative eventually reveals that Boy Charles, Bernice and Boy Willie's father, later lost his life in an act of self-appropriation when he liberated the piano from the Sutter household because he believed the family would never be free of its slave past as long as their former owners were in possession of it. But after burning alive the escaping Boy Charles with a group of hobos in the boxcar of a train called the Yellow Dog, the whites responsible for the massacre began to suffer mysterious deaths. The legend of the Ghosts of the Yellow Dog soon developed, as blacks in the area attributed the avenging acts to the spirits of the men who died on the train. One by one, reports began to circulate concerning the deaths of the white vigilantes who were all allegedly pushed down their wells, culminating with Sutter, whose 340-pound body was found in his well only three weeks before Boy Willie's rambunctious arrival at the start of the play.

Both Bernice and Boy Willie have lost their sacral connection to the instrument. From the moment of his arrival in Doaker's house, Boy Willie plots to remove the piano for the purposes of peddling it as a mere musical instrument. For Boy Willie, who has traveled up from Mississippi with his friend Lymon in a broken-down truck full of watermelons that they hope to sell, the piano represents economic opportunity and potential power. He wants to sell it and use the money along with his profits from the watermelons and prior savings to pay for a parcel of land back in Mississippi that had been owned by the Sutter family. He needs only the portion of the money that he would receive from the sale of his and his sister's inheritance to assume ownership of the land that his family once labored upon as slaves. He feels as though his father would have supported his efforts since possession of the land would put him on equal footing with the white men of the South. Being a man who perceives materialism as wealth, Boy Willie believes his plan of turning the family heirloom into land would do more to honor their father, who started out in life with nothing, than having it sit in Doaker's house practically unused, except by Bernice's young daughter and on occasion by Winning Boy, their transient, blues singing uncle. Like his father, he believes a tenacious act—buying a plot of land in the Jim Crow South to work as an owner instead of as a slave—is the next step in the family's procession from commodified objects of possession to equal citizenship. Ironically, the person he seeks to sell the piano to is a white man who combs the black community seeking all of the instruments he can appropriate from the people in the area. In the context of other Wilson plays, including *Ma Rainey's Black Bottom* and *Joe Turner's Come and Gone*, it seems as if Boy Willie is willing to sell his family's heritage outright to a man who is intent on separating African Americans from their most important mode of expression: their music. Bernice, on the other hand, has refused to touch the piano since her mother's death, because it is a reminder of the senseless loss of her father, her mother's death, and even the death of her husband who was involved in a scheme with Boy Willie and Lymon. Both Boy Willie's effort to use the piano for commerce and Bernice's refusal to play it are dangerous and place both the past and present members of the family in jeopardy.

To Bernice, who has been in custody of the instrument since their mother's passing, the piano represents the narrative of her family's pain and oppression. For her, the piano's legacy includes her father's senseless death over what she calls "a piece of wood" and her mother's resulting "seventeen years worth of cold nights and an empty bed" (52). The piano itself is what provides key links to the past in what Michael Morales calls "its interrelated, dual ritual functions" (106), as both a sacred object and as a functional piece of property. It is a means used to transmit oral history through a pictorial narrative, and it serves as an ancestral altar bridging the world of the living to that of the dead. Its power, however, in this regard, is only potent when it is played, for even Sutter's ghost plays the piano in an effort to make it an instrument of his own melodic design. Similar to the legendary Joe Turner in the previously discussed play, Sutter's ghost threatens to steal the family's song.

According to Morales, if the piano as a shrine is considered in the context of many West African ritual practices, "the spiritual and physical consequences of [Bernice] forgetting her past and not using the piano are very serious" (109). He adds that in the ancestral worship of many African cultures, especially those that represent the former cultures of the majority of slaves, "neglect of the ancestors and the ancestral altars results in loss of their protection and threatens the destruction of the entire community" (109). In fact, by neglecting one's shrine, especially through the failure of offering requisite prayers or gifts, a person's ancestral spirits will either leave or become estranged from those they left behind in the realm of the living. Such neglect eventually reduces these deities to mere idols. This lack of diligence by living members of the clan can result in their loss of protection by the ancestors, making them all susceptible to destructive forces, such as Sutter's ghost. In the play's climatic scene, Bernice's suitor, Avery, an aspiring preacher, attempts to cleanse the house through a ritual of water purification and scripture recitation. Although the mystical dream he relates to Boy Willie and Lymon about how he received his calling to be a preacher is a fascinating narrative, his efforts fail, because, as Pereira notes, "Christian rites are insufficient to dispel the ghosts of Christian oppressors" (101). To Boy Willie and Lymon, Avery's powerful testimony has less to do with his belief in supernatural signs and wonders than in his desire to gain the economic advantages that any shepherd with a flock of giving sheep might expect to receive. The absence of music in the ritual of exorcism is of importance since both in African *and* Old Testament context music has the transcendent qualities of a phantom limb and might have served as a conduit to supply Avery's words with metaphysical power.

Lacking the aid of a Christi-conjure figure such as Binder from *Joe Turner's Come and Gone* or Aunt Ester in *Two Trains Running*, the family finds itself faced with the dilemma of having to overcome the presence of its hunted past on their own. Boy Willie attacks the ghost physically while Bernice comes to his aid by playing a call to the ancestors on the piano, uttering the names of family members from previous generations of slavery and freedom. The phantom limb conjured up through her musical exhortation succeeds in bringing forth the combined spiritual presence of the ancestors whose images are carved in the wood and the more recently passed family members such as Bernice's and Boy Willie's parents, whose blood and tears were spent either to free it from the Sutters or to cleanse it in ritual sacrifice. Thus, at the end of the play, Sutter is banished and the family is redeemed through the process of ritual renewal. Although Boy Willie goes back to the South without the money he needs, there are signs that he realizes the bond of kinship that has been healed through the ordeal are much more important than Sutter's land. For Bernice, playing the piano has helped her overcome the wounds of bitterness that have haunted her through most of her life, and her reconnection with the ancestors allows her to find sacred value in the deaths of family members that she had previously viewed only in secular terms.

Throughout the play, especially in its final scene, the Charles's house in Pittsburgh shares a strong connection with the house on 124 Bluestone Road in Toni Morrison's *Beloved*. This is especially true when Grace, a woman whom both Boy Willie and Lymon try to court, senses the presence of the ghost in the climatic scene and says before fleeing "Something ain't right here" (103). Boy Willie's physical assault of the ghost is also reminiscent of Paul D's onslaught against the baby ghost near the beginning of Morrison's novel not long after he entered Sethe's home. Even the singing, chanting, and praying by Ella and the other women from the community in *Beloved* is similar to Bernice's piano playing and chanting, as they come forth to banish the ghost from the house and out of Sethe's life in the world of the living. The transcending essence of musical song in concert with Sethe's attempt to confront physically the white man she saw riding up on her yard helped to revise a moment from eighteen years before when the community ignored her plight and allowed Sethe to take her daughter's life to keep the child from being taken into slavery. Sethe's existence in the years following her act of infanticide might be characterized best by Orlando Patterson's concept of the "social death" endured by blacks *during* slavery, but it is also important to remember, as Marilyn Sanders Mobley attests in writing about *Beloved*, that for Morrison "the complicated psychic powers one had to exercise to resist devastation" was not relevant only to slaves and their experiences, "but of the Black experience in America after slavery as well" (197). Just as the social death of slavery lingered in Sethe's life and haunted her even in the years after the system's legal abolition, the lives of many in African American communities continued to be affected by its debilitating effects even well into the twentieth century. Wilson's exploration of twentieth-century African American life in his cycle of plays that touch upon each decade is, in essence, an examination of the ways African Americans have attempted to cope with the continued reality of social death in their lives.

In these works of spiritual realism, characters whose lives are affected by the lingering decay of social death must be redeemed as vital beings through a ritualistic process that results in what might best be thought of as secular resurrections. It is only through ritualistic acts or performances that include music that the spiritual renewal necessary to achieve this form of mortal redemption can be achieved.

According to Amadou Bissiri, Wilson's worldview is informed by an African sensibility that he "consciously seeks to integrate" into his plays and which "recognizes the reality of the invisible world (gods, spirits, the unborn, the dead—the ancestors) whose forces determine the lives of humans" (100). Through the aid of the ritually conjured or evoked phantom limb, the forces of the invisible world are able to manifest themselves in human life. The worldview and aesthetic sensibilities informing Wilson's plays have often led to indifferent responses from mainstream critics who insist on judging black expressive art solely by their own traditions and values. For example, Peter Wolfe, in a discussion of the critical responses to *The Piano Lesson*, states the resolution of the plot with Boy Willie confronting an actual ghost "offended some playgoers" (105). He cites Mimi Kramer as a critic who complained "the play's ending 'takes refuge in mystical and melodramatic event,'" and also cites Gerald Berhowitz's claim that Boy Willie's fight with Sutter's ghost is "a theatrically weak climax, since the mystical element seems imposed on the essentially realistic play" (105). But the intersection of the mystical and realistic in African American culture is endemic and plays an important role in black vernacular expression. As Levine has noted of the blues, it successfully blends "the sacred and the secular" (237). The integration of the spiritual and the real in *The Piano Lesson*, just as it is in *Joe Turner's Come and Gone*, was a goal—not a mistake—in that the spiritual realism that serves as the play's foundation and gives it depth supports what Wolfe calls its "realistic foreground" (105). The plays' mystical elements serve as much more than easy plot resolution, since the exploration of spiritual realism in both *Joe Turner's Come and Gone* and *The Piano Lesson* are much more important to Wilson and his goals as a storyteller than are the realistic elements in these dramatic works.

Typical modes of critical analysis that are used to read realistic drama are inadequate when confronted by works of New World African spiritual realism because the phantom limb that conveys the essence of such works to readers and viewers actually serves to interrogate conventional reality. If the phantom limb occasions a "shift in perspective between the real and unreal"(Mackey 33), those who are too heavily grounded in the materiality of American culture to participate in what Mackey terms an "exchange of attributes between the two" are figuratively limited by their critical perspectives to a dead end road. Conversely, those who are able to open themselves up for the possibility of exploration upon a Dixie Pike that not only connects Africa to African America but also the ethereal to the real are better able to discern the often conflicting worldviews that are at the center of the African American psyche.

WORKS CITED

Anderson, Douglas. "Saying Goodbye to the Past: Self-Empowerment and History in *Joe Turner's Come and Gone.*" *CLA Journal* 40 (1997): 432–457.

Bell, Bernard W. *The Afro-American Novel and Its Tradition.* Amherst: University of Massachusetts Press, 1987.

Bissiri, Amadou. "Aspects of Africanness in August Wilson's Drama: Reading *The Piano Lesson* through Wole Soyinka's Drama." *African American Review* 30 (Spring 1996): 99–113.

Boan, Devon. "Call-and-Response: Parallel 'Slave Narrative' in August Wilson's *The Piano Lesson.*" *African American Review* 32 (Summer 1998): 263–271.

Dash, Michael J. *The Other America: Caribbean Literature in a New World Context.* Charlottesville: University Press of Virginia, 1998.

Gates, Henry Louis, Jr. *The Signifying Monkey: A Theory of African-American Criticism.* New York: Oxford University Press, 1988.

Harris, Trudier. "August Wilson's Folk Traditions." *August Wilson: A Casebook.* Ed. Marilyn Elkins. New York: Garland, 1994. 49–67.

Harrison, Paul Carter. "August Wilson's Blues Poetics." Afterword. *August Wilson Three Plays.* Pittsburgh: University of Pittsburgh Press, 1991. 291–317.

——— "Mother/Word: Black Theatre in the African Continuum: Word/Song as Method." Introduction. *Totem Voices: Plays from the Black World Repertory.* Ed. Harrison. New York: Grove, 1989. xi–lxiii.

Levine, Lawrence. *Black Culture and Black Consciousness.* New York: Oxford University Press, 1977.

Mackey, Nathaniel. "Sound and Sentiment, Sound and Symbol." *Callaloo* 10 (Winter 1987): 29–54.

McDowell, Deborah E. "Negotiating between Tenses: Witnessing Slavery After Freedom." *Dessa Rose. Slavery in the Literary Imagination.* Ed. McDowell and Arnold Rampersad. Baltimore: Johns Hopkins University Press, 1989. 144–163.

Mobley, Marilyn Sanders. "A Different Remembering: Memory, History, and Meaning in Toni Morrison's *Beloved.*" *Toni Morrison: Modern Critical Views.* Ed. Harold Bloom. New York: Chelsea House, 1990. 189–199.

Morales, Michael. "Ghosts on the Piano: August Wilson and the Representation of Black American History." *May All Your Fences have Gates: Essays on the Drama of August Wilson.* Ed. Alan Nadel. Iowa City: University of Iowa Press, 1994. 105–115.

Morrison, Toni. Interview with Bill Moyers. "The World of Ideas." PBS. WTTW, Chicago, September 14, 1990.

Olson, Ted. "Folklore." *Oxford Companion to African American Literature.* New York: Oxford University Press, 1997.

Pereira, Kim. *August Wilson and the African-American Odyssey.* Urbana: University of Illinois Press, 1995.

Plum, Jay. "Blues, History, and the Dramaturgy of August Wilson." *African American Review* 27 (Winter 1993): 561–567.

Shannon, Sandra G. *The Dramatic Vision of August Wilson.* Washington, D.C.: Howard University Press, 1995.

Toomer, Jean. *Cane.* New York: Norton, 1988[1923].

Williams, Dana A. "Making the Bones Live Again: A Look at the 'Bones People' in August Wilson's *Joe Turner's Come and Gone* and Henry Dumas's 'Ark of Bones.'" *CLA Journal* 42 (1999): 309–319.

Wolfe, Peter. *August Wilson.* New York: Twayne, 1999.

10

Speaking of Voice and August Wilson's Women

Tara T. Green

Much has been written about the male protagonists of August Wilson's plays. Wilson himself admits to making men the focus of his work. In an interview with Sandra Shannon, the award-winning playwright was asked, "How do you perceive women's roles in your work? Are you concerned that, so far, women have not been the focus of your plays?" Wilson responded, "No, I am not concerned, and I doubt seriously if I would make a woman the focus of my work simply because of the fact that I am a man, because of *the ground on which I stand* and the viewpoint from which I perceive the world" (Shannon, "Blues" 8 [emphasis mine]). Wilson suggests that his focus on males is as natural as his focus on black characters. Though Wilson primarily centers on the plight of male characters in his plays, these men are usually not unaffected by the relationships they have with women who are their mothers, lovers, or friends.

The ground on which he stands is not only his male perspective, as he states in the interview with Shannon, but is also informed by his cultural experiences. In his speech, "The Ground on Which I Stand," Wilson calls for black playwrights to come together and to discuss ways to "develop guidelines for the protection of our cultural property" (6). Arguably, Wilson's desire to preserve and celebrate his African American culture stems from the influences of his mother:

> Growing up in my mother's house at 1727 Bedford Ave. in Pittsburgh, PA, I learned the language, the eating habits, the religious beliefs, the gestures, the notions of common sense, attitudes towards sex, concepts of beauty and justice, and the responses to pleasure and pain, that my mother had learned from her mother, and which you could trace back to the first African who set foot on the continent. (Wilson, "The Ground" 3)

What Wilson makes clear is that his observations of the daily cultural "performances" of his mother informed his point of view. Further, Wilson attributes the fruits of the culture as stemming from the collective experiences of the ancestors, and, in his experience, the legacy of the culture was passed through his maternal lineage. Thus, women have played a significant role in molding his perception, and subsequently, his art.

Wilson continues, stating that there are two kinds of black art: "art that is conceived and designed to entertain white society, and art that feeds the spirit and celebrates the life of black America by designing strategies for survival and prosperity" (3). There is an important distinction between the two kinds of art: the impact on the audience. While in the first form white audiences are merely entertained, in the latter form, black audiences are not only "spiritually fed" but are provided with a strategic plan needed for survival. Wilson prescribes to the latter of the two kinds of art he identifies. Emerging from Wilson's call for black artists to refrain from simply entertaining in order to self-define their culture is a call for voice ownership. For Wilson, theater is a voice that has the "power to inform" ("The Ground" 7). If theater is the voice of the culture, by extension, each character speaks to certain aspects of the culture. Ownership of voice is ownership of the culture's expression or the unimpeded claim that the culture has to communicate ideas vital to its survival.

Within the artistic performative space where black Americans design strategies for survival and prosperity, Wilson says that he stands on the "self-defining ground of the slave quarters" made "fertile by the blood and bone of men *and women*" (emphasis mine). To adequately speak for and celebrate the lives of black men *and* women, the playwright of performative black art is charged with the responsibility of presenting not only male, but female characters whose voices express the ideas of the culture's people. According to Wilson, when he attempted to write a play just about men, a woman's voice emerged and said: "How are you going to write this play about these guys and not include me in it? I'm part of it. They didn't get to be *who they are without me....*" (Shannon, "Blues" 10 [emphasis mine]). Notably, this insistent female voice speaks for the women of Wilson's collective works, all of whom make a place within male-dominated spaces as does the woman described above—demanding to be heard.

Wilson's female characters represent his perception and *conception* of art as an expression of African American culture. However, the women in Wilson's plays commonly do not play dominant roles. In fact, they are usually outnumbered by the men, as there may be only one woman amongst a cast of several men. As a result, the women's *act* of speaking—what they say, how they say it, and how their words affect their male associates—is vital when assessing the characterization of Wilson's women and the role they play in plot development. How does what they say affect the other characters and perhaps the outcome of the play? Further, keeping in mind that for Wilson, black art is to design "strategies for survival and prosperity," do his female characters contribute to this design? More importantly, how does what they say affect their positions within Wilson's male-dominated culture? As they negotiate the male-dominated spaces of the site of performance, Wilson's female characters demonstrate the importance of voice ownership.

Perhaps the most prominent of Wilson's female characters are Ma Rainey of *Ma Rainey's Black Bottom* and Rose of *Fences*. Ma Rainey, the "Mother of the Blues" is in the unique position of being able to exert power during the 1920s because of her voice. A woman who makes a living speaking for the people of the African American culture, she demonstrates what Wilson means when he says, "We have voice and we have temper" (4). In contrast to Ma Rainey, Rose does not become aware of the importance of her voice until near the end of the play. She is the "I" in the "we" of the culture that Wilson celebrates, and her journey to self-awareness demonstrates the necessity of voice ownership. On the other hand, Risa of *Two Trains Running* demonstrates the consequences of lack of voice ownership. She expresses herself through self-mutilation and not through her voice. These women's successes and failures to own their voices prove the significance of what Wilson identifies as black Americans struggle for "self-determination, self-respect and self-defense" ("The Ground" 2).

Ma Rainey of *Ma Rainey's Black Bottom* is a superb example of the struggle and importance of voice ownership. Set in March 1927, the play begins with Rainey's band awaiting her arrival so they can record songs for a company owned by a white man. As they do so, they dialogue about a number of issues ranging from religion to racism. In the center of their interactions is Levee, a black man in his early thirties who wishes to be his own bandleader. When Ma Rainey enters the stage with her lover, Dussie Mae, and her nephew, Sylvester, the three bring with them a flurry of chaos. But since the occasion for the gathering is to record Rainey's voice, any trouble she brings, her white agent reluctantly fixes, ensuring that the recording session will proceed.

From the moment of her entrance, Ma Rainey demands that all treat her with respect, particularly white men. She, Dussie Mae, and Sylvester have been involved in an altercation that required police intervention. According to the police officer, while he was investigating their car accident, the three tried to flee the scene in a cab, but the cab driver denied them service. Consequently, Ma Rainey hit the cab driver. Having no power on the street, she moved to the place where she has limited power—the recording studio. Here she can issue commands with the expectation that they will be met. In order to appease her, Irvin, her white manager, must obey Ma Rainey when she insists that he "tell the man [police officer] who he's messing with." Irvin is reluctant to follow instructions: "...Give me a chance! Officer, this is one of our recording artists...Ma Rainey." Ma Rainey quickly corrects Irvin: "Madame Rainey! Get it straight!" (Wilson, *MaRainey* 49). Rainey demands that the white male not identify her as "Ma"—a term of familiarity, but she insists that she be identified with a title of respect not given to black women of the 1920s era. While she may have been accused by the white police officer of stealing her own car and may have been denied taxi service because of her race, she will be vindicated by being identified as "Madame" by the one white male she can dominate, if only for a short while. She uses her power further by calling him Irvin and not *Mr.* Irvin as the black band members must do in this 1920s era.

Irvin and Sturdyvant resent the power that Ma Rainey's voice has over them. Aware that her voice is a commodity, they must allow her to occupy a certain space in their world. The audience may note that in an earlier discussion Irvin had with Sturdyvant, the white owner of the recording studio, Sturdyvant expresses his displeasure with Ma Rainey who acts like she is a "Royal Highness" and marches in "like she owns the damn place" (18). The "damn place"—the recording studio—is a space he must share with Ma Rainey, an African American woman. What Sturdyvant makes clear is that her "uppity" attitude is offensive to him, especially since both men are powerless to curtail it for her talent allows them a lifestyle they most certainly enjoy.

Ma Rainey vehemently protests against whites who attempt to "take her voice and trap it in one of the fancy boxes..." (79). As she indicates to Cutler, Rainey is aware that Irvin only tolerates her because they can benefit financially from her talent. Thus, she is aware that her status as a paid entertainer does not prove to give her racial equality. As characteristic of a blues singer and blues writer, she compares the music industry executives to men who use women for sexual gratification and once done "its just like if I'd be some whore and they roll over and put their pants on. Ain't got no use for me then" (79). What she expresses is disrespect on two fronts—gender and race. On one hand, she is a woman in an industry dominated by men. Consequently, she must claim her own place when they would prefer to designate a place for her. On the other hand, she is subject to whites who own the recording studios and the rights to her songs, her words. Ma Rainey's struggle to sing the blues songs as she wills is expressive of Wilson's call for the protection of the culture:

> We need to develop guidelines for the protection of our culture, our contributions and the influence they accrue. It is time that we took responsibility for the talents in our own hands. We cannot depend on others. (6)

Ma Rainey, as do her band members, depends on "the others"—Sturdyvant and Irvin—to pay them and to market their talents. Through Ma Rainey's struggle to keep her voice—the mouthpiece of the culture—free from the control of others, the play becomes a statement about white executives' exploitation of black entertainers/black voices, and it demonstrates the need for the culture's protection.

White men are not the only ones who try to "trap her voice." Levee, a young, black man, is guilty of trying this as well. His insistence that she sing his version of the song, "Ma Rainey's Black Bottom" makes him complicitous with her enemies. She will not sing, "Levee's Black Bottom," but she will sing "Ma Rainey's song" (62). In an attempt to have Ma Rainey overruled, Levee has solicited the support of Irvin and Sturdyvant, men who otherwise have no use for him. Rainey responds by asking Irvin to explain who was included in the decision-making process: "Who's this 'we'? What you mean 'we'?" Rainey implies that Levee cannot rewrite a woman's song, thus usurping a woman's voice. Indeed, the song is about Ma Rainey's Black

Bottom. A dance, as she relays in the song, that she learned from the black people of the South. Further, Ma Rainey has an awareness of the people that Levee, Sturdyvant, and Irvin do not have. Angela Davis describes Ma Rainey's music as being "socially oriented music [that] constituted an aesthetically mediated community-building and assisted in developing a specifically African-American social consciousness" (*Blues* 92). To trap Ma Rainey's voice would amount to stifling the voice of the people she speaks for and to:

> White folks don't understand about the blues. They hear it come out, but they don't know how it got there. They don't understand that's life way of talking. You don't sing to feel better. You sing 'cause that's a way of understanding life. (Wilson, *Ma Rainey* 82)

Wilson explains the relationship of blues to the culture: "You get the ideas and attitudes of the people as part of the oral tradition. This is a way of passing along information" (Adell 52). Further, he says that blues singers are "carriers of ideas" who engage in the sacred tasks of "disseminat[ing] this information and [of] carry[ing] [the] cultural values of the people" (Shannon, "Blues" 2). As "Mother of the Blues," Rainey's songs project this understanding about life that "articulate the burden of marginalization" (Bogumil 22). While Levee is interested in being in the white men's good graces, Rainey is interested in using her voice to speak *for* and to the people of her community. Her voice is a projection of the awareness that she has, and her refusal to have it edited by males represents her attempt at cultural preservation as well as female independence. Ultimately, like Wilson's mother and grandmother, Ma Rainey is a cultural conduit.

Rainey's inner voice plays an important role to her sense of self and of others. She explains the value of her inner voice to Irvin: "Ma listens to her heart. Ma listens to the voice inside her. That's what counts with Ma" (63). As she argues that "white folks don't understand the blues," which also suggests that white folks don't understand her, Rainey is conscious that Irvin will not fully understand what she means about "the voice inside her." Her inner voice accurately tells her that Levee "ain't nothing but trouble," and "He ain't nothing but bad news" (78). As they record, Ma praises all the players but Levee, whom she criticizes as going off by himself and playing what he wants (101). Levee is on the outside of the culture yearning for power, even the limited power that Rainey possesses: "Ma tell Mr. Irvin she gonna leave...and Mr. Irvin get down on his knees and beg her to stay! That's the way I'm gonna be! Make the white man respect me!" (94). Rainey's assessment of him will prove to be correct, and it is an assessment that none of the other characters make.

But Levee is not Ma Rainey. The earlier presence of the police is mirrored at the end of the play when Levee, who is angered by Sturdyvant's rejection of his music, kills fellow band member, Toledo. There is a significant difference between the two scenes. While Levee does not express his anger to

Sturdyvant, the one who offended him, he unconsciously chooses to project his anger on a member of his own race. In Ma Rainey's case, she consciously hits the one who has offended her—the prejudiced cab driver. Even though she denies touching the man, it is likely that she intentionally opened the door, causing it to hit him: Rainey says, "Said he wasn't gonna haul no colored folks...if you want to know the truth of it" (51). While Levee deludes himself into thinking that he is in the white men's favor (Shannon, "The Good Christian's" 131), Rainey remains aware of where she stands with the whites. Levee does not possess the survival techniques that Rainey has mastered. She knows to go to the studio when she is faced with being arrested; she knows to demand payment for Sylvester before she signs the contract; and she knows to fire Levee after the recording session. As Kim Pereira notes, Levee is motivated by pride resulting in "a defiance of tradition as he pursues his own destiny" (18). Since Levee has attempted to sell his songs/voice to whites and to stifle Ma Rainey, the voice of the culture's collective consciousness, he will suffer the consequence of not claiming ownership of his voice. As such, his only outlet of expression is the act of murdering one of his own race. What Levee does not know is that Rainey's power comes from her keen sense of awareness and her refusal to be defined by others. In this Wilson play, hers is the voice that speaks to "strategies for survival and prosperity."

While Ma Rainey enters the stage conscious of the power of her voice, Rose of *Fences* enters unconscious of her power. Rose is a member of the culture Ma Rainey speaks for, but Rose proves that speaking for herself is vital to her own survival. Rose represents the importance of voice ownership for the self. Through her transformation from a state of unconsciousness to consciousness, Rose will claim ownership of her voice and use it as an instrument to claim the identity she allowed her husband to overshadow.

Fences begins in 1957 and focuses on the Maxson family. Troy Maxson is a refuse collector who has been married to Rose for eighteen years and is father to their seventeen-year-old son, Cory. When the play opens, he has protested against the fact that black men have not been allowed the opportunity to be truck drivers. As a result of his protest, he is later promoted to truck driver even though he is illiterate and, therefore, does not have a driver's license. Troy appears to be happily married to Rose, but after eighteen years of marriage he confesses to her that he has impregnated a woman. When Troy's mistress dies in childbirth, Rose agrees to raise the child. *Fences* ends in 1965 with Troy's funeral.

When Rose enters, she uses her voice to disrupt the confines of a male-dominated space—the yard. The play begins with Troy and Bono standing in the Maxson's yard engaged in dialogue while drinking liquor. Rose is said to be an "integral part of the Friday night ritual" (2414). Although she is an "integral part" of the ritual, Troy attempts to isolate her from the ritualistic space: Rose asks, "What you all out here getting into?" Troy's response is curt: "What you worried about what we getting into for? This is men talk, woman." Peter Wolfe notes that Troy's language "shows that he does not view her as a full and equal partner" (63). Troy places restrictions on the yard as being a place for men, and he emphasizes his command to her by identifying her as "woman." Rose's counteractive response serves to dismiss her husband's attempt at rhetorical domination while subsequently re/claiming her place in the ritual: "What I care what you all talking about? Bono, you gonna stay for supper?" Troy remains persistent, however, and a few lines later he tells Rose to go back into the house "and let me and Bono finish what we was talking about. This is men talk. I got some talk for you later. You know what kind of talk I mean" (2415). Although he changes his tactic of simply issuing an order, his language still reeks of patriarchal dominance. Troy implies that Rose is to remain in the domestic space as cook and sexual gratifier. Significantly, Rose rejects these labels by remaining present in the "men's space," ignoring the fact that she has been told two times that she is interrupting "men talk." She is a part of the ritual because she insists on being part of it.

Troy continues by conveying how he courted Rose, but Rose counters Troy's story by telling how she allowed him to be a part of her life: "I told him if he wasn't the marrying kind, then move out the way so the marrying kind could find me." According to Troy, he came back two or three days later; but according to Rose, he was back the same night (2418). The space Rose claims in the storytelling session is reminiscent of Zora Neale Hurston, the remarkably talented storyteller who told of storytelling. In *Dust Tracks on a Road*, Hurston describes how both men and women would sit on the porch of Joe Clarke's store and tell each other the town's gossip. As Hurston tells the stories of the porch, readers will never know whether they are stories that she actually heard and is therefore retelling or if these are stories that Hurston, herself, is telling, making her a participant of the communal storytelling ritual rather than a mere observer. Either way, Hurston, who was too young to sit on the porch with the adults, is in control of the narrative, and she writes herself into the restrictive space of the porch:

> I was not allowed to sit around there, naturally. But, I could and did drag my feet going in and out, whenever I was sent there for something, to allow what was being said to hang in my ear. (46)

Rose likewise refuses to be simply a part of Troy's story about their lives or a mere observer. She insists on telling the story. Consequently, her voice, not simply her presence, is an integral part of the ritual. However, while it is true that she interrupts the male-dominated ritual, the role she assumes is a respondent to Troy. He initiates and she supports.

Troy also engages in the telling of folklore, as the three stand in the Maxson's yard—Wilson's version of the urban porch. Troy tells about his bout with Death: "We wrestled for three days and three nights" (2418). Rose notes that "Every time Troy tell that story he find different ways to tell it. Different things to make up about it" (2418). He continues his storytelling by describing his experience with the Devil. This Devil is a "white

fellow . . . [who] got on good clothes" who came to Troy's house and offered
him a line of credit so that Troy could purchase furniture. According to Troy
the Devil said, "If I miss a payment the devil was coming back and it'll be
hell to pay. That was fifteen years ago. To this day . . . the first of the month
I send my ten dollars, Rose'll tell you." Rose's response is simple, "Troy
lying" (2420). Hurston describes this ritual of "lying" sessions: "That is,
straining against each other in telling folk tales [about] God, Devil, Brer
Rabbit, Brer Fox, Sis Cat . . . ," as being restricted to the "menfolks" (47).
Each woman would be at home, calling for her husband's return but would
be ignored, as the ritual would not be disturbed by women. However,
Hurston, once again, writes herself into this cultural ritualistic space that is
both gender restrictive as well as age restrictive. In the case of *Fences*, Troy
is the one who dominates the session as he is the one who tells the stories for
the entertainment of his friend, Bono. Although Bono, like Rose, recognizes
that Troy is engaging in a "lying session," Bono does not question or refute
him. In contrast, Rose who, like Hurston in her community is younger and
is female, refutes her husband by calling his stories "lies." While her husband
protests racial restrictions, Rose defies gender restrictions.

Though she resists restrictions, Rose is unaware of the importance of her
voice. To Troy, part of her role as his wife is to be his loyal supporter. This
is suggested when he "jokingly" calls her like she is his servant: "You supposed to come when I call you, woman" (2434). He expects Rose to be his
respondent, and this is a role that she accepts. So consumed by this role, she
is unable to recognize that Troy has been lying to her by maintaining a relationship with another woman. In fact, it seems that Rose is unable to discern
the difference between his lies and his stories, and her naïveté proves to be
problematic for her. When she tells her husband, "I know you like I know
the back of my hand" (2424), she unknowingly admits that she knows herself about as well as she knows her husband. In other words, she does not
know herself well at all. Rose will not be able to realize the full meaning of
her life with her husband until she realizes the full meaning of her own.

Not until Troy confesses his indiscretions does Rose begin to see how
much she has lost by not claiming a more prominent place in their relationship. When Rose asks Troy if he plans to continue seeing Alberta, he says,
"I can laugh out loud and it feels good. . . . I can't give that up" (2446).
Implicit in Rose's question is that she is still willing to be a supportive wife
if *he allows her* to be. Since the beginning of the play, Troy has defined Rose's
role as wife. As wife/woman she is not privy to certain conversations, rather
she is his cook, his lover, and the mother of their son. Now Rose voices what
it is to be a wife: "You should have held me tight. You should have grabbed
me and held on" the way she did to him. What Rose makes clear is that as
his wife, she was supposed to be his sole supporter. If all of the characters,
including Rose, have revolved around Troy until this point (Wolfe 58), the
consequences of his actions will serve to give rise to Rose's development. She
admits to him that she has invested herself in him: "I planted myself inside
you and waited to bloom. And it didn't take me no eighteen years to find

out the soil was hard and rocky and it wasn't going to bloom" (2447). Her name signifies that she does bloom, and the audience must remember that at the onset of this conversation, Gabriel interrupts them to hand Rose a "same rose like you is" (2445). Her realization that she has buried her identity in another, specifically a man, will empower her to claim an identity outside that of Troy's dedicated, supportive wife.

Rose's gradual transformation is seen in the way she uses her voice, particularly when she speaks for Gabriel to Troy. In Act I, Rose consoles Troy when he expresses his guilt for taking his brother's money to buy their home: "Ain't no use in you blaming yourself for nothing. Gabe wasn't in no condition to manage the money. You done what was right by him" (2426). Again she acts as a respondent, intent on supporting her husband. However, after Troy reveals the news of his affair and the coming of a child, Rose's responses to Troy are based on his actions and not on his words. Specifically, in response to Troy's action of signing papers that authorize the state to hospitalize his brother and to give part of his brother's check to him, Rose expresses her disappointment by directly confronting Troy (2449). Further, she is not moved by his excuse of illiteracy. "You went back on yourself, Troy. You gonna have to answer for that" (2449). Rose's use of her voice to challenge her husband's actions proves her transformation.

Rose does not instantaneously claim a separate identity; rather, her rise to consciousness is gradual. Even when Rose knows about Troy's affair with Alberta she continues to play the role of a respondent, one who supports Troy despite his faults. Six months later, when the hospital calls to inform Troy that his daughter has been born and that Alberta is dead, Rose offers her support: "I am your wife Troy. Don't push me away" (2450). She is still willing to be supportive of her husband, but he rebuffs her offer of support. Troy's dilemma is now solved. He no longer needs to decide between his wife and his mistress. Fate has made the decision for him, so he thinks. Three days later, when he brings the baby home and asks his wife for her help, she agrees to be supportive, but the support he now seeks comes from a new woman, not his wife. Rose's response to Troy makes her stance clear: "From right now ... this child got a mother. But you a womanless man" (2451). She now has realized the importance of voice ownership, for this statement places her in a position of control. Rose has now bloomed into a woman who defines herself and is subject to no one.

The Maxson's yard has been a transformative space, the place where Rose claims ownership of her voice and the place where Troy looses the power of his. In the beginning of the play, Rose was second to Troy and by the time Raynell is born, the Friday night ritual is no longer as Troy and Bono rarely see each other at work or after work. Further, it is Troy, not Rose, who seeks inclusion. Near the end of Act II, Rose leaves home with Troy's child—now her child—to go to church. God has become Rose's other man and Troy, who has by now built the fence that keeps him in, asks the questions that Rose earlier asked of him: "What time will you be back?" She does not answer this question, much to Troy's chagrin, and the audience can see his powerlessness: "I just asked you a question, woman. What's the matter...can't I ask you a question?" She still refuses to answer and this time she directs *him* to the kitchen: "Your dinner's in there on the stove" (2452). She has come to realize the importance of her voice, an expression of her being. Rose is no longer Troy's respondent and supporter. His job as husband is to turn over his pay, to eat Rose's cooking, and to keep out of her way.

To be sure, Rose has found herself. And so she declares, "You can't be nobody but who you are" (2459). As she articulates at the end of the play, her gravest mistake was letting her husband "fill up the house" and not making him leave room for her. She assumed the role of "cooking his supper and keeping clean sheets on the bed" (2460). Notably, this is the role that we see Rose filling earlier in the play, much to the enjoyment of her husband who wants both his sexual and physiological appetites satisfied. Comfortable in her role, Rose was unconscious of the effect this had on her: "I didn't know to keep up his strength I had to give up pieces of myself" (2460). Her role as supporter allowed Troy to live, while she was consumed by his living. Rose's transformation has come full circle. She not only realizes the importance of speaking for the self to maintain identity, but she is able to impart this wisdom to her son. Rose has moved from a state of unconscious being to a conscious one.

While Ma Rainey and Rose serve to show the importance of voice ownership, Risa of *Two Trains Running* demonstrates the consequences of lack of voice ownership. Risa is the cook and waitress in a black-owned diner that will be soon bought by the government. The diner is the place where several men, including a mentally disturbed man, Hambone; a funeral home owner, West; a paroled ex-convict, Sterling; and Wolf, a numbers-runner, meet everyday to discuss a variety of topics. As Risa's boss, Memphis, orders her to serve them, she mostly remains quiet and speaks only when a statement is directed toward her or piques her interest.

Though she rarely uses her voice to speak about herself or to assert her opinions, she does attempt to speak on behalf of women who have been emotionally and mentally misused by their companions. Early in Act I, she suggests to Memphis that the reason why his wife left him may have been in reaction to his treatment of her: "Maybe she didn't like the way you was treating her." Memphis dismisses her revelation by saying, "I treat that woman like she was a queen...." He continues by telling of the things he bought her. Risa remains adamant in her unsolicited assessment of the woman's feelings: "Maybe she don't see it like that. She had to leave for something" (Wilson, *Two Trains* 4–5). Rather than considering that Risa may be correct, Memphis defends himself by describing their final interaction:

> I ain't don nothing but ask her to get up and make me some bread. And she got up and walked out the door. I know she didn't expect me to make it myself....She told me she was tired....Now, how you gonna get tired than I am? I'm the one going out there wrestling with the world. She ain't got nothing to do but stay home and take care of the house. (5)

Memphis's defense is a dismissal of a woman's attempt to express herself for the purpose of being understood. Unfortunately, Risa is unable to respond to Memphis because Holloway interrupts them. This act of interruption by a male is symptomatic of the underlying problem represented in this play: The dominance of powerful voices over that of less empowered voices. Perhaps if Risa had been given the opportunity or if she had interrupted Holloway to continue the conversation, she could have explained to Memphis that his wife's problem was not that she was physically tired, but perhaps mentally tired. Having to do nothing but stay home and take care of the house or in other words, perform any duty—like make the bread—when she is "asked," clearly was not satisfying to Memphis's wife. His refusal to acknowledge this, instead placing the blame of their union's demise on her, forces his wife to seize her only outlet of expression—to flee the scene of discomfort. She was clearly "tired" of her life with him.

Like Memphis's wife—she is never identified by her name—Risa is expected to perform all duties he assigns to her. This would be an acceptable expectation for Memphis is Risa's employer, but Memphis's habit of dominating his wife by use of his voice is extended to his treatment of Risa. Throughout the play, he orders Risa to clean the chicken, cook the food, and serve the customers: "Risa, get on back there and get that chicken ready, you ain't got time to be standing around." As she "exits into the back, Memphis takes his papers and goes to the booth" (15). When next Sterling enters, Memphis calls Risa from the kitchen to serve him and is astonished to find that she has been occupied with cleaning the chicken. It would seem that his only job is to see that Risa does all the work. Though Risa expresses awareness of why Memphis's wife left him, she does not protest his unfair treatment of her. Risa remains voiceless in the community of the diner, where she is outnumbered five to one by the male characters.

Certainly, Risa is able to speak on Memphis's wife's behalf for she is also tired of the way she has been treated by men. Risa is a beautiful woman with one physical abnormality: She has intentionally scarred her "legs with a razor," according to the playwright, in "an attempt to define herself in terms other than her genitalia" (3). In other words, Risa's scars represent her desire to attain self-definition. Later, when Sterling asks Risa why she has scarred her legs, she asks him to explain why he was looking at her legs. Implicit in her question is the answer to his question. She hopes to make a man appreciate her character and not her beauty.

Risa's tendency to self-mutilate herself is motivated by more than just a desire to force men to overlook her outer beauty and to value her inner beauty. She is likely attempting to protect herself from the problems that can arise from failed relationships with men. According to psychologist, Steven Levenkron, self-mutilators act in an effort to cope:

Like other disorders that result from failed trust relationships and attachments—eating disorders, obsessive-compulsive disorders, alcoholism, drug dependence—a behavior or a substance is used as a coping mechanism for the pain of the original wound. Self-mutilation is just the most bizarre and paradoxical example, in which pain and self-damage are used to bring about relief, safety, and security. (39)

Levenkron's assessment may be applicable to Risa. A flat character, Risa is not given the opportunity to speak about her background as are Sterling or Memphis, for example. In fact, the audience knows why Hambone recites the mantra, "He gone give me my ham," but we do not know exactly what events motivated Risa's decision to engage in the act of self-mutilation. Wilson does not give her voice; thus her lack of voice and her desire to have a voice is projected through the act of protecting herself from the men who seek to dominate her in some way, either emotionally, socially, or mentally.

Sadly, Risa appears to be as powerless as she is speechless. Her failed attempts to keep Sterling, a smooth talking criminal, at bay are expressive of her inability to use her voice to defend herself from the emotional pain a relationship with Sterling would undoubtedly bring. Though Sterling says that he does not care about how her legs look, he does not acknowledge her inner beauty. He states, "Quite naturally when men see you that big ass and them pretty legs they gonna try and talk you into bed somewhere...Ain't no sense in you getting upset about that. You ought to take it as a compliment. All you got to do is say no and keep on stepping" (100). Risa's response is significant. She states, "That just what I done" (100). Despite her efforts to remain independent and her acknowledgment that a future with him would be disappointing, she falls into his arms a few lines later.

Risa's greatest character flaw is that she does not speak strongly for herself. Unlike Ma Rainey and the transformed Rose, even when Risa knows better, she does not say and act. Part of voice ownership is the act of speaking and performing the act spoken. Ma Rainey sings and does not sign the contract until she gets everything she can for the act of performance. Rose says that Troy is a womanless man, and she supports her declaration by moving about while intentionally ignoring his pleas for attention. But Risa speaks and does not follow through. She does not "keep on stepping" as Sterling suggests.

Though a flat character, as a representative type, Risa is important. Risa represents humans' innate desire to express themselves and to have that expression respected. "For me," explains Wilson, "the scarring of her legs was an attempt to define herself in her own terms rather than being defined by men...for me it was her standing up and refusing to accept those definitions and making her self-definition" (Shannon, "Blues" 8). As he makes clear in the interview and in his speech, "The Ground on Which I Stand," self-definition is vital to the culture's prosperity and survival. Thus, Risa's inability to articulate her feelings and to protect herself suggests the consequences of what happens to the African American culture, and any culture, that does not speak for its self. Through Risa's self-scarification, Wilson suggests not speaking for the self—claiming ownership of the voice—is self-destructive.

Wilson's female characters, particularly Ma Rainey, Rose, and Risa demonstrate why it is important for African Americans to define themselves through use of their voices. Notably, both Ma Rainey and Rose use their voices to assert themselves in the culture that at times places constraints on them. Arguably, the characteristics of strength, consciousness, respectability, and nurturing can be found in all of Wilson's middle-aged black female characters. As the audience sees with Ma Rainey and Rose, they speak even when not invited to and act not when asked to but because they can and must. Young and beautiful, Risa's scars are a visible reminder of the consequence of not speaking for one's self as a matter of protection and survival. Wilson's women are the voice of the culture.

Works Cited

Adell, Sandra. "Speaking of Ma Rainey/Talking about the Blues." Ed. Alan Nadel. *May All Your Fences Have Gates.* Iowa City: University of Iowa Press, 1994.

Bogumil, Mary. *Understanding August Wilson.* Columbia: University of South Carolina Press, 1999.

Davis, Angela. *Blues Legacies and Black Feminism.* New York: Vintage, 1999.

Hurston, Zora Neale. *Dust Tracks on a Road.* New York: HarperPerennial, 1991.

Levenkron, Steven. *Cutting: Understanding and Overcoming Self-Mutilation.* New York: Norton, 1998.

Pereira, Kim. *August Wilson and the African-American Odyssey.* Urbana: University of Illinois Press, 1995.

Shannon, Sandra G. "The Ground on Which I Stand: August Wilson's Perspective on African American Women." *May All Your Fences Have Gates.* Ed. Alan Nadel. Iowa City: University of Iowa Press, 1994.

———. "Blues, History and Dramaturgy: An Interview with August Wilson." *African American Review* 27.4 (1993). *Expanded Academic ASAP.* InfoTrac. Southern Univ. Lib., Baton Rouge, LA. October 8, 2002 <http://web1.infotrac.gale-group.com/itw/infomark/224/959/28071920w1/purl=rc1_EAIM_0_A15342272&dyn=5!xrn_5_0_A25342272 &bkm_5_?sw_aep=lln _louis>.

———. "The Good Christian's Come and Gone: The Shifting Role of Christianity in August Wilson Plays." *MELUS* 16:3 (1988–89): 127–142.

Wilson, August. *Ma Rainey's Black Bottom.* New York: Plume, 1985.

———. *Two Trains Running.* New York: Plume, 1992.

———. *Fences. Norton Anthology of African American Literature.* Ed. Henry Louis Gates, Jr. and Nellie Mc Kay. New York: Norton, 1997. 2411–2462.

———. "The Ground on which I Stand." *American Theatre* 13.7 (1996). *Expanded Academic ASAP.* InfoTrac. Southern Univ. Lib., Baton Rouge, LA. October 8, 2002 <http://web1.infotraccustom.com/pdfserve/get_item/1/Sac57f0w1_1/SB704_01.pdf>.

Wolfe, Peter. *August Wilson.* New York: Twayne, 1999.

11

Using Black Rage to Elucidate African and African American Identity in August Wilson's *Joe Turner's Come and Gone* (1911)

C. Patrick Tyndall

Introduction

With his speech, "The Ground On Which I Stand," delivered to the Theatre Communications Group's Eleventh National Conference in Princeton, New Jersey, in June 1996, August Wilson galvanized a national debate on race and culture. In this speech, he all but demanded fully funded African American theaters for African American actors, directors, and other theater practitioners. Wilson pointed out that of the sixty-six theaters that are members of the League of Resident Theatres, only one could be considered African American—the Crossroads Theater in New Brunswick, New Jersey (Wilson, "The Ground On Which I Stand" 16; Gussow, "Energizing the Future of Black Theater" E3; Gussow, "Plea Heeded for Meeting on Black Theater" B1). As of this writing, the Crossroads Theater has closed but intends to reopen. Wilson hoped to bring attention to this sad state of theater by highlighting the reality of economics and race: "Black theater in America is alive...it is vibrant...it is vital...it just isn't funded" ("The Ground On Which I Stand" 16). Wilson expected that his speech would activate African American theater practitioners' rage, motivating them to change the sorry condition of African American theater on a national level.

As a result of and testimony to Wilson's cultural power, Dartmouth College sponsored a conference in March 1998, where black theater artists came together, as Wilson asked, to "'address questions of esthetics and to defend ourselves from naysayers'" (Gussow, "Plea Heeded for Meeting on Black Theater" B1). His incendiary speech also led to a highly publicized

Town Hall meeting in New York City on January 27, 1997, between Wilson and critic Robert Brustein, titled "On Cultural Power" (Gussow, "Plea Heeded for Meeting on Black Theatre" B1; Jefferson, "Oratory vs. Really Talking About Culture" C11). Between his plays and his cultural criticism, Wilson has given voice to the African American experience, leading to further examination of African Americans' placement within American society.

In retrospect, one can see how the ideas in Wilson's speech resonate in *Joe Turner's Come and Gone*. In the speech, Wilson calls for the support of black art (his and others) in order to improve the standing of the African American community in general. In the play, Wilson uses *his* black art to show how black rage can positively impact the African American community. Thus, Wilson's black art functions as a healing tool and guide for the African American community.

In *Joe Turner's Come and Gone*, Wilson uses his protagonist, Loomis, to clarify the connection between oppression, self-image, and black rage. According to African American theater scholar Paul Carter Harrison, by creating the Loomis character, Wilson is "placing a face on the Invisible Man while refiguring the turbulent angst of Bigger Thomas into gestures of liberation" (299). Like the Invisible Man, Loomis faces issues of identification because of his recent imprisonment via forced labor. And rage clearly connects Loomis with Bigger Thomas, whose rage has led to his downfall.

For Africans in America, one major legacy of slavery and emancipation was the loss of identity. During slavery, slaves did not possess any individuality; they were simply the master's property. After emancipation, the slaves were free, but they did not know who or what they were. What did it mean to be free? Wilson answers this question using Loomis's story. How is Loomis's identity impacted once his confinement is over? Wilson is able to use Loomis and the largest metaphor in the play—the search/journey for self—to personify the ethereal Invisible Man. Wilson also uses Loomis to show that rage does not have to lead to tragic events, as with Bigger Thomas but, instead, can be triumphant.

How is black rage used to determine and elucidate identity? Oppression created Loomis's black rage, which literally fuels his trek up North where he discovers his true image as an African in America. Though Wilson demonstrates how the suppression of one's song can result from rage, he also uses Loomis to show how black rage can be used as a motivating force, leading to self-awareness. Thus, Loomis's rage is positive because if it were not triggered by his coerced drudgery, he would have never realized his connection to Africa. Loomis will use his rage to advance toward accepting his slave ascendants and, within his own shining light, discover himself to be a leader for his people.

In discussing why he wrote *Joe Turner's Come and Gone*, Wilson states:

"Joe Turner" was born from a painting [...] in a magazine. [...] It was a boardinghouse scene, and I began to wonder who one of the figures was, a man [...] in this posture that I call *abject defeat*. He eventually became the character [and protagonist] Herald Loomis. [...] the song called "Joe Turner's Come and Gone" [...] and the painting [...] fueled what I wanted to say about the separation and dispersal of blacks. (Brown F11; emphasis added)

Wilson's use of the terms "abject defeat" and "separation and dispersal of blacks" both connect to the suppression of self present in the play, in that it takes a broken and displaced man to repress who he is. Though slavery, both literally and metaphorically, is a major catalyst for the action in this play, according to theater critic Clive Barnes, "Wilson's play is not about slavery. It is about the results of slavery; it is about separation. Separation from roots, separation from kith and kin, *separation within one's own psychic self*" (320; emphasis added). I agree with Barnes as the play is not about Loomis's unjust imprisonment; it is about what happens *after* Loomis is released. Wilson shows his audience that African Americans are intricately connected to Africa. Thus, in some ways the play is also about reunion (Hornby 518) and in other ways about disconnection (Barnes 320). Characters are separated from their Africanness and then reunited with it, resulting in a hero (Loomis) who will "show the way" for blacks (Marra 138). This champion should also show the way to Wilson's audience, heralding Wilson's message that African Americans need to know who they are and accept their African historical identity and connections, whether they are painful or not (Herrington 85). Specifically for his contemporary African American audience, Wilson demonstrates through his characters that an African American cannot truly realize who s/he is until s/he accepts her/his African roots (Savran 296). This is especially accurate if the African American in question is experiencing black rage (Plum 565). Thus, Wilson's art is also informed by a "healing black rage," and is functional, as he seeks to educate and to improve the standing of the African American community.

Wilson sets *Joe Turner's Come and Gone* in a boardinghouse in August 1911 in Pittsburgh, Pennsylvania to facilitate the presentation of various types of black people; the one thing all of the boarders have in common is that they are searching for something, oftentimes their own identities, in an oppressive American society (Rich 318; Watt 319). Thus these transient characters are archetypal characters representing all blacks in America who do not, have not, cannot enter Wilson's boardinghouse (Pereira 63). Wilson contends that his black characters are isolated, "cut off from memory, having forgotten the names of the [African] gods and only guessing at their faces" (*Joe Turner's Come and Gone* xvii). In addition to finding their memory, as with most of the characters in Wilson's plays, these characters are trying to find their worth in American society.

When Loomis first enters the Holly boardinghouse, he is not ready to face his past; he needs a guide, and that person is Bynum. Sixty-something Bynum is a boarder who is known to the other characters to be a root worker/conjure man. Root workers and conjure men, also known as medicine men, have the ability to tap into the force of spirits (Mbiti 16). This is an ability that will allow Bynum to help various characters throughout the course of the play. Though Bynum helps other characters, his biggest project is Loomis. Upon meeting Loomis, Bynum realizes that he is going to have to shepherd Loomis to his identity. Bynum first takes an interest in Loomis because he looks like Bynum's Johnstown shiny man. Bynum and Loomis have a symbiotic relationship; Loomis is saved from his own insanity and confusion by Bynum (Mills 32). Loomis's salvation commences with the Juba, continues through a song and storytelling, and ends with a revolutionary discovery of self.

LOOMIS'S JOURNEY BEGINS WITH THE JUBA

Bynum attempts to bind Loomis to his progenitors in two ways, both of which trigger Loomis's rage: first, he uses the Juba. The Juba is defined as a species of dance that often includes the reenactment of a mental breakdown (Bogumil 466). It is also a ritual dance that involves drumming and singing; the goal of the dance is to invite the presence of ancestral spirits (Nobles 116). The Juba is heavily influenced by African circular dance ceremonies, called the ring shout—the dancing and singing are directed to the gods and those who came before. The tempo and revolution of the circle quickens during the course of movement. Once Loomis sees the boarders engaging in the Juba, he begins to insult them and the spirits they are calling. In addition, Loomis begins to unzip his pants, speak in tongues, and dance around the room. Loomis reacts the way he does because he does not have a connection to any type of spirit, neither African nor Christian. Bynum presumed that Loomis would be deeply affected by the Juba, and he was correct. The Juba is a major example of how Bynum challenges Loomis's notion of his own identity.

Toward the end of Act One, before Loomis reenters the boardinghouse, the following dialogue leads into the Juba:

> SETH: Come on, we gonna Juba.
> BYNUM: You know me, I'm always ready to Juba [...]
> SETH: You said it! Come on, Bertha, leave them dishes be for a while. We gonna Juba.
> BYNUM: Alright. Let's Juba down! [...]
> ([Bynum] calls the dance as others clap hands, shuffle and stomp around the table)
> (Wilson, *Joe Turner's Come and Gone* 51–52)

Although Bynum does not begin the initiation of the dance, the Juba actually begins when Bynum gives the "word." He calls the dance because he is the character most connected to Africa and Yoruban culture, both of which are heavily linked to the Juba.

Mary L. Bogumil, in "'Tomorrow Never Comes': Songs of Cultural Identity in August Wilson's *Joe Turner's Come and Gone*," explains what the Juba means to the characters in the play: "The juba signifies the recurrence (in memories, in deeds, and in visions) of remote ancestral ties—a [...] cultural legacy from the characters' African [...ancestors]" (465). The ring in which Africans danced and sang, the ancestral tie, and "cultural legacy" are all keys to understanding the means by which the boardinghouse residents achieve oneness in America (Anderson 452; Pereira 75). These Africans in America achieve unity with the help of the Juba/ring because the Juba connects them to Africa while they are in America (Harrison 312).

The characters are bisected as they try to navigate religion and their own respective histories. The characters are trying to connect with their African roots, as well as an American Christian God, as evidenced by the characters calling on the Holy Ghost (Hayes 202). Referring to these dual connections, Kim Pereira determines:

> Their road to self-fulfillment begins by reconnecting themselves with their past through music and rituals. This reunion provides them with a proper perspective of their tumultuous history, as they discover their true origins not in the plantations of slavery but in the *rich and varied cultures* of Africa [...] They discover their real identities to be African, not Christian, though this "African-ness" is transfigured with multiple images drawn from a Christianity in which they may find truth and *affirmation* of their deepest beliefs. (83; emphasis added)

The characters are searching in and for their collective identities; what they find is rooted in the past—in music and dance from Africa—as well as the present—American Christianity. The characters achieve a oneness, a unity that is twofold: one, the characters are engaging with each other at the same time in the midst of this ritualistic event (Hayes 201; Rich 318). Two, within the Juba, the characters are able to straddle their own dualities—the fact that they are Africans in America. In other words, the Juba allows the characters to engage in both of their worlds—the "Americanness" symbolized through the Holy Ghost and the "Africanness" represented by the singing, dancing, and circularity of the Juba (Hatch 27). In the midst of this bonding, partially with Mother Africa, Loomis's rage is triggered, which Bynum suspected would happen.

The Juba triggers Loomis's rage as the dance represents the two conflicting spiritual aspects of his life—his former Christianity (when he was a Deacon) and his more recent African Traditional Religion. Harrison describes the Juba dance and its relation to Loomis:

> Herald Loomis [...] is drawn [...] by a frenzied, improvised [...] ritual call of the Holy Ghost, which was generated in the remnants of a ring shout retrieved from African memory and now configured as the Juba dance. Loomis [...] who seeks salvation without submission to powers larger than his own, challenges the authority of the Holy Ghost. (311–312)

In light of Loomis's resistance to submit to a higher power, it is not surprising that Loomis cannot be a part of the Juba (Bogumil 467). Loomis is out of rhythm and harmony with other human beings; it makes sense that he would not be able to partake in an activity that brings the characters together. Though Loomis's rage will eventually engender healing, he is not ready to heal, as he himself is not whole yet. Because of this, by the end of Act One, Loomis is not prepared to be a part of a community. Bogumil explains Loomis's resistance to group activities:

> Perhaps what disturbs Herald Loomis about the characters' participation in the dance is that sense of community, of solidarity, of an atavistic legacy of Africa, but sadly also of the bondage still in the consciousness of the post–Civil War generation—all of which are in sharp contrast to his desire for autonomy. Why do they laud it over him? Why do they wish to be reminded of their cultural past? [...] Is not the juba a connection to that unwanted past or tradition? (467)

At this point, Loomis does not know his own identity; he cannot be part of a group celebrating duality, even though he himself is a man split in two (Herrington 90). Bogumil continues:

> Herald Loomis, a member of the post–Civil War generation, attempts to *sever* that *native African connection* to the earth and to *break free* from that past American connection to Joe Turner enslavement in order to become Americanized in post-Emancipation Proclamation America. Surrounded by what he perceives as a conspiratorial group [the other boarders], Loomis even degrades his own ancestry with his vociferous attack against the religiomagical elements of his African American ethnicity, including physical and sexual stereotypes, to further his insult upon others present. (469; emphasis added)

Though the characters are calling on a Christian Holy Ghost, they are encasing their Christian call in an African context; thus African spirits come into the Holly boardinghouse as well, and, like Bynum, help Loomis on his pilgrimage. In an interview with Kim Powers, Wilson explains Loomis's vision and how it connects to his identity:

> [Loomis] is witness to bones rising up out of the ocean, taking on flesh and walking up on the land. This is his connection with the ancestors, the Africans who were lost during the Middle Passage and were thrown overboard. He is privileged to witness this because he *needs most to know who he is*. It [the vision] is telling him, "This is who you are. You are these bones. You are the sons and daughters of these people. They are walking around here now and they look like you because you are these very same people. This is who you are." (54; emphasis added)

These people are now spirits; these African spirits enter the Holly boardinghouse because they were called by the characters engaged in the Juba; the spirits stay because Loomis not only disparages Christianity when he interrupts the Juba, but he also denigrates Africa. It is at this moment that the spirits recognize they have to intervene. Once this happens, the Juba has connected the past to the present, which is its original function. According to Sandra G. Shannon, the African spirits use Loomis at this particular moment to be their "spokesperson" because:

> As the symbolic equivalent of black America at the turn of the century, Herald Loomis also reveals the changing place of Christianity in the lives of former slaves and the progeny of slaves. The tension between certain residual African religious ideas and Christian doctrines to which his slave ancestors were exposed by their masters detonates in him an explosion of opposites. (130)

Thus the setting becomes ripe for a spiritual intervention since the Juba riled up the African *and* Christian spirits (Pereira 73). It is at this time that Loomis really begins his self-discovery. So the Juba triggers Loomis's rage, which leads him to a connection with his forbearers; but he is not ready to face them at the end of Act One, as Loomis has just begun to move toward healing, fueled by black rage. The next signpost on Loomis's path is a song about Joe Turner.

SONG + BLACK RAGE + STORYTELLING = HISTORICAL IDENTITY

The second way Bynum binds Loomis to his past and future is by singing about Joe Turner. Loomis again responds with rage. In order for Loomis to know where he is going, he has to acknowledge where he came from. Bynum gets Loomis to do this when he sings about Joe Turner. In Act Two, Bynum continues to push Loomis's buttons, only this time Wilson does not use a dance to inspire rage; he uses a song. The mention of Turner's name leads to Loomis's triggered rage and causes Bynum to state openly that Loomis does not know who he is. Basically, Bynum tells Loomis all he has to do to solve his identity dilemma is sing his song. Of course, Loomis does not trust in this, as he still believes that all he needs is Martha.

As a result of Loomis's reaction to the song, Bynum tells a story that subtly tells Loomis that he has to mine what came before if he wants peace. In response to Bynum's story, Loomis delivers a monologue that tells the audience (and reiterates to himself) where he has come from and to whom he is connected. Loomis does not recognize at this point that he is housing an internal battle over his identity, with Martha on one side and Africa and Bynum on the other. Thus, Wilson uses storytelling and monologue to get Loomis closer to his identity. Bynum's story instructs Loomis as to how he can accept who he is, while Loomis's monologue will give the character an opportunity to express his pain. Once Loomis realizes he has to stand on his own two feet, he becomes shiny and moves out into the world to help other lost souls who do not know their songs, their history, or their stories.

Using black rage, monologue, and storytelling, *Joe Turner's Come and Gone* revives the connection between Africans and African Americans that was lost during slavery; the connection between African Americans and

Africans, in this case, is synonymous with one's identity/song. Alan Nadel argues that, for Wilson and African Americans in general, recovering the song becomes a truer form of archives than written European chronicled text, and the song allows Loomis a historical identity as a human being (102). Toward the end of Act Two, scene two, Bynum is storytelling; he informs Seth and Loomis how he learned how to accept his song. In addition to telling his story, Bynum is demonstrating how the act of storytelling can serve as a healing agent. Bynum states that when a man forgets his song and goes off in search of it, the song is usually *with* the man all the time (Wilson, *Joe Turner's Come and Gone* 71). Bynum's point refers to Loomis having his song—the song of self-sufficiency—with him all along, even when he suppressed it so that Joe Turner would not be able to take it from him (73). Thus, Bynum argues that the cure usually begins with the self. Bynum purports that Loomis (read: the African American community) can heal himself if he will just acknowledge and accept his song. Nadel elaborates on how Wilson's use of song connects to Loomis's journey:

> It [Loomis's song] is the authority upon which rests Loomis's claim to human rights. To steal that song is thus to deprive Loomis of the claim and thereby to legitimize the treatment of him as property. At the same time, Loomis's attempt to protect his song, in the way he was unable to protect his body, has forced him to suppress that song [...] In denying Joe Turner access to the source of his claim to human rights, he has also had to deprive himself of that access. In consequence, now that Joe Turner has come and gone, Herald Loomis doesn't know whether he is coming or going. The figurative source of his claim to human rights, his song, has turned into a literal search for logistics, the walkin' blues. Hence he searches for his lost wife not to recapture her—which would replicate Joe Turner's enslavement—but rather to recapture the history he lost when he suppressed his song. (101–102)

Though Loomis spends most of the play trying to find his place in the world ("searching for logistics") and raging, it is his rage that finally leads him to realize who Herald Loomis is, a man with a story to tell.

Use of Storytelling and Monologue

Thus we can see that Wilson uses storytelling and monologue (Bynum's storytelling, Loomis's monologue, and both characters' oral tradition) to recuperate African/African American song/identity. Though Loomis will eventually find his song, he must first tell his story (Nadel 102). Loomis does not reveal his history through written text, but rather through monologue, a type of oral text. Likewise, Bynum conveys his past using storytelling. Monologue and storytelling are both oral traditions and significant in Wilson's works. In addition to being significant to Wilson, a reverential regard for the spiritual world and an exceptionally high regard for storytelling are also African traits (Shannon 127). Thus, storytelling and monologue are African *and* Wilson trademarks. Hap Erstein identifies these trademarks and declares: "A consummate storyteller, he [Wilson] often gives his characters that gift too and has them wander off with tangential monologues that could be likened to blues solos" (E10). Wilson uses storytelling to illustrate Bynum's historical identity and to show how Bynum reached back to the Africa to move forward in America. Bynum intends to help Loomis do the same thing. For example, Bynum tells Loomis:

> Now, I used to travel all up and down this road and that . . . looking here and there. Searching. Just like you, Mr. Loomis. I didn't know what I was searching for. The only thing I knew was something was keeping me dissatisfied. Something wasn't making my heart smooth and easy. Then one day my daddy gave me a song. That song had a weight to it that was hard to handle. That song was hard to carry. I fought against it. Didn't want to accept that song. I tried to find my daddy to give him back *his* song. But I found out it wasn't his song. It was *my* song. It had come from way deep inside me. *I looked long back in memory and gathered up pieces and snatches of things to make that song.* [. . .] And that song helped me on the road. (Wilson, *Joe Turner's Come and Gone* 71; emphasis added)

By telling stories, Bynum is able to illustrate who he used to be and to show that it was an oppressive existence until he connected with Africa ("looked long back in memory") and accepted his identity. Once he was able to do this, Bynum began to carry the enslavement of his ancestors within himself, and this strengthened him because he now knew who he was (Herrington 92).

Responding to Bynum's story, Loomis also uses storytelling to expose his historical identity. In order for Wilson's message—black rage can act as a healing tool, leading one to uncover his/her concealed identity—to resonate, it is necessary to understand who Loomis was, including the America in which he lived. It is essential to comprehend what happened to Loomis before the play begins. Not surprisingly, Loomis's history is connected to his black rage and to his ascendants. Just as Loomis's progenitors were enslaved, he was also held captive. Because Loomis cannot go back to Africa at this point in the play, his history, rooted in America, rooted in negativity, is packaged within a monologue that is full of rage, the subject of which is Joe Turner. Through convict leasing, Joe Turner is able to capture Loomis and make him a slave, despite the fact that some thirty-six years earlier, the 13th Amendment had abolished slavery. It is this convict leasing that originally triggered Loomis's rage and caused him to suppress his song from Joe Turner and from himself. Though Wilson uses Joe Turner as a metaphorical representation, the real man Joe Turner is based on—Joe Turney—and his connection to government facilitates Wilson's depiction of convict leasing. Since Joe Turney was the brother of Peter Turney, the governor of Tennessee, it would be easy for him to tie up Loomis in a statewide system (Kroll 82; Daniel 24).

Historically, the American black male at the turn of the century, as Wilson demonstrates, led a life that made it difficult to maintain an identity because of state, country, and judicial constructs like convict leasing. The convict-lease system was devised as a post-Reconstruction socioeconomic advantage for white southern landowners to further exploit black labor (Bogumil 469). Before Loomis was captured, he was a deacon at the Abundant Life church; after, he was a slave/prisoner. As was the case with actual convict leasing, when Loomis was seized, he was forced to work Joe Turner's land (Daniel 24–25). In "Saying Goodbye to the Past: Self-Empowerment and History in *Joe Turner's Come and Gone*," Douglas Anderson connects Loomis to convict leasing and his ancestors:

> Before Loomis can claim the legacy of empowerment left him by his ancestors, he must confront and understand his own experience of oppression: seven years of false imprisonment and forced labor on the chain gang of Joe Turner [...] Though this experience is part of Loomis's personal past, it is not one that he has suffered alone, but with the men imprisoned with him, those who lived in fear of imprisonment and the families deprived of their men. Loomis's experience, then, is once again part of a collective past, a past preserved for collective memory in a song [of self-sufficiency]. (455)

The men Anderson refers to all suffered under convict leasing. When Loomis's black rage causes him to slash himself, go out into the world, and show blacks the way, the blacks he will lead are his fellow "convicts." Thus, Wilson uses his art, specifically through Loomis and his black rage, to show those who feel like convicts in American society that there is a way to heal their pain and to gain a deeper understanding of self. Though Loomis's triumphant exit from the Holly boardinghouse implies he is going to pursue retribution, he is also seeking vindication for his fellow convict-leasing survivors—his brothers. Anderson argues that Loomis's experience was part of a collective past, and his healing should be as well. Though Loomis was not an actual slave, his imprisonment serves as a metaphor for slavery: while Loomis was under Joe Turner's control, he had no authority over his life, no freedoms (Burton 9, 10; Anderson 433). A black man could become a white man's property at any moment under convict leasing. It is this lack of autonomy that feeds Loomis's rage.

After Bynum sings the song "Joe Turner's Come and Gone," and engages in storytelling, Loomis tells *his* story of how he was captured and how his rage was triggered:

> Joe Turner catched me when my little girl was just born. Wasn't nothing but a baby sucking on her mama's titty when he catched me. Joe Turner catched me in nineteen hundred and one. Kept me seven years until nineteen hundred and eight. [...] I was walking down this road in this little town outside Memphis. Come up on these fellows gambling. I was a deacon in the Abundant Life Church. I stopped to preach to these fellows to see if maybe I could turn some of them from their sinning when Joe Turner, brother of the Governor of the great sovereign state of Tennessee, swooped down on us and grabbed everybody there. Kept us all seven years. [...] Got out from under Joe Turner on his birthday. [...] Martha's gone. [...] We [Zonia and Loomis] been looking

for her ever since. [...] That's the only thing I know to do. I just wanna see
her face so *I can get me a starting place in the world.* [...] I been wandering a
long time in somebody else's world. (Wilson, *Joe Turner's Come and Gone* 72;
emphasis added)

Loomis's black rage is, unbeknownst to him, leading him to his future; at
this point in the play, he believes it is Martha. Loomis's storytelling elucidates the connection between black rage and historical identity in that
Loomis's story gives further insight into his past, why he is raging throughout the play, and his currently repressed and thus unknown self.

THE REVOLUTIONARY DISCOVERY

Loomis's last visible instance of triggered rage leads to a revolutionary discovery about his identity—via an ancestral blood sacrifice—he does not *need*
Martha; nor does he have to hide from Turner. He can stand on his own.
Loomis's rage, fired up because of American oppression, is the gas that drove
him to the Holly boardinghouse and fueled his determination, as he looked
for Martha; this rage will also support Loomis when he realizes that Martha
is not his starting place. Loomis's encounter with Bynum helps him understand his rage, his connection to his ancestors, and his calling. After Loomis
finally sees Martha and realizes that she is not his salvation, his rage explodes.
It is logical that if Loomis's rage were used to propel him toward Martha,
when he recognized that this had been a mistake, his rage would seemingly
spin out of control. When Martha and Loomis reunite in the Holly boardinghouse, this leads to a reversal for Loomis (Burton 21). Loomis realizes
that he can no longer say Martha is his starting place when she is standing
right in front of him, and he is still lost. Loomis has reached the end of his
trek and believes he has nothing to show for it. As a result, Loomis has to do
something; he needs to engage in some action to combat this ineffectiveness.

When Martha mentions the blood of the lamb, referring to Jesus, Loomis
instinctively knows what he must do—he has to show himself and the others
that depending on a white savior instead of one's own history or oneself is
problematic. The fact that Loomis's most heightened instance of rage
involves a ritual sacrifice speaks to the Africanness that was always within
him, but simply suppressed. Within that moment, when his grief and pain,
over not knowing who he is, overtakes him, Loomis's rage and the physical
action of slashing himself forces him to realize who he really is. Loomis realizes he can bleed for himself, and he does not need anyone to do it for him.
Loomis recognizes that the Christianity he had been following before his
imprisonment failed him; thus he falls back on the African Traditional
Religions that led him to this point and gives him the strength to stand up.

When Loomis slashes himself, he becomes whole. The act might seem to
be violent, but it is not; it is more of a sacrificial action, resulting from his
black rage (Burton 16). The "shedding of his own blood is a baptism and a
resurrection that sweeps over him with a transcendental force and finally sets

his spirit free. [...] the African wins" (Hayes 203–204). This act releases his rage, at least a part of it (Burton 16). At this point in the play, this part of Loomis's spiritual expedition is over. He is healed.

In addition to cutting himself, Loomis also cleanses himself. As Harrison argues, "If renewal of spirit is to be made possible, the body must become transfigured. The ritual sacrifice of Loomis's body becomes the seeding of the new soul, the body gilded with the precious life force—blood—until it shines like the armor of pure song/spirit" (314). At the end of the play, when Loomis cuts himself, he is truly free; he drops the shackles that Joe Turner placed on him and embraces his African identification (Herrington 85). Thus, Loomis's bloodletting is not violent, but rather a crucial sacrifice of the lost Loomis, in favor of a shiny man. When Loomis exclaims that he is standing, this is the same thing as Loomis saying he has found his strong, African identity.

In an interview with Nathan L. Grant, Wilson defines identity as understanding one's political and social history (108). Wilson utilized this definition as he wrote Loomis's story and resultant actions. At the end of the play, Loomis understands and accepts that his identity is intricately tied to his political and social history, which is connected to Africa, his ancestors, and Joe Turner (Herrington 92). Loomis is a product of American oppression, but the release of Loomis's black rage is a *healing* response to exploitation (hooks 12). This response to racism should not be silenced (as Seth tries to do in the play), because it can lead to revolutionary action that can change a society. Once Loomis understands his victimization (political history) and rejects the claim of worthlessness that American society (specifically Joe Turner) placed on him (social history), he has to say "Good-bye" to what he lost at the hands of Joe Turner. Loomis also has to reclaim and embrace what Joe Turner was not able to take away from him—his song (Anderson 456).

Loomis is unable to stand up at the end of Act One because, as Joan Herrington writes, he "is unable to accept what the vision is revealing to him—that slavery is his history, too, that these are his people, and that he must acknowledge his past if he is to establish his place in the world and move efficiently into the future" (88). Loomis is going to show black folks their history and how to embrace it, even the bad parts. When Loomis leaves the Holly boardinghouse, he is going to go out into the world to show black folks the light (Burton 17). Thus, triumphant black rage motivated and provoked Loomis to find his song.

Loomis's transformation strengthens all of the black characters, thus making Loomis's black rage a victorious emotion, not only for him, but also for the other black characters in the play (Burton 17). When Loomis realizes and accepts his identity as a shiny man, this action motivates the other characters to embrace their Africanness to a larger degree and to figure out where Africa fits in their lives (Hayes 204). Thus, Loomis's realization becomes not an individual event, but rather a communal event. One example of how this is actualized in the play is Mattie running after Loomis after he leaves the Holly boardinghouse and goes out into the world (Wilson's, *Joe Turner's Come and Gone* 75–76). Though Mattie was presumably searching for her husband throughout the course of the play, what she was really searching for, according to Bertha and Bynum, is a man who has discovered himself (Pereira 76). This is why she runs after Loomis at the end of the play. He is this man. Once Mattie sees Loomis's self-empowerment, she now knows they can make room in their lives for each other (80). Mattie finds her identity as Loomis finds his; she is strengthened because of his renewed strength. Though Bynum led Loomis to shiny man status, even Bynum is able to solidify his identity because of Loomis. Anderson explains that "for Bynum to see the shiny man 'again' means [...] acting as the shiny-man guide to another. Seeing the shiny man again does not entail Bynum's deliverance from the world but confirmation of his contribution to it" (449). When Loomis becomes a shiny man, Bynum now knows his song is accepted, and his work with Loomis is complete.

Black rage and finding one's song are used as healing tools—the kind of response to oppression and exploitation that bell hooks writes about in *Killing Rage: Ending Racism* (Shannon 121). Pereira argues,

> people are doomed to wander through life aimlessly, unaware of who they are or what their purpose may be. This song is the music of each person's essential nature, his or her *true identity*. And that identity, with its special rhythms, dictates the course of each one's destiny. Each song is unique, with its unique power that derives from the unique mix of each person's characteristics. (63; emphasis added)

Wilson's message to his audience is to champion the positive aftereffects of black rage. In effect, he urges us—in spite of racial grief—not to repress our song or identity, because only by embracing our past can we move on to a triumphant future.

WORKS CITED

Anderson, Douglas. "Saying Goodbye to the Past: Self-Empowerment and History in *Joe Turner's Come and Gone*." *CLA Journal* 40.4 (1997): 432–457.

Barnes, Clive. "O'Neill in Blackface." Rev. of *Joe Turner's Come and Gone*, by August Wilson. *New York Theatre Critics' Reviews* March 28, 1988: 320–321.

Bogumil, Mary L. " 'Tomorrow never Comes': Songs of Cultural Identity in August Wilson's *Joe Turner's Come and Gone*." *Theatre Journal* 46.4 (1994): 463–476.

Brown, Joe. "Staging the Black Experience." *The Washington Post* October 4, 1987: F1 ff.

Burton, Nefertiti C. " 'Joe Turner's Come and Gone': an African Odyssey." Thesis. University of Massachusetts at Amherst, 1993.

Daniel, Pete. *The Shadow of Slavery: Peonage in the South, 1901–1969*. Urbana, IL: University of Illinois Press, 1972.

Erstein, Hap. " 'Joe Turner' is a Piece in the Puzzle of Identity." Rev. of *Joe Turner's Come and Gone*, by August Wilson. *Washington Times* October 9, 1987: E1 ff.

Grant, Nathan L. "Men, Women, and Culture: A Conversation with August Wilson." *American Drama* 5.2 (1996): 100–122.

Gussow, Mel. "Energizing The Future Of Black Theater." *New York Times* March 9, 1998: E1, E3.

———. "Plea Heeded for Meeting on Black Theater." *New York Times* February 2, 1998: B1, B3.

Harrison, Paul Carter. "August Wilson's Blues Poetics." *Three Plays.* By August Wilson. Pittsburgh: University of Pittsburgh Press, 1991. 291–318.

Hatch, James. "Some African Influences on the Afro-American Theatre." *The Theatre of Black Americans.* Ed. Errol Hill. New York: Applause Theatre, 1980. 13–29.

Hayes, Corlis Angela. "A Critical and Historical Analysis of Five Major Plays by August Wilson." Thesis. Southern Illinois University at Carbondale, 1993.

Herrington, Joan. *I Ain't Sorry for Nothin' I Done: August Wilson's Process of Playwriting.* New York: Limelight, 1998.

hooks, bell. *Killing Rage: Ending Racism.* New York: Henry Holt, 1995.

Hornby, Richard. "New Life on Broadway." Rev. of *Joe Turner's Come and Gone,* by August Wilson. *The Hudson Review* 41 (1988): 512–518.

Jefferson, Margo. "Oratory vs. Really Talking About Culture." *New York Times* February 4, 1997: C11, C14.

Kroll, Jack. "August Wilson's Come to Stay: A Major Writer Illuminates the Black Experience." Rev. of *Joe Turner's Come and Gone,* by August Wilson. *Newsweek* 111.15 (1988): 82.

Marra, Kim. "Ma Rainey and the Boyz: Gender Ideology in August Wilson's Broadway Canon." *August Wilson: A Casebook.* Ed. Marilyn Elkins. New York: Garland, 1994. 123–160.

Mbiti, John S. *African Religions and Philosophy.* Oxford: Heinemann, 1990.

Mills, Alice. "The Walking Blues: An Anthropological Approach to the Theater of August Wilson." *The Black Scholar* 25.2 (1995): 30–35.

Nadel, Alan. "Boundaries, Logistics, and Identity: The Property of Metaphor in *Fences* and *Joe Turner's Come and Gone.*" *May All Your Fences Have Gates: Essays On The Drama of August Wilson.* Ed. Alan Nadel. Iowa City: University of Iowa Press, 1994. 86–104.

Nobles, Vera Lynn. *Emi: The Concept of Spirit in Selected Plays of August Wilson.* Thesis. Temple University, 1995. Ann Arbor: UMI, 1998.

Pereira, Kim. *August Wilson and the African-American Odyssey.* Urbana: University of Illinois Press, 1995.

Plum, Jay. "Blues, History, and the Dramaturgy of August Wilson." *African American Review* 27.4 (1993): 561–567.

Powers, Kim. "An Interview with August Wilson." *Theater* 16.1 (1984): 50–55.

Rich, Frank. "Panoramic History of Blacks in America in Wilson's 'Joe Turner.'" Rev. of *Joe Turner's Come and Gone,* by August Wilson. *New York Theatre Critics' Reviews* March 28, 1988: 318–319.

Savran, David. *In Their Own Words: Contemporary American Playwrights.* New York: Theater Communication Group, 1988. 288–305.

Shannon, Sandra G. *The Dramatic Vision of August Wilson.* Washington: Howard University Press, 1995.

Watt, Douglas. "Second Thoughts on First Nights." Rev. of *Joe Turner's Come and Gone,* by August Wilson. *New York Theatre Critics' Reviews* April 8, 1988: 319.

Wilson, August. "How to Write A Play Like August Wilson." *New York Times* March 10, 1991, Sec. 2: H5 ff.

———. *Joe Turner's Come and Gone.* New York: Plume Book, 1988.

———. "The Ground on Which I Stand." *American Theatre* 13.7 (1996): 14–16, 71–74.

IV

Current Unpublished Interviews
that Speak to Aesthetic
Issues Raised in "The Ground on
which I Stand"

12

THE GROUND ON WHICH HE STANDS: CHARLES S. DUTTON ON AUGUST WILSON

Yolanda Williams Page

Actor, director, and producer Charles S. Dutton has had the opportunity to work extensively with August Wilson, from their humble beginnings at the Eugene O'Neill Playwright Conference to Wilson's Tony and Pulitzer Prize winning Broadway performances. Dutton played the lead male character in three of Wilson's most successful plays, *Ma Rainey's Black Bottom, Joe Turner's Come and Gone*, and *The Piano Lesson*, and with the exception of *Joe Turner's Come and Gone* in which he only performed in the Yale Repertory production, he was the driving force in both the Yale Repertory and Broadway performances.

I had the opportunity to interview Dutton in October 2002. What follows is a transcript of that interview in which Dutton discusses his experience working with Wilson and offers insight into the motivations of the characters he has had the opportunity to portray: Levee, Herald Loomis, and Boy Willie. In addition, Dutton candidly speaks about Wilson's dramatic vision and Wilson's idea for an institutionalized African American theater.

WILLIAMS PAGE: What was it like working with Wilson?

DUTTON: August and I first worked together in 1982 when his play *Ma Rainey's Black Bottom* was accepted for work-shopping at the Eugene O'Neill National Playwright Conference. I was still a student at the Yale School of Drama. I was in my second year.

When I first read the play and someone pointed the playwright out to me, I said, "That is not the person who wrote this play. It can not be." I said that because August was so unassuming and laidback. The play seemed like it should have been written by a guy who was loud and more assertive.

At that point it was just a staged reading, so we pretty much just said hello to one another and that was it. But in 1984 there was the production of *Ma Rainey's Black Bottom* at the Yale Rep; that's when I got to know him better. At that moment I guess you can say that we were both in awe, not of one another, but of the moment, that destiny and fate had brought he, Lloyd Richards, and I together. Thinking that twenty-five years earlier in 1959 Lloyd had done the same thing with another young, promising playwright and actor, Lorraine Hansberry and Sidney Poitier. Then twenty-five years later here he was doing the same thing with another young, exciting playwright.

WILLIAMS PAGE: And actor, right?

DUTTON: Yes, and actor. So it was kind of beautiful to revel in Lloyd's destiny. That kind of thing does not happen often in the theater, so it was a magical time.

For us to come together that way and launch each other's career was wonderful. I can only describe it as one of the greatest times I have had in the theater, and I am sure he would say the same thing.

WILLIAMS PAGE: Had you been in any other plays before you did *Ma Rainey's Black Bottom*?

DUTTON: No, *Ma Rainey's Black Bottom* was my first professional job. Actually, I became a member of the union while I was working with the play.

WILLIAMS PAGE: You have had the opportunity to portray the lead male character in three of Wilson's plays, *Joe Turner's Come and Gone*, *Ma Rainey's Black Bottom*, and *The Piano Lesson*. What was it like to play each of those characters, for they are completely different as far as personalities and life perspective are concerned.

DUTTON: Different personalities they do have, but as far as life perspective is concerned, I'm not sure they are so different.

Let's start with *Ma Rainey's Black Bottom*, and why other actors fail to realize or capture that part. The character Levee is thirty-three years old, but he is very much a man–child, so there has to be some imbalance with him. Now when I say imbalance, I don't mean that he is mentally challenged, but that he is severely, emotionally scarred.

WILLIAMS PAGE: Are you referring to the scene in the text where he talks about his parents?

DUTTON: Yes, the sense of his father being killed and his mother being raped, all of that. He is so emotionally scarred that there has to be some imbalance to him, and the imbalance is pretty much the man–child aspect of him. Levee is a character who can talk about your mother all day long, but the minute you start talking about his mother he wants to fight, and that is because of his past, what he has seen. But on a deeper level if Levee is played as the big, strong, know-it-all villain who can take care of himself and knows what he is doing, then the murder of Toledo at the end of the play is indeed an act of murder and not a crime of passion. I have seen it played post-Broadway where either the actor or the director do not know this and you do not see this Levee. He is a hoodlum. But he has to be played with almost a boyish, childlike, lovable quality, where the audience just wants to take him, hug him, and love him despite what he does or says.

WILLIAMS PAGE: I would describe Boy Willie that way as well.

DUTTON: Yes, but in a whole different way. Boy Willie can take care of himself; Levee cannot. Boy Willie would not spend a whole week's paycheck on a pair of shoes. Boy Willie is looking for something very practical, 100 acres, and Levee is chasing a pipedream—that this white studio executive is going to give him a record deal. The three older guys try to tell him this the entire play, "Man, don't trust that white man," but he does not listen.

Boy Willie has an ability to take care of himself, a history of his own. Boy Willie has what Levee does not have—that family structure of support.

WILLIAMS PAGE: Family support with the exception of Berniece, wouldn't you say?

DUTTON: Yes, but it is still family. He has somewhere to go. They may be at odds with one another, but she is still family. For example, she has been telling Boy Willie to leave since he got there, but does he leave? No. Does she insist that he leave? No, because he is her brother; he also has uncles, but Levee does not have any of that. His family is the band; his blood family has been wiped out.

WILLIAMS PAGE: But he ostracizes the members of the band and Ma who could possibly be a surrogate family for him.

DUTTON: I do not think he ostracizes them so much as this. It is that beautiful thing black men have, the dozens. The band plays the dozens throughout the entire play, and if the play is done right, the banter between them is always light, with a lot of love for one another and not viciously. Now I have seen it done viciously where you would think that they hate each other, but they do not. It is just the way band members are. "Ah, man shut-up. You ain't nothing. Nothing but an old trumpet player that come a dime a dozen." But all of that is said with them enjoying one another, and when the play is directed with them seeming like they do not enjoy one another that is when it does not work. Those four guys should have as much of a good time together when they are talking about one another as they do when they are not talking about one another. When the play is done that way, in the sense that the other band members really do love Levee and he really loves them, he is not ostracized.

Now Ma's problem with Levee is not one to write volumes of critique about. Ma is Ma. Ma does not take shit. Play the songs you have been told to play and that is it. The only reason Ma has a beef with Levee is because he is after her girl. If Dussie Mae was not in the equation, they would be okay because Ma is the type of person who would not pay Levee any attention anyway. He is just a member of the band. Notice, the only person she talks to in the band on a serious level is Cutler. The others she will talk to if she has to, but it is Cutler who she talks to about personal things.

WILLIAMS PAGE: Let's talk about Herald Loomis, whom I would say is the darkest character of the three. What was it like playing him?

DUTTON: He is probably the most difficult character I have ever done. That is a difficult role to play. It was so difficult that I did not want to take it to New York.

WILLIAMS PAGE: Really?

DUTTON: First of all it was two years before it even went to New York. It was produced at regional theaters for two years, and I said I would go out of my mind if I had to do that character for two years. Herald Loomis is probably one of the most difficult characters to play in literature, period. He is as difficult to play as any Shakespearian, O'Neill, or Tennessee Williams character. As a matter of fact, I would compare the level of difficulty to playing a Greek character rather than a Shakespearian character.

If the character were on stage all the time it would be less difficult to play him, but because he is on and off the stage so much, he is difficult. With him you cannot go offstage, have a cup of tea, read the newspaper, and be ready to go back on stage twenty minutes later. You have to stay in character even when you are not on stage. With him you have to leave the stage, go backstage, find a corner, and stay in that corner until it is time to go back on stage. Otherwise, when you go back on stage you will not be the same intense character you were twenty minutes ago. You would have to regenerate the character. So, playing Herald Loomis is a very lonely life.

WILLIAMS PAGE: Because he is so intense?

DUTTON: Yes. All the things that motivate him are very intense. Loomis is one of those people in the world who has seen things. Whether they are on the other side of the spirit world or whatever, Loomis has seen things and nobody understands him. Loomis cannot go up to people and say, "You know I saw bones coming up out of the water." People would not listen because they would think he was crazy. The only person he can talk to about that is Bynum because Bynum has seen things. When you walk around not knowing whether the person who walks besides you is a real person or a bones person, that makes you intense.

That is what Loomis's problem is. He does not know who is who now because as soon as those bones came out of the Atlantic Ocean they became human beings. They got flesh and clothes and started walking around everywhere, so Loomis does not know if a person is a bones person or a regular person, and he carries that all the time. Consequently, when he looks at people that is what he is trying to find out, "are you one of those people?"

It takes a certain kind of actor to play that role because you have to have a lot of discipline.

WILLIAMS PAGE: Well, let's go back to Levee. How did you prepare to play this imbalanced role, as you call it?

DUTTON: By making him a man–child. If you are given that direction, that he has to be a man–child, then it is easier to play him. Levee is also a boundless character. He is full of fun and frolic; he is fearless, uninhibited, lovable, mischievous, deceptive, and conniving; he can be vicious, but at the same time apologetic. He is the complete package to play, but at the same time if he is played as a gangster, a guy with a knife, then the murder at the end of the play is not justified.

WILLIAMS PAGE: In what way?

DUTTON: There is a difference between a guy who has a switchblade in his back pocket versus one with a pocketknife in his back pocket. A guy with a switchblade has a weapon and is looking to stab somebody. A guy with a pocketknife has a tool, not a weapon.

Anybody who worked on a farm had a pocketknife. You could use it to open something if you were on the road, a can of beans; if you had to screw something in, you could use it; you could use it to clean your fingernails; or you could use it to cut something like a piece of string, so it was a tool, rarely used as a weapon. You could use it as a weapon, but to pull it out, un-do it and all that is time consuming.

On the other hand, with a switchblade you are looking to cut somebody. That is what it is for. It is not a tool. You try to screw something with it, and it will break. So, when I played the part, I made the decision that Levee would not carry a switchblade but a pocketknife and that makes the difference in how he is perceived, the guy who is looking to hurt somebody versus the guy who has a tool. Although it is not said, all of the band members have a pocketknife. That is a part and parcel of men, especially men back then.

Part of Levee's man-childness informs why he is so gullible about certain things. For example, why he believes that Sturdyvant is going to produce his records when the others tell him Sturdyvant is not.

Levee does things in the play that are classic Greek tragedy. First he comes into the play with all kinds of hubris. He is on top of the world, he cannot be told anything, and nothing can stop him or stand in his way. Then in a moment of revelation he challenges the gods and after that challenge everything is downhill. The beauty of the play is that in the moment of killing Toledo it is about the amount of self-hatred we all have within ourselves. At that point he hates Sturdyvant for reneging on his promise to cut him a record deal, and he hates himself for believing Sturdyvant's promise, but he cannot do anything to Sturdyvant because Sturdyvant is a white man. When Toledo steps on his shoes, all those years of self-hatred start to surface, and he reaches out and hurts the next best thing, his own people.

WILLIAMS PAGE: Kind of like a transference of anger?

DUTTON: Yes, as a culture we have had a history of doing this. We could not do anything to the oppressor so we would lash out and hurt ourselves.

WILLIAMS PAGE: Like the rioting in L.A. after the Rodney King verdict?

DUTTON: Exactly.

WILLIAMS PAGE: Let's talk more about Boy Willie. I have read Wilson said he wrote the character of Boy Willie with you in mind as playing the role. How are you similar and/or dissimilar to Boy Willie?

DUTTON: I do not think he wrote it because of any likeness between the character and me, but he wrote it for the actor. If a playwright writes a play and the actor has the capacity for him to realize that character completely and fully, then he is going to write for that actor's voice or capacities. As a matter of fact, he is going to say, "Well, I can stretch myself as a writer because I know this actor has the physical and vocal stamina to do this work." So, he was not writing based upon any similarities between the character and me. He was writing based upon the type of acting talent I have been blessed with, that I am the type of actor who understands the physicality of the theater and has the emotional depth required.

Had I not done *Ma Rainey's Black Bottom* or *Joe Turner's Come and Gone*, I do not think he would have made that statement. He just would have been writing a play, but because he had seen what I had brought to Levee and Herald Loomis, he knew that I could do the same thing with Boy Willie. And he hasn't done that since then because I haven't been available. Now if I were to say, "Come on August, it is time for me to get back on the stage." He would probably write a character for a play with me in mind. It has been said, not by him but by other people, that he has not written those types of epic characters since that play because I have not been available to do them. This is not ego, but August became very spoiled in his early days. He had James Earl Jones and myself doing his plays, so he became very spoiled.

People may refute this, but there is a wide river of stage actors and trained artists, but there is only a tiny pond of real talent, and what I mean by real talent is, yes, everyone can walk and talk on the stage, but not everyone can realize a playwright's work; everyone cannot make the audience leave the theater wanting to change their lives after witnessing and experiencing a true theatrical event. Everybody cannot capture an audience that way. There are only a handful of actors on the entire planet who can really play King Lear. Just because you are an English actor does not mean you can do Shakespeare, and just because you are a black actor does not mean you can do August Wilson. If that were true, every performance of an August Wilson play would be monumental. I do not think the rest of the United States other than New York has really seen August Wilson done the way it should be done.

I think he wrote the play for what he saw in me as an actor because I do not know what Boy Willie and I have in common. I certainly do not dress like him, but I am sure there are some things. For example, I guess you could say that we are both lovers of life, but I am not the kind of actor who looks for similarities between the character and myself. To me you have only done the role, the play, and the playwright justice when you as a performer leave an ounce of your internal essence on that stage floor every night. If you have not done that, you have not done the play.

WILLIMAS PAGE: With that in mind, for the sake of this interview would you repeat what you said during a previous discussion about the difference between the entertainer, the actor, and the artist?

DUTTON: Certainly. An entertainer will do anything regardless of the image he or she is portraying or depicting; it does not matter. An actor will do most things; he or she will not do everything the entertainer will, but he or she will do just about anything. The artist will only choose to do those things he or she feels will advance civilization. He or she expects to change the lives and minds of the audience.

WILLIAMS PAGE: Wilson has described his dramatic vision as teaching African Americans we should not avoid our past, but face it and learn from it because our past holds lessons that can help us succeed in the present and future. What is your opinion on looking to the past and learning from it?

DUTTON: I agree with that totally. If I had to put into a sentence or a paragraph, I would just simply say that in the larger scheme of things, we are only on this planet a couple of seconds, life goes by extremely fast, and as an artist you have to leave an epithet. Mine would simply be that you have to respect the African tradition of lineage. There were many who were entertainers decades ago who had to be buffoons. They had to play clowns and demeaning characters because that was the only venue available to them, but they would be turning over in their graves to see that people are still doing those kinds of things today. The sad part about it is that you make the same kind of money doing intelligent work as you do doing unintelligent work, so you might as well make it intelligent.

Who would have thought we would see the day when black music would demean women, promote killing one another, and glorify individualism and disunity? The artists of yesterday did not struggle for that. To me that is sacrilegious, an un-African thing to do. It is a total disrespect of your cultural lineage. I know many of those artists say they are only speaking from experience, but that is bullshit. I used to rob banks, so every time I write or direct something is it going to be about robbing banks? No. To me it is about what I would like to do in my lifetime, to get people to understand that you are supposed to progress in culture, not digress.

WILLIAMS PAGE: Does that sum up who you are as an artist?

DUTTON: Yes. I have always considered myself an artist, since the day I got out of the penitentiary. If I were to let that go I would probably be richer and more famous, and I would probably being doing some of that buffoonish, clownish work on television I just finished talking about, or I would be doing anything in the movies just to be rich and famous. But, that is not who I am, what my chemistry make-up is. I have always been an outlaw, since I was twelve years old, and I am still an outlaw, just in a different way.

I may not get to be the richest or most famous person in Hollywood, but I have never cared about that. I have always cared about whether or not I would be able to look at something I had done five years earlier and not be embarrassed about it, so I have always tried to choose what I do extremely carefully. Now, though, I don't have to choose as much because I am only given or sent those things that people know I would be interested in.

WILLIAMS PAGE: Do you think you will work with Wilson again?

DUTTON: I recently received a phone call from August's people about performing in his latest play *King Headley*, which is playing in L.A. I read it, but it didn't have a strong protagonist.

WILLIAMS PAGE: Is it the latest play in his ten-play cycle?

DUTTON: Yes, it is set in 1980. It is about the son of Headley from *Seven Guitars*.

WILLIAMS PAGE: Wilson has said that one of the problems of African American theater is that it is not institutionalized. Do you agree with that assessment?

DUTTON: Yes, that is true, but we [African Americans] also do not have a history of theater. There is also no culture of theater in America like there is in Britain. Yes, there is Broadway and regional theater, but the regional theater movement is only about thirty-five years old. Without a culture, it is every man for himself. White people will create their own personal, public and private endowments to ensure their theater is taken care of. We do not, and that is because for us life has always been a struggle. We have not had the extra money to set aside for those type things. Another problem I see is that black theater management does not possess the organizational skills needed to keep the theaters afloat.

WILLIAMS PAGE: So how do we move toward institutionalization?

DUTTON: As I said, first we need people with good organizational skills. In the heyday of government liberalism in the arts, a lot of the money given to black theaters was squandered, so we need people who will be able to run the theater as well as keep the books. Second, we need people who will be committed and sincere about running the theater, people who have an interest in creating a culture of theater and passing it on. Next we need to find playwrights who are writing serious works, nurture them, and give them the venue they need.

WILLIAMS PAGE: Do you think part of the problem is that as a people, historically, we tend to not patronize those plays that are serious, like *Joe Turner's Come and Gone*, but patronize those that are less serious and more comical such as *Beauty Shop* and *A Good Man is Hard to Find?*

DUTTON: Those type plays, and to call them plays is a stretch, have their place and audience, and they prove my point about the difference between the entertainer, the actor, and the artist. Those people are only out to make a dollar. The only thing I can say about those "plays" is they do get people to get out of the house and spend $25 or $30 to see them. Now if we could cultivate the people who go see those types of plays for some serious drama, then we would be getting somewhere. Now I believe that can be done; it just will take some time; it will have to be a process.

WILLIAMS PAGE: As I am sure you are aware, in 1990 Wilson was criticized when during the search for a director for the screen version of *Fences* he stated he would prefer a black director for the film and would stand firm on that preference. His reason for that stance was he wanted someone who shared the cultural sensibilities of his characters. Do you support that belief?

DUTTON: To a degree I think it has more to do with the kind of director a person is rather than whether he or she is black or white. There are some black directors who could not do *Fences*, to be honest; who would screw it up just as much as a white director would. John Singleton cannot do *Fences*. He wasn't around during the 50s. He has no idea about that decade. It takes a certain kind of human being, and I do not mean Spielberg, who would really understand the dynamics of the individual struggle of Troy, and not necessarily the cultural scope of it.

I agree with August in that that whole scenario has been forced by the lack of the industry's diversity. August Wilson is not a race-baiter because he insists that black directors do black work. It is Hollywood that says, "We will let white directors do all the work, whether it is a white or black work." So, the reaction to that is "okay, if the white directors get to do the majority of the work at least let the black directors do the black work."

WILLIAMS PAGE: Well Mr. Dutton those are all the questions I have for you. Do you have any final thoughts?

DUTTON: To really realize August Wilson's work takes just as much emotional commitment, physical commitment, and overall sacrifice as it does with any other play or playwright. You have to be just as tireless and fearless to do August Wilson as you would Shakespeare. For August Wilson's plays to retain their classical affinity, one must be committed when he does them. Now, of course, kids in college should do August just as they do Shakespeare, but once you're on a professional level you have to realize that that is some beautiful stuff you are spewing out, and that at this point it is the only African American historical record of literature in the theater. When he finishes all ten plays, we will have a decade-by-decade volume of works that is ours. Unfortunately, the plays are pretty much male dominated, but nevertheless they are ours. If we can find a black female writer who is going to chronicle the black female experience in the last century, then we have to grab and nourish that person just as much as we have August Wilson.

13

A CONVERSATION WITH AUGUST WILSON

Sandra G. Shannon and Dana A. Williams

This interview with August Wilson (AW) was conducted by coeditors Dana A. Williams (DW) and Sandra G. Shannon (SS) on Friday, September 26, 2003 at the Edison Hotel in New York City.

DW: We interpret *black aesthetics* broadly in our collection. Can you speak a little about your interpretation of *black aesthetics*?

AW: I interpret *black aesthetics* as broadly as you do. As you know, you can write entire books on just the word *aesthetic*. I would say that the black aesthetic is black thought that is organized into conventions, and what those conventions are would be based on your ideas about the world. Translating that into art, its dimensions would be the aesthetic expression of those ideas. Now exactly what that aesthetic is we are still trying to find out, especially as it relates to black theater, which is still in its infancy. When you look at European theater, Europeans have been developing their aesthetic over thousands of years. So, we've been at this for a relatively short time. And we're still in the process of developing our conventions. So when you talk about conventions of black theater and a black aesthetic you have to say that they are still in the process of being developed.

SS: Your aesthetic, based on the plays that you've written and the poetry as well, is informed by the blues, Africa, some aspects of cultural nationalism...a combination of those things. Are there any other things that inform your aesthetic?

AW: I think you would have to add to that Aristotle's *Poetics*. Here again, the art form that I work in is a European art form. So that would have to be included. But if you go to the Greeks or to the white American theater they will have Aristotle's *Poetics*, but they don't have the black nationalism, or the blues, or those other things that make black aesthetics unique. But this black aesthetic is still based on a European art form until it's defined otherwise, until some other form or method of what theater is and some new conventions are developed by black Americans. And I think that if you look at literature you'll see that black Americans are in a very unique position. They may be the only ones who are in a position to develop an American litera-ture. And that includes theater. When the European came to America to set-tle here, they brought with them European conventions. And so the literature that was created on this continent was not American but European with European conventions. The African, who came to America, stripped of his culture and his language, didn't have any conventional bag-gage. And that's what allowed the blues and jazz to be developed; those conventions had to be developed. And so I think if you're going to have an *American* literature, an *American* theater, then it has to include and prob-ably be lead by African Americans. So when you see black theater, some of it is not based on Aristotle, and I think that is good.

SS: Black theater is writing against these conventions?

AW: Well, I don't know that it's so much against it. But we're in the process of developing different ideas about what theater is and in the process of devel-oping those ideas. And here again, this is all very new. And in order to do theater you have to have the tools, and the tools are theaters. So the more theaters you have the more you are able to develop the tools. I think there is in the process of being developed a black theater that is not based on Aristotle's *Poetics* and European conventions.

DW: Sybil Roberts's *A Lovesong for Mumia*, which we've included in this collec-tion, is among those plays that are not based on European conventions. *A Lovesong for Mumia* is very ritualistic and is birthed out of the concept of theater activism. In her essay detailing the development of the play, Roberts comments that there already is a constituency in black theater that is exactly what you call for—theater for the people and by the people—in "The Ground" speech. In addition to calling attention to this cadre of writers, what do you see as the most significant advance of the speech and the sub-sequent conference at Dartmouth?

AW: The African Grove Institute for the Arts (AGIA) came out of that. But the concrete results of black gains—I don't see any, none. I think it's been the opposite. These are not always the things by which we measure. But the important thing is we started with one black LORT theater, and we don't have any now. Jimandi Productions in Atlanta, a city that is something like 73 percent black cannot support a black theater. They closed. It's not there anymore. I'm willing to bet that if you go back and look that after the speech there was less money given to black theaters than before. And there are reasons for that. And I think it's because in certain ways there's not a value for black theater. As long as the club doesn't close, we're doing all right. We just had the Black Roots Festival here in New York. It was myself and Derek Walcott, and we had a conversation. And the turnout was not a very large crowd. But if Teddy Pendergrass, Ice Cube, or Fifty-cents were here, or if they had said, "We're going to have some music afterwards. Wynton Marsalis is going to come done and play his trumpet," then it would have been a larger crowd. But a conversation with two playwrights...

DW: How do we change that? How do we promote both music-as-culture *and* theater?

AW: I think one has been more valuable to us, which is why we readily embrace the music. We understand the music as the thing that has enabled us to sur-vive. So, we know what that is. But then this other thing? What is that, which I think is crucially important? I think when we look back in history, we'll see that in rap, it's the words *and* the music. That's very similar to the blues, where you have words to provide you with the information and music to give you the emotion. It's an emotional response to the information, and when you put those two things together, it's one of the unique things about the blues. The entire philosophical system is contained in the blues, and the emotional reference is provided in the music. So when Derek [Walcott] talked about Bob Marley and "No Woman No Cry," he pointed to the line "In the government yard in Trenchtown." Just that one line, and I thought, "Oh man, that's the line that gets me too." But the line without the music doesn't matter. It's the music that provides the emotional reference to the line that just grabs at you. If you heard the music without the line, it doesn't mean anything. It's the combination. And that may be the very thing that rap provides. So the whole future of theater may be based on some conventions of theater that rappers are developing now. It's like back in '65 when we used to have poetry readings and jazz concerts. The jazz musicians would tell us we could read while they set up. People would come in and see us reading, and they'd walk right out until the music started. So, you can't compete with music if all you have is words.

DW: Well now, most poetry readings have poets read with music behind them like in the 60s.

AW: That's what Baraka tried to do. He put out a couple of albums, but he got confused. They were trying to put jazz to poetry, but it was the beat, not the jazz. And the rappers sell the beat. And what I've found about rap is it's where we're going. I was talking to some kids at a school, and they were talking while I was talking until I said, "Anybody rap?" And that got their attention. So, I said, "Everybody come on up." And one kid comes up and says, "I'm the beat man." And I asked, "What does that mean?" And he says I keep the beat. He was a big guy, and he said, "Most of us big guys keep the beat." And we played around. But the teacher got mad because rap is playground activity, and I had brought it in the school and legitimized it. And I was thinking, "You can use this to teach these kids how to read."

SS: You're on play number ten. How does ten fit into the aesthetic you've already created?

AW: Well, it's cut out of the same cloth. It's a summation, if you will. It tells where we are at the end of the century as we prepare to go on to the next century. It looks at what this 100 years have meant and how we have fared. So, I think to do that I'm going to make use of some of the offspring of some of the characters from *Gem of the Ocean*, which is the first play. But so far, the play is tentatively titled *Radio Golf*. The structure of the play is relatively simply. Aunt Hester dies [in *King Hedley*] in 1985; her house at 1839 Wylie is abandoned, and they want to tear her house down. It's surrounded by empty lots, and they want to tear the house down and build a little shopping mall. And there's a question of who owns the house. And then the city battles to tear it down.

SS: After the tenth play, are you going to start experimenting with different forms?

AW: Well, I have some ideas about plays that did not fit in the cycle. And I want to explore those ideas. One thing I know I'm going to do is to participate in this playwright series at Signature Theater [in New York] in '05 to '06 I think. I'm having a series at the Signature Theater. They select a playwright every year, and they do three or four of the artists' plays. They have done a series on Adrienne Kennedy, Lanford Wilson, and Arthur Miller. They are going to do three or four of my plays in their season, one of which is going to be *Seven Guitars Too,* which is another way of telling the story of *Seven Guitars.* It's a five-minute-vignette kind of thing. Originally when I started *Seven Guitars,* I started doing it like that. But I realized it wasn't cut out of the same cloth as the rest. So, I want to go back to that. And it's very much different from what I do now. I think I'll do the one-man show ["How I Learned What I Learned"] again. I may have stumbled onto something because I only did two years of my life in the first show. So, I can foresee "How I Learned What I Learned . . . Reloaded" [laughter].

SS: Fiction?

AW: Oh yes. I have an idea for a novel. I've got about forty-two pages or something. When I actually sit down and write it, I'll just do it. But I'm tuning up my fiction muscle by writing and publishing a collection of stories before I tackle the novel just to limber up a little bit.

SS: I saw a comment from you about Susan Lori-Parks that you tip your hat to her. Could you talk about her work?

AW: She's a very good playwright. She has a very unique use of language, which attracts me. Her work is unlike mine, but it's like mine since she's dealing with the black thematic thing. But I just love her language and how she writes. So many playwrights write small. And small things don't interest me. I like big things. And she tackles big things.

SS: Are there any other playwrights you would take your hat off to?

AW: I'm sure there must be. But I don't like doing that because I'll leave somebody out. There are a lot of good playwrights out there. So, I don't want to say that Parks is the only one I'd tip my hat to, but then I don't want to name four or five because what you'd come up with is the list of the "usual suspects." I will say that I haven't seen anyone just blaze across the scene, but I imagine they are out there.

DW: Have you worked with Javon Johnson, who is often billed as "August Wilson's protégé?"

AW: I haven't worked with him, but I know Javon. And I support his work. What happened was *USA Today* had different artists, and they wanted the artists to sit down with a younger person in their field and to have a conversation with them. And they approached me about this. And I knew Javon, so I said I'd sit down with Javon and have this dialogue. So they published it side by side, and that's how the "Wilson protégé" thing came to be, which I think is unfortunate for Javon. If I were him, I wouldn't want to be tagged with being anyone's protégé. I say, "Let me do my own thing." And it's unfortunate for me also because it locks me in a certain support of his work, some of which I know and some of which I don't. But I think he's a very talented writer, which is why I chose him to sit down with.

SS: Why is it that the urban circuit theater, not theater about "big" things as you say, has large audiences now more than ever?

AW: I'm not sure that some folks know that there is any other kind of theater. That's what theater is to them. Let me say this—there is nothing wrong with it. That may in fact be the future of black theater. That aesthetic we're talking about may in fact come right out of there. But in order for that to happen, there has to be critical attention brought to bear on that. Some of that stuff, they shouldn't be able to get away with. And the audience has to demand more. Until they demand more, you aren't going to get more. And that audience doesn't know that there is more to be gotten from a play. And I think critical attention will drive that and lift the audience. And you'll have a whole new way of doing theater—black folks' way of doing theater that has its own conventions. Folks will say, "Well, where did they get them from." And they'll say, "We made them up."

SS: What kinds of subjects are worthy of theater, worth putting on stage?

AW: Love, honor, duty, betrayal, the human condition...those things. How we respond to the world...

SS: So the urban circuit plays would fit the bill?

AW: Well, my understanding of them, and I could be wrong, is that they are driven by the church. The Christian church has been the one institution that has enabled us and contributed tremendously to our survival. It's the most stable organization in the black community and has been for years. "My grandmother prayed for me." Well, my grandmother prayed for me too. Now that becomes a play. But to me, that's still pathology driven. It's driven by the lowest common denominator that connects everybody, and it's influenced by television. So, they make it a sitcom. The only problem I see with that though is that is the black pathology. It's like writing about all the horrible things that happened. Well, what about your grandfather who didn't do all that? The guy who wasn't on drugs...let's deal with that stuff. And in the process of doing that, other stuff will emerge as part of who we are.

SS: But it seems like those plays have hit a moneymaking formula.

AW: Because people are starved to see themselves. So, the church organizes a trip, and you have 3,000 people in the audience. And they get something out of these plays. It's almost like a church experience, which is where black people have traditionally gotten their theater from. They've consolidated the experience. Church functions for black folks the way theater functions for European Americans, who don't have that church-as-theater experience. For them, church is very quiet. So, they developed a theater to get that experience. But we already had that. So we didn't need theater. All we had to do is walk into a church. And the emotions Aristotle talks about are played out every Sunday...pity, fear, anger.... It's right there. Of course, that's not what they call it in the church, but theater's what they're doing.

DW: Does black theater, then, have to have a different function from white theater?

AW: I think the function is the same—to create art that responds to or illuminates the human condition. In other words, I don't think they are any different. And I don't want to force a writer or an actor into "this is what you should be doing." I don't want to say that what you're doing should fit this set of rules. Art should be liberating; it should be functional. This is from the 60s—art has to be functional, collective, and committing. Well, maybe it does. Let's assume it does. But you can't force that on anyone. If it doesn't emerge from the people, you can't lay that on them. You can't tell people "you guys are doing that, but you should be dealing with black liberation or that which presents positive role models to our kids." Maybe that's not the way the artist sees it. And I don't want to tell anybody what to do, and I don't think you can force it on the people. The people decide, and if that's what the people want, that's what the people get. And you can't let down the people. All you can do is expose them to other things so that when they are making their decisions about what black theater is supposed to be they can see what black theater is capable of first before figuring out where they should be going.

SS: What would you tell a class of aspiring playwrights about being a part of black theater?

AW: I'd tell them to walk on the other side of the street. And that's simply saying you have to get out of the usual mode of viewing the world. If you walk on the other side of the street, you'd be surprised at what you see over there. So, that's the first thing—walk on the other side of the street, and know that there are other things in the world than what you think is in the world. The difficulty is in getting to the thing that is inside you or finding something worth writing about. Everything is not worth writing about. I personally do not want to see any more novels written by a young black person talking about their dating experiences in New York. No more. I've had it up to here. There's got to more stuff to write about than that. It's sad when people have talent and don't put that talent to any use. So, I'm assuming that all the writers have talent. Now, let's find a way to put the talent to some use other than just saying you wrote a play. So, I would say to them that they are all potentially talented writers. But unless they claim it, claim being an artist, they're just a writer, which means you'll write anything for anybody. But if you're an artist, then you're not for sale. You have to have a belief in yourself that's larger than anybody's disbelief, and find something to say.

SS: What's the critic's role in what you find to say?

AW: I don't allow criticism to influence my art. Sometimes critics will give you a different way of thinking about a play. They'll describe a character a certain way. And I'll say, "Well, I never thought of him that way. I haven't thought of him as a subversive vagabond." But I've always placed my own value on my art. Now, do I read the critics? Yes, and I think that any playwright who tells you they don't is being at least intellectually dishonest. It might be true, but I don't believe it. Do I pay attention to what the critics are saying? Yes.

SS: I remember in "The Ground" speech, you challenge critics to evolve just as the aesthetic evolves.

AW: Absolutely. Let's say I'm reading this critic who is responding to a play, and it's a white play, but he's still responding to a play as having a neoclassical German influence. You recognize that. And that's good. So if you can do that, when you come to a black play, you should be able to say, "Oh, that's the blues" or whatever the influence is. And if you aren't able to do that, accept it on those terms, then you have the wrong analytical tools when you come because you're not going to find the neoclassical German influence. You have to be aware of what's going on. You have to know something about black culture and be able to say, "Oh that's a jazz influence." And I think you should be able to do that. But generally critics develop a single set of analytical tools, and they apply them to everyone. And all the references are mostly to Europeans—white critics, black critics, myself included. Generally, your first reference is to a Western piece of literature. So the critic has to develop a single set of analytical tools, and I think that's where you start. You have to have that in your tool bag. But if you're a music critic, and we have this thing called rap now, and you haven't paid any attention to it, you're out of step. So you're looking at rap and saying "that's new R&B or doo-wop" when it's this other thing that's going on. So the critic has to keep adding to his tools. But I think the responsibility of critics is to do two things—they drive the art, or they should drive the art. And they are the keeper of the gate, so to speak; they work at what [Robert] Brustein would call "preserving thought." So that if you're a critic and you're going to maintain a certain quality, then the critic has to demand that you [the playwright] come up to the bar. They have to maintain that quality. As a playwright, it's a privilege to stand here in this art form, and along with that privilege comes some responsibility and duty to the art form. And if the playwright assumes that then the playwright has to do the work. And the critics can't let them get away with anything else.

SS: And that's different from what race you are. I think the issue of the black director [for the film version of *Fences*] was another issue for you that was blown out of proportion. The individual ought to be sensitive to the culture, right?

AW: It's not just that. No matter how sensitive you are, no matter how well meaning you are, you're an outsider. I'm sensitive to all the issues of Italians, but I'm not qualified to direct *The Godfather*. You have to go and get an Italian. You cannot learn the Italian experience. No matter how well meaning I am or how long I study, I cannot learn it. And everybody in the world knows I'm right, and it's been proven. Steven Spielberg did not direct *The Godfather*. And when they decided to make the movie about the holocaust, they didn't go get Spike Lee. They got Steven Spielberg. When you have a situation where a film is about the culture of the people like *The Godfather* or *Schindler's List*, then you go get someone who has lived the culture, except when it's black. And I just said, "Wait a minute. That ain't right." Why can't I get a black director? There are occasions when a movie is about a car chase, and you can get anybody to direct that because it's not about the culture. The problem you run into is times when people are trying to prove that race doesn't matter. I was in L.A. a few months after I first made the comment, and a guy came up to me and said, "I'm a director. And I've been out here telling these folks for fifteen years that it doesn't matter that I'm black. And here you come along telling them that it does. So, I direct your movie. Then what." If he were to accept the fact that he could only direct black movies, then he'd only work every five years or whenever they decided to put out a black movie. He told me not to do him any favors. And I responded that I wasn't trying to do him any favors. I was just trying to get my movie made in the best possible way I can. I wasn't out there carrying a banner saying "hire black directors," and I'm still not. But I am saying, as a black playwright, if you want to make a movie of my work, I want it to be done in the best possible way, with a black director. And that's the way I want it done.

DW: But you've had white directors for your plays. What's the difference between that and having a white director for the film?

AW: I've had white directors work on my plays. In fact, the guy who directed my one-man show is white—Todd [Kreidler]. But I think there is a difference. The difference is that the film is forever. There was a production of *Ma Rainey's Black Bottom* in London that I saw. They didn't do too bad. There were a few things that they didn't understand, but I corrected them. But that's over and done with. A film will be here 150 years from now. I would want that permanent record to be best reflected by a person of my culture.

DW: The film version of *Fences* is also likely to be used as a reflection of the culture, much more so than someone going to theater. Someone going to the theater is not likely going to the theater specifically to look at the play's representation of the culture. But in teaching moments, especially, people are looking at a film expressly to identify the culture and the social context of out which the text emerges.

AW: Here again, it is a permanent record. It can be used for anything. So it has to be a good reflection of the culture.

SS: Do you consider *Fences* your signature play?

AW: I want to say here for the record [laughter], of the plays that I have written, it is my least favorite play. It's not my signature play.

DW: Oddly, in spite of your point about why you want a black director for the movie version (because it's so specifically about the culture), *Fences* is also considered the most universal of your plays. What do you say to an all-white production of *Fences* that misses the cultural underpinnings of the play?

AW: An all-white production *would* miss the cultural underpinnings, but there is nothing I can do about that. My signature play would be *Joe Turner's Come and Gone*. Most of the ideas of the other plays are contained in that one play. So, if I had to pick one play as my signature play, that would be it but certainly not *Fences*. *Fences* is the only one that's not an ensemble play. The rest of them are ensembles. *Fences* has Troy Maxson in every scene, and all the other characters revolve around him. But with *Joe Turner*, there are like ten people, and they are all involved in the scenes.

SS: But *Fences* has been done more widely. I know of the all-Chinese production, for instance. And the audience got it from what I understand.

AW: It was also done in Ghana. And even though they were Africans, it was different because they were British. For instance, one of the things that they did was Gabriel was a chorus. He would talk to the audience. He would say the same things that were in the play—they didn't add lines, but he would talk directly to the audience. And I thought that was interesting. And I would have said that black culture is black culture until I went over to London and they were doing *Ma Rainey's Black Bottom*. And I found out that the black folks over there are very influenced by British culture. So, the kinds of mistakes that a white director might make because he isn't familiar with the culture, I found the black cast making the same mistakes because they are British. Toledo [from *Ma Rainey*] was sitting around reading a newspaper, and Levy is saying something. And then Levy jumps up on the table and kicks the newspaper out of Toledo's hands. And I said, "No, you can't do that."

DW: That's a fight waiting to happen [laughter].

AW: Yes, that's an assault that would call for a different response in the text. So, he can't do that. And I thought that a black cast should have known that. The guy playing Toledo should have known that. So, they took it out. Other than that it was fine.

DW: What are some diasporic aesthetic ideas that do cross geographical boundaries?

AW: Music, for instance. My assumption would be that music is cross-cultural. One of the driving things of any black aesthetic is improvisation or the idea of improvising. It's the thing that enabled use to survive—the ability to think on our feet. We're essentially the same people. For instance, I was watching these Japanese guys in a hotel, and there was a jukebox in the restaurant. And they didn't play the jukebox. It never occurred to them to play the jukebox. But if six black guys walk in there, the first thing one of them is going to do is go over to the jukebox. And it's the aesthetic. Music is more important to them maybe. I don't know what it is exactly. I just know the black guys would have played the jukebox.

SS: If you had to do the speech again would there be any changes made?

AW: I think so. I think I would leave the colorblind casting alone.

SS: But that wasn't really the big picture.

AW: That's why I would leave it alone, because that became the lightening rod that everyone focused on as if that was the only thing I was saying. I think it muddled the speech. So leaving that aside would force people to focus on what I was really saying because that was not it. That was an addendum to it and part of it all, but I think I would say some things differently. I would still have said it, but I would have talked about that the next week.

SS: Well, thank you very much for the interview.

DW: Yes, thank you for the interview and for the inspiration for *August Wilson and Black Aesthetics*.

AW: You're welcome.

APPENDIX

A LIBERATING PRAYER: A LOVESONG FOR MUMIA

Sybil J. Roberts

PROLOGUE: A SLIDE OF SAGE AT A GALLERY OPENING SURROUNDED BY HER ALTAR CREATIONS AND DOZENS OF WELL-WISHERS. SOFT JAZZ IS HEARD PLAYING. (OPTIONAL: A CHORUS SINGS A JAZZ A STANDARD.) SUDDENLY, THE SOUND OF DOORS SLAMMING BUZZERS AND BELLS IS HEARD. A SLIDE OF MUMIA ABU-JAMAL APPEARS. A CLOCK TICKS LOUDLY BY THE END OF THE SCENE TO SILENCE.

SAGE:
a single cowrie shell ... a mother's cry ...
a cotton blossom in fertile soil ...

MUMIA:
I stand poised gracefully at the edge of leaving this life. Where
waiting is an art ...

SAGE:
the smell of honeysuckle on a warm summer night ... a length of rope ... a
piece of my granddaddy's spiritual ...

MUMIA:
We are all here lining cell blocks from one coast to the the other ...

SAGE:
scraps of time from other
places ... Boston ... Scottsboro ... Soledad ... Attica ...

MUMIA:
America's latest version of the slaveship ...
no rough-hewn wood and crisp trimmed sails. All metal and concrete.
Sleek and new.

SAGE:
Our men are dying their deaths are slow and horrible ...

MUMIA:

You won't hear the rattle of chains, the crashing of waves, or the moans of the dying. Even sound is sanitized.

SAGE:

Only beauty can save them. Call them by their
names. Chant down the hunger of their would-be murderers...

MUMIA:

My father. My brother. My sons. The men of my village. We are all here.
Taken by force. Taken by arms. Taken by law.

SAGE:

I build altars. I give my hands to struggle. Speaking kindred speech in
sign and symbol. Piecing together our story...

MUMIA:

Brought to this place to await Justice. Once a wizened elder. Now a senile old man obsessed with time.

SAGE:

My hands calling warriors onto the field of battle saying "never
forget... never forget..."

MUMIA:

We are all here in this place where death is a promise.

SAGE:

Until... until they discovered a slow-moving madness chasing us across
centuries.

**THE CHORUS ENTERS AND BEGINS EXAMINING HER ALTARS.
THEY WALK AROUND AS IF THEY'RE IN ATTENDANCE AT HER
GALLERY OPENING.**

MUMIA:

I give my hands a ritual. Praying.

SAGE:

Catching us tired... running... so we wait... wait to die by the hands of
our own children. Perhaps this is our fate.
I would give my hands a ritual. But they are still.

CHORUS:

We meet in this place of prayer. Loving here is an invocation and spirits do come.
We are the ones who crossed the Middle Passage with sweet tears of resistance
beating back our blood-dreams. We are the ones who refused to be silenced by the
ride of history. Connected by breath... touch... and knowing... we... wandering
through time giving our hands to struggle. They are raw nerve and bone now. Their
softness gone. We heard our children praying... we are gathered around them.
They will be the last ones. Mumia, this man who loves like faith and new days will
show Sage the way... back to herself. Then our hands will rest.

MUMIA:

"The death chambers of America are not as tightly sealed as many may suspect for how can spirit be kept out..." (**MUMIA, DEATH BLOSSOMS, p. 32**)

MOVEMENT #1: A SLIDE OF A WHITE-WASHED CHURCH FOLLOWED BY A SLIDE/VIDEO FOOTAGE OF PARKS AND NATURAL ENVIRONMENTS (I.E. FORESTS, STREAMS, ETC.) THE SOUNDS OF NATURE ARE HEARD...GIVING INDICATION OF A HOT SUNNY URBAN DAY. THE CHORUS ENTERS DRESSED AS MUMIA PROTESTERS. THEY CARRY SIGNS AND BANNERS WEARING "FREE MUMIA" T-SHIRTS. THEY ARE CHANTING "FREE MUMIA" SLOGANS. THEY HAND-OUT FLYERS AND RIBBONS TO AUDIENCE MEMBERS. SAGE SITS ON A BLANKET SURROUNDED BY ARTIST'S MATERIALS.

SAGE:

First Congregational Church...I would give my hands a ritual...but I take them to church instead. Well not to church, but to the park across the street to escape my studio-tomb. I would will my hands to give full voice to this sorrow that has silenced me. But I am not that strong. If I could go back...back to the beginning...when I first heard the madness speaking and stand...stand without fear. I would give my hands ritual...dig deep into the earth...to find something blessed...hallowed...something to lead me back to...

CHORUS:

We are mothers and daughters, fathers and sons, brothers and sisters. We are dancers, singers, seers, and sayers. We are the warriors who refused to lay down our swords and shields by the riverside. No. We study war...still.

THE CHORUS SINGS CIVIL-RIGHTS ERA PROTEST SONGS SUCH AS "STUDY WAR NO MORE..."

SAGE:

First Congregational Church. A hot August day. I watch them coming. All of them coming to save the life of Mumia Abu-Jamal. In the cool mahogany sanctuary of the church. Our collective energy would be a prayer...a prayer to save the "voice of the voiceless". My hands digging deep into earth...

CHORUS:

Hand in prayer: an extremity...reaching...open-palmed...offering destination...smooth and clear as the mirror of time...Who are you?

A SLIDE OF PAM AFRICA WITH THE FRENCH DELEGATION. (A NOTE: ANY GUEST ACTIVIST MAY BE SUBSTITUTED HERE

WHICH WOULD MEAN USING DIFFERENT IMAGES...AND INDICATIONS OF GENDER IN THE LINES.)

SAGE:

A question sung in the round melody of prayer-circle. I took a flyer and a ribbon. Gifts from my sister. My sister...a little brown woman...commanding all of Europe...America...and the children of Africa to free Mumia! I'm impressed but I'm thinking about all the other revolutionaries that fear to save themselves and this country.

CHORUS:

Nat Turner rising up one August night. Blood announcing his presence.
John Brown rising up one hot August night. Blood and gunpowder
announcing his presence. George Jackson going down in blood and
defiance in San Quentin one hot August day.

SAGE:

I decide August is not a good month for revolutionaries. But they don't know that. I take the flyer. I don't know why.

THE CHORUS RELEASE MUMIA FROM PRISON. HE STANDS BEHIND HER WHISPERING SOFTLY IN HER EAR. SAGE HEARS HIS VOICE IN HER HANDS. SHE STUDIES THEM CLOSELY.

MUMIA:

"Let the thump, thump, thump of countless feet resound, as they crumble
the walls of the ancient caged city a chains! A nation of prisons,
where political prisoners and Prisoners of an Eternal War sit shackled,
in a place that dares to claim to be the home of the Free! Let the
marchers come and let their voices resound the entire world around, and
let the people know the time of freedom is now." **(TEXT COPYRIGHT
1988 MUMIA ABU-JAMAL)**

SAGE:

Mumia was speaking...right here...in my hands.
A strip of bright blue kente circling the words like a prayer-cloth...

MUMIA:

Wear a piece of Africa everyday in memory of all our brothers and
sisters who gave their lives because they believed in something.
Something that made them alive like children.

SAGE:

"Mumia Abu-Jamal...award-winning journalist...former Black
Panther...who in 1982...convicted in a frame-up trial for murdering a
white police officer...sentenced to die...
There was a faint calling of drums...

CHORUS:

Hand...a woman promised...a considered source
of knowledge...

MUMIA:
Something this system couldn't crush, kill, or take away...

SAGE:
A strip of bright blue kente circling an image...
like a rainbow lying down...resting...cool
against my fingers...frayed edges like Sunday
school ribbon...I'm a girl again praying in this place where yearning
becomes art.

CHORUS:
Remembering touch...your hands gathering light...
finding language...

MUMIA:
Wear a piece of Africa...

SAGE:
African-beautiful this brother...

MUMIA:
For those who never stood empty-handed before some blind woman begging
for justice...

SAGE:
Whose life I know as well as my own. I study his hands.
Raised. Shackled. Reaching...

MUMIA:
For those...who knowing Africa...was more than a place
took God's hand and accepted their destiny...

SAGE:
And for a moment...just for a moment...he reached for me...

MUMIA:
No matter what we may lose...and our losses will
be many. Wear this cloth that is a prayer. Say to them
I'm still here...I'm still here...

**MUMIA RUMMAGES AMONG SAGE'S ART SUPPLIES AND FINDS
A PIECE OF KENTE CLOTH...BLUE LIKE THE RIBBON...WHICH
HE LAYS ACROSS SAGE'S HAND.**

SAGE:
He reached for me. But my hands held the bones of all our dead. Jagged. Sharp.
Cutting clean through all my knowing laying me open to myself...places too raw
to be birthed into beauty. Hands hold truths that tongues refuse to speak. I'm trying to find a way to love Black people again. Love them through my doubts and
their terribleness. The origin of my art is now lost. My hands are empty.

MUMIA:
Can we make beauty in a place that steals time and makes an altar of
sorrow and regret?

SAGE:
I took the flyer ... I don't know why.

CHORUS:
Your hands gathering light ... finding language ...

MUMIA:
Wrap your passion around my life. Make beauty dawta.
I was in search of a woman who could love like a prayer.
I saw her and made a gift of my hands.
I saw her and made an altar of my heart.

**MUMIA TAKES SAGE'S HANDS IN HIS OWN. HOLDING THEM AS
TO KEEP THEM WARM ... AND SAFE AGAINST HIS OWN HEART.**

CHORUS:
Hand in prayer ... a circle of memory reaching back ...

SAGE:
My hands have an ear for memory.

**SAGE EXAMINES HER HANDS STILL NOT QUITE SURE OF WHO
OR WHAT IS SPEAKING TO HER THROUGH THEM.**

MUMIA:
There is power in beauty.

SAGE:
I'm always collecting things. Bringing things home.
Bits of summer love songs ...

CHORUS:
Pieces of my granddaddy's spirituals. A child's night prayers. Scraps of time from
other places. Boston ... Scottsboro ... Soledad ... Attica ... Philadelphia ...

SAGE:
This is my resistance ... I protest ... making beauty in the face of it
all. Making beauty ... forcing me to remember what I should forget. But
no more ... no more.

CHORUS:
Memory is strong medicine ... don't be afraid to taste it's bitterness.

**MUMIA THREADS THE STRIP OF KENTE THROUGH SAGE'S
FINGERS.**

MUMIA:
You're safe here dawta.
Give me your stories and I'll make you a crown.

**MOVEMENT #2: SLIDES OF THE TERENCE JOHNSON CASE MAY
                    APPEAR. PHOTOS OF YOUNG TERENCE AND ALL
                    THE HEADLINES AND ARTICLES. WHICH**

**SLOWLY FADES TO THE MARCH ON SELMA...
WHICH SLOWLY FADES TO SLIDES OF VIETNAM
SOLDIERS. BY THE END OF THE MONOLOGUE
THEY ARE REPLACED BY SLIDES OF VARIOUS
LYNCHINGS THROUGHOUT U.S. HISTORY. THE
CHORUS SINGS A ROUND OF SPIRITUALS AS AN
ACT OF MOURNING AND RESISTANCE. EVERY
NOW AND THEN THEIR SONG IS PUNCTUATED
BY CLENCHED FISTS OR A SHOUT!!!**

SAGE:

I'm remembering the one time my father took us to a protest, my brother and me.
Daddy come home with all this posterboard and told us to get the magic markers.
Told us we were gonna make some signs and go down to that courthouse...raise
our voices to a shout and demand our brother's freedom. It was for a boy who had
just shot and killed 2 county police officers. A boy who went to the jr. high right
down the street from mine, a boy I could've played basketball...kickball...dodge
ball with at the rec center. We were making signs...gonna demand our brothers
freedom...

MUMIA:

"People say they don't care about politics; they're not involved or don't want to get
involved, but they are. Their involvement just masquerades as indifference..."
(MUMIA ABU-JAMAL, DEATH BLOSSOMS, p. 11) His freedom would be
yours.

**SAGE BECOMES HER CHILDHOOD SELF IN HER STORY. OTHER
CHORUS MEMBERS MAY PLAY HER FATHER AND LITTLE
BROTHER.**

SAGE:

'Cause that's what we do...stand up for each other...fight for each other. Isn't
that what he taught me and brother to do? My father always saying..."I'ma tell
you something...3 things...I want you to remember all your life"...he said
"don't never let nobody call you out your name...don't ever let nobody hit you
and walk away...don't never let nobody force you to tell a lie."

CHORUS:
There is beauty in truth.

SAGE:

Nobody...ever...cause once a person can do that...they own you.[2] He said that
the first time cause somebody stole my brother's bike and we all knew who did it.
So when my father asked the boy about it he said my brother gave it to him. Then
he looked at my brother like...My father said, "is that true?" My brother just
stood there looking at the ground. I didn't say nothing either. My father told him
say "get your little black ass up off that bike!" Then took us home and whipped
both of us. Said "don't nobody own you but yourself." And Daddy would know
cause he marched in Selma with Dr. King, then turned around and fought in
Vietnam.

MUMIA:

"Remember, the system is not a true reality, but an idea which can be fought and dismantled . . . We need only the things God gave us: love, family, nature . . . " (**DEATH BLOSSOMS, p. 76**)

SAGE:

So we making signs and I'm all proud thinking I'm just like daddy going to Selma. Doing what we do. He said we could save him. Had to save him . . . get enough of us in the street saying no.

CHORUS:

There is beauty in struggle.

SAGE BECOMES TERENCE JOHNSON.

SAGE:

There are many versions of what happened. How those 2 officers came to be dead. The facts are these . . . a 15 year-old boy was stopped along with his 19 year-old brother for some alleged traffic violation. The officers then discovered a sock full of change in the car. His brother had supposedly robbed some coin-operated laundry mats at a nearby apartment building. They were taken to the precinct. The facts end here. They took them down to the station for "questioning." They were not under arrest. They placed them in separate rooms. They didn't call the boy's mother. They didn't let him call either. They handcuffed him to a chair. One beefy red-haired officer, and his blonde partner. Much loved symbols of the "force." They took turns beating him. They opened up his skull. He could feel his blood running warm down his face. Soaking the collar of his shirt. He could feel the bones of his nose give way . . . taste the blood on his upper lip. Once one eye was swollen shut they decided to play a game with him. "We're gonna put this gun on the table nigga and if you can get it before we get to you . . . you might live. Uncuff him." The boy was scared. He was fast. He grabbed the gun . . . the red-haired one went down first . . . the blonde one tried to help . . . too slow. The boy scared. Crying for his mama. They finished opening up his skull. Put him in a cell. A black officer walked by. "Help me brother . . . ," the boy cried. "I ain't your brother!" He got his face smashed through the bars. After days of protest . . . all of us lining the streets . . . saying no. . . . He was tried as an adult. No death penalty though because something did happen. The boy did need some forty stitches to close his skull. Something happened. He was cuffed . . . then uncuffed. Something happened. The red-haired one was something of a hot dog . . . not known for following procedure. Something happened. My father said we could save him . . . said we would save him . . . we had to . . . it's what we do. The boy was convicted of manslaughter. Sentenced to 25 years to life in prison.

MUMIA:

But not in silence!! "Many people say it is insane to resist the system, it is insane not to . . ." (**DEATH BLOSSOMS, p. 11**)

SAGE IS HERSELF AGAIN.

SAGE:

Later that night my father called me and my brother to the basement. He was sitting with one hand resting on the Miller Pony next to him the other on a stack of books balanced on his knee. He was sitting there so quietly. So quietly it created a stillness around him. A stillness you could see. I wondered where he learned to do that to become part of silence so completely. He had a stack of books mama kept locked in something she called a "commode" which I always thought meant toilet. He opened one of those books. His old college yearbook. Said "look at this..." We looked. My brother and me. Pulled back. Looked away. Looked again. This time our eyes...riveted...studying...swallowing the image whole,...then picking it apart...swallowing it again piece by piece. A black man hanging from a tree with what look like it could've been my old jump rope tied around his neck. Not a heavy rope wit a big loopy noose. You know like the kind you see in old westerns. But a thin rope pulled so tight the skin on his neck seemed to fold over it...hide it. His face set. Lips apart. Eyes not bulging but closed. Like he willed them shut. A bushy head tilted forward. Hands limp at his sides...not tied. His shirt shredded...but you could see it was once long-sleeved. On the front of his pants...a dark...dark spot. A group of men with light...light blonde hair... almost white...standing under him. Still holding shotguns. They were scared of the dead. Like me. "Look at this..." My father handed us another book. A man tied to a tree...a rope around his neck...near kneeling. Almost like he was praying. Hands tied this time. Charred tree bearing witness. Hair burned clean off one side of his head, memory jump-curve-wrapped around me. It lived. It breathed. I could smell smoke. My father hands us another one. A magazine this time. "Jet." Pictures of a boy. Bloated. Head...face...all mashed up...then resigned. Resigned to whatever happened to it. A woman in white standing there. Staring down at him. Crying. Daddy say "she made them take those pictures. She wanted the world to see. To see what this country would do to just a little boy. I was twelve. My brother was eleven.

My father looked at me and my brother and said... "it doesn't matter a black man can lay down his life..." Then he stopped. Held the words in his mouth. Tried to swallow them back down. There was that silence again. Finally, in the stillness he whispered "You all be sure to put them signs in the trash. Trashman be here in the morning..."

MUMIA:

But he taught you the language of resistance. Use it!
"The choice, as every choice is yours to fight for freedom or to be fettered,...Hold your heart open to the truth." (**DEATH BLOSSOMS, p. 121**)

CHORUS:
Who are you? Listen for the truth in your hands.

SAGE:
I took the boy's image...cut it into little tiny pieces...and kept it.

CHORUS:
Don't be afraid...don't be afraid...don't be afraid...

MOVEMENT #3: SLIDES OF MUMIA ABU-JAMAL IN VARIOUS STAGES OF LOCKING. SLIDES/VIDEO FOOTAGE OF OTHER DREADLOCKED WARRORS SUCH AS BOB MARLEY...PETER TOSH...ANGELA DAVIS... ALICE WALKER.

SAGE:
I don't know whether I conjured him...dreamed him...or both.
A simple man standing in the midst of Babylon committed to living the
life he made. I give my hands a ritual...trying to remember...to
forget...to find a place to make beauty...somewhere....somewhere...

CHORUS:
Theirs is a love story...loosed from bits of concrete...the heat of
summer days...and sanctuary...

SAGE:
I study his roots...an old-growth forest laying roots in cramped sun-
starved spaces.

MUMIA:
"[My hair]...I wear it as a conscious African, I wear it to show
oneness with the first man, an African, who wore his hair that way."
**(MUMIA ABU-JAMAL "MOVE: DREADLOCKS WITHOUT A
STATEMENT" PHILADELPHIA INQUIRER, 1/15/80)**

SAGE:
I study his roots and see the
first sweet dark African to give us life being celebrated there...a
covenant...a vow to return again and again.
I give my hands a ritual. Understanding that speaking
is really an act of touch. That at least a thousand
words reside in our fingertips alone.

MUMIA:
"Many hear the term 'radical' and automatically begin to think the
worst. Such is the power of the mass media projection and the forces of
social conformity, that this is so. Who or what is a radical? The word
literally means 'root.'" **(TEXT COPYRIGHT 1998 BY MUMIA ABU-JAMAL.
ALL RIGHTS RESERVED.)**

SAGE:
Hands hold the residue of stories that sometimes seep out before their
birthing time...

MUMIA:
My sister there may come a time when I will live only in your soul's
memory. When the sound of my voice can only be conjured by breath and
knowing. My sister...making beauty with deft hand and hungry eye...it
is you who will celebrate the sweetness of my life...or death with your
own life.
Your hands are not empty.

SAGE:
I give my hands a ritual. Finding the furrows of my scalp. Twisting
deep. Tiny circles of hair curling 'round my
fingers. Folding time between them creating sacred space as we move.

MUMIA:
Finding the furrows of her scalp. Twisting deep.
Tiny circles of hair curling 'round our fingers.

CHORUS:
Keeping ancient confidences in song and secret. The wisdom of the
multiverse making itself known through the mystery of touch.

SAGE:
I give my hands a ritual. Making locs. I take a few drops of sweet
almond oil scented with sandalwood and cedar. A warm smoky smell
charting a path from my third eye to my crown.
Fingers finding the furrows of my scalp twisting deep.
My roots unearthed naked and glorious.

MUMIA:
Her roots unearthed naked and glorious. Twisting deep. Tiny circles
curling 'round our fingers.

CHORUS:
Folding time between them creating sacred space as we move . . .

SAGE:
Tiny circles of hair curling 'round my fingers. Each circle birthing
circle. Making revolution. Calling to me . . . saying "if you love
me . . . follow me . . ."

MUMIA:
Creating sacred space as we move.

CHORUS:
Twisting. Deep.

SAGE:
And it was his voice . . . his hands making these locs.

MUMIA:
Spread yourself wide and let yourself come through . . .

CHROUS:
Spread yourself wide and let yourself come through . . .

SAGE:
I wet my fingertips with sweet almond oil. I could hear the ancestors
riding the whispers beneath his words.

MUMIA:
If you love me follow me . . .

CHORUS:
If you love me follow me . . .

SAGE:
a circle of voices making revolution.

MUMIA:
Can we make beauty my sister?

SAGE:
This surrender would be raw-honey dangerous.

CHORUS:
Theirs' is a love story unfolding knatty ringlet by knatty ringlet.

MOVEMENT #4: SLIDES/VIDEO FOOTAGE OF 19TH CENTURY AFRICAN-AMERICAN COUPLES LIVING AND LOVING IN SPITE OF....

SAGE: (NOTICING HIM FOR THE FIRST TIME)
Mumia, this isn't the first time is it?

CHORUS:
Scraps of time from other places. I remember being a woman...circa 1870...this quilt...a double-wedding-ring pattern made up of them old indigo overalls of yours...and that flannel nightshirt of mine...the one what ride up over my wanting thighs what catch the seat in the small of my back where it be all balled up while I'm all stretched out and you be studying me. Be scraps of pleasure what make up this quilt. At the edge of the cotton field at night where the cotton look like so many stars on the ground...good stars. At the edge of the cotton field where the black earth seem to reach up and grab hold to the sky like a woman reaching for her man when the time comes. Like me reaching for you. This little part of God's earth be ours when we ain't got nothing else. It be ours 'cause our love done consecrated it. Like holy ground. We bury all the things that hurt us there. And know it go to rest. Easy. All them nights I lay down beside your bringin' all them sore places I been patching up all week. The only places I got left after all of me done gone and got lost in somebody's elses wants. How I take that tired rag off my head and give myself to the moon and you. You let your fingers dance counter-clockwise over all them rough circles. I am a simple altar. Calling forth Africa. You smelling all good...like coming rain. You start'rubbin. Gentle-touching all them found places inside me. Leavin' that good kind of heat. Helping me gather up all what's been lost. Healing all them wounds it leave. Then I go to trembling. It be sweet sleep after that. We be making beauty right there.

MUMIA:
I saw her roots. Unearthed. Sprouting promise.

SAGE:
He saw my roots. Unearthed. He smelled good. Green-leaf crisp. Like coming rain.

MUMIA:
Dreaming her...Conjuring her. I heard her spirits singing...

SAGE:
My roots exposed. Growing from the top of my head. Pushing into earth.
My roots ancient women. Praise-house women.
Feet marking time rhythm to sound of breath-song. Arms spiraling to heaven.

A marching of God's army. Chanting down the walls of Babylon with drylongso courage and clarity. The grace of their song said they were older than time. I'm gathered among them. Naked before the altar of their hands.

MUMIA:
Can I touch you?

SAGE:
I believe you already have.

MUMIA:
Give me your stories. Take me with you.

SAGE:
Where Mumia? Where do you want to go?

MUMIA:
Take me to the place where you make beauty.

SAGE:
That place is lost.

MUMIA:
No Sage...it isn't.

SAGE AND MUMIA:
I was in search of a woman/man who could love
like a prayer.

SLIDES/VIDEO FOOTAGE OF "DREAD" LOVERS...THAT IS COUPLES WITH LOCKED HAIR. THE CHORUS SINGS BITS OF SUMMER LOVE SONGS FROM SUCH WELL-KNOWN R&B GROUPS AS THE DELFONICS...THE STYLISTICS...THE DRAMATICS...THE CHI-LITES...ETC.

MUMIA:
There is a faint calling of drums. Praying in one breath...long and unbroken nurturing her resolve...keeping her safe...so that she might fulfill her mission. Kneel here.

SAGE AND MUMIA:
It was war that brought us to this place of poetry. We had lost the peace of morning's music. We had fashioned the enemy's words into weapons. Which we've turned on ourselves. But my locs are not faggots or a molotov cocktail. They are prayers wrapped in the tensile strength of our ancestors.

SAGE:
It was Mumia praying.

MUMIA:
Fingering each of her locs...intricate lines filled with good stars.
She was wearing Africa inside her.

SAGE:

His hands dark honey sweet.

MUMIA:

Intricate lines filled with good stars. Laying a trail of ancient
voices. I followed...

SAGE:

I was in search of a man who could love like a prayer. I studied his
face. Intricate lines curving to enjambment around eyes...ears...nose.
Like earth and sky.

MUMIA:

Fingering her locs I tasted her sweetness...

SAGE:

This is no wincing-weak medicine. It is a reconfiguration of the
senses. A conjuration of touch. The smell of sound. The taste of color.
A powerful healing.

MUMIA:

Tasting her sticky sweetness...

SAGE:

The salt-sweet secrets of late-night love...

MUMIA:

Caressing her baby locs...

SAGE:

Blessing them into beingness...

MUMIA:

They sing love in a forgotten language...

SAGE:

Caressing my baby locs...

MUMIA:

Mapping a path to pleasure. My fingers mark the spot again and again.

SAGE:

Taking me to a place where I remember that water is always sacred.

MUMIA:

She is woman of shadows. Too much darkness where there should be light.
Her thoughts centuries old. I could see them.

SAGE:

His hands were a gift. I was listening...gathering...remembering...

MUMIA:

I give my hands a ritual.

MOVEMENT #5: SLIDES OF TREES AND TRANQUIL WOODED
AREAS IN VARIOUS SEASONS WHICH FADES TO

AN IMAGE OF 13TH AND LOCUST STS. WHICH
FADES TO AN IMAGE OF 6221 OSAGE AVENUE.

SAGE:

I fell in love with his hands. Chained. Weighted. Callused hands. Hands remembering love. The moments that brought me to this one. Hands as beautiful as the words of Senghor and Marley. Hands that crave my kind of closeness. That can cook . . . clean . . . wash dishes. Hands that can understand how I make my work and appreciate it. Hands that know my woman-fullness but still love me like a little girl . . . you know like my mama. Hands that speak to me like Hartman singing "Moonlight in Vermont." Hands that can love me like a slow Sunday afternoon.

CHORUS:

Hands that were like lips of Pandora's box. Opened. Hell breaking through tender crusts of fertile earth. Surrendering him to its secrets. And he stands there still. Hands that walked back to Osage Avenue all by theyself. Sifted bone from ash. Calling the names of his dead. Pouring libation with sacred breath. John. Frank. Conrad. Phil. Tomaso. Theresa. Rhonda. Raymond. Delisha. Netta. Tree-Tree. He called the names. Giving shelter to their spirit in the nap of his hair. Keeping them safe amongst the dense curl and dark. Hands that tasted his own blood. Clutching air when a policeman's bullets gave him wings. But Mama Earth held him fast.

SAGE AND CHORUS:

Hands that give us the courage to face this circle that is history.

SAGE:

What else could I do? I had to save him. Let him speak the truth he
held in his hands.

MUMIA:

My hands a lullaby.

SAGE AND MUMIA:

It was a song of hands . . .

MUMIA:

Palm-smooth swirling . . .

SAGE:

I'm unfolding. Spreading myself wide . . .

MUMIA:

Like one in prayer.

CHORUS:

And spirits come . . . and come . . . and come . . .

MUMIA AND CHORUS:

Then . . . the dance stopped. The music of hands now silent. Each circle
stilled. Revolution stalled. There are days when beauty just walks away
from us and we are left to see ourselves in the wake of what remains.

MUMIA:

I come here because I wanted to touch you . . . to prove these hands . . . won't . . .
can't hurt you . . . to whisper to you in the voice of John Africa saying "each

individual life is dependant on every other life, and all life has a purpose..."
(25 YEARS ON THE MOVE) My breath is your breath...my life is your life...
my prayers are yours. But my hands were stopped...stilled...

MOVEMENT #6: SAGE AND MUMIA ARE ACCOSTED BY A YOUNG THUG IN THE PARK WHO COMES INTERRUPTING THEIR "FLOW." SAGE LIVING IN THE MOMENT BECOMES THE THUG...THE VERY FEAR BLOCKING HER PATH.

SAGE:

Because I was walking back to the beginning and there he stood. The boy
with the stocking cap and the oversized Jordans. Who would save him?
The boy who spent his childhood bearing witness to evil then let his
eyes die.

> He watched me. Watched me and avoided my eyes. He was singing... "baby
> let me rub you up from behind..." He was loud. Loud and wrong. A love
> song? An invitation to intimacy? I saw him.

MUMIA:

To whisper to you in the voice of John Africa saying "when you are committed to
doing what's right the power of righteousness will never betray you..." (DEATH
BLOSSOMS, p. 3) LIFE will protect you.

SAGE:

I tried not to pay him any attention. But I couldn't help it. He hunched himself all
up beside me. I thought of a line from one of my favorite Gwendolyn Brooks'
poems. "When you set out for Afrika you did not know where you were going
because you did not know you were Afrika." I thought of all the things he
didn't know.

MUMIA:

Whispering in the voice of John Africa, "... don't ever allow yourself to be
confused about true strength..." ("MOVE'S BELIEF IS LIFE" by Debbie,
Janet, and Janine Africa FIRST DAY #22)

SAGE:

I could hear death talking to him like the father we never had. The mesh skullcap
boring Nike or Tommy Hilfiger into his brain. The only evidence of Africa a few
scraggly braids spread over his head like dried bush over drought stricken earth.
What could've been handsome legs sprouted up from unlaced Air Jordans.
They looked like cheap meatballs at a tacky cocktail party. Planting his feet firmly
in front of me. My eyes staring the question "when you look in the mirror what
do you see?"

MUMIA:

Whispering in the voice of John Africa "Revolution starts with the individual.
It starts with a person making a personal commitment to do what's right..."
(25 YEARS ON THE MOVE, p. 69)

SAGE:

Death still talking to him. "I'm the greatest hustler of 'em all.

Ain't been killed or caught yet." "Who's your daddy?" Death seducing
him like a cheap trick.

MUMIA:

Whispering in the voice of John Africa, "To understand revolution you must be
sound" **(25 YEARS ON THE MOVE, p. 69)**

SAGE:

I could've gansta-pimp slapped him with Jacob Lawrence ... bludgeoned him with
Romare Bearden ... took some Bettye Saar and kicked him all up in his ass. But my
hands are still. He licks his lips not because they're dry. But because the presence of
his tongue gives him power. Then he had the nerve to say "so how you today?
ummm ... you look good ... almost good enough to eat ..." Would I save his life?
Could I save his life?

MUMIA:

Whispering in the voice of John Africa, "... Revolution is not a
philosophy, it is an activity." **(25 YEARS ON THE MOVE, p. 69)**

SAGE:

I looked at him. Leave me alone!!! "I'm just trying to talk to you! I
can talk to you bitch! Oh no he didn't! I stood facing the man-child who
would bring us all our deaths.

MUMIA:

Whispering to you in the voice of John Africa, "Revolution is not war,
but peace. It does not weaken. It strengthens.
Revolution does not cause seperation, it generates togetherness ..."
(JOHN AFRICA, STRATEGIC REVOLUTION)

SAGE:

Do you know me? Haven't we learned the lessons of our foremothers?
Don't we hear their cries raped ... in
fields ... barns ... plantation houses ... and churches? Being entered like a
waiting market instead of a sacred space.

MUMIA:

No. Listen to the voice in your hands. Hear me.

SAGE:

Legs pried open in darkness ... clinched teeth set against tender nipple
demanding silence.

MUMIA:
Hear me ...

SAGE:

We just don't remember. The overseer's voice is now the voice of our
sons ... fathers ... husbands.

MUMIA:
But I'm still here. I'm still here.

SAGE:
I wanted to save him from history. His own. **(EXAMINING HER HANDS)**

MOVEMENT #7: SOUNDS OF THE OCEAN. LIGHTS FADE TO REPLICATE THE DARKNESS OF A SLAVE SHIP. CRIES AND GROANS ARE HEARD AS SAGE AND MUMIA AND THE CHORUS LIE NEXT TO EACH OTHER SPOON FASHION. AS THEY SPEAK THIS MEMORY AFRICAN RHYTHMS ARE HEARD. ***SLIDES OF A SLAVE SHIP AND VARIOUS OTHER RENDERINGS OF THE MIDDLE PASSAGE ETC. CAN BE USED.

MUMIA:
It wouldn't be the first time. I saw her roots unearthed.

CHORUS:
The Middle Passage circa 1858. I saw you when they brought you in . . . stole you in . . . clean as night and death. Illegal good. We all went to the barn. Standing there naked as a newborn baby. Don't look like you knowed nothing at all. Carrying the stench of that ship all over you like something dead. The one with wet-sea eyes. Holding silence in your throat like a precious gift. You huddled in that in that barn yes trying to forget and remember. Bone-numb. Except for the wildness. Wildness . . . your hair . . . it was in your hair. The gnarled clumps fighting each other . . . where lice and ringworm compete for available space . . . where pine tar burned out the rest. Wildness. I saw your eyes jump-curve wrap around something long since lost. Wildness. Scaring people the way you moved your lips without saying a word. Your tongue caressing ancient songs causing you to smile like you were alone even when you were not. Wildness . . . you scared them. Scared them all. In your wildness I saw a place to lay my hands. I needed to speak to you from that quiet persistant place between my thighs that makes me know I'm a woman. That's how I come walking into that barn. Kneeled before you and offered myself like a prayer. For months you would only speak one word . . . "Wanderer . . . Wanderer . . ." It would even spill out in the air surrounding your dreams. I came to take that away. Wildness that tangle of hair on your head. Matted with burrs. Ate out by ringworm in patches. I take some of that lye soap, part your hair, and rub it deep down to the scalp. Soon I don't feel that grit sticking under my nails. I take out that rosemary water I make with new rain and wash out the last of that soap. You close your eyes. That be a good thing. 'Cause next I got to cut off what's already been hurt to bad to heal. Feeling the tears on my own face. I start thinking that hair be the last thing left you got free. So I let it be.

SAGE AND MUMIA:
We give our hands a ritual.

CHORUS:
A circle of memory reaching back . . .

CHORUS:
Their's is a love story . . . a womb . . . a beginning . . . And yes
Sage it is you who will save his life.

SAGE:
It had been 2000 seasons and I was spring water returned.

MUMIA:
Can we make beauty make sister?

SAGE:
I am clean. Laid open. It is a song of hands. The naked soul of my head
is honored. I'm becoming...

MUMIA:
Give me your stories...

MOVEMENT #8: VIDEO FOOTAGE OF THE MAY 1985 BOMBING OF THE MOVE HEADQUARTER IN PHILADELPHIA.

SAGE:
The memory of this night came wedging itself perfectly between my history and
my becoming. My father stood transfixed by the image of night and flame. Hands
still in his back pockets. He stood still in his uniform...a gray summer wool suit
with the pink shirt my mother picked out, and the burgundy tie he added for himself. "They bombing black people!" I eased up beside him. Drawn into what first
seemed like awe. In the original sense of the word. But that wasn't it. Not at all.
I sat there in that space between the recliner and the television. The images crackled
and flame-danced on the screen in front of us. Long arms of orange flame stretched
through what was once doors, walls, and windows of the seemingly tiny rowhouse
on 6221 Osage Avenue, cupped its hands and reached up toward heaven offering
up the lives of its occupants.

CHORUS:
Forgive us children. For we have sinned. You have forgotten those who crossed the
Big Water chanting cries of war and peace. Remembering only silence. Forgive us
children. For we have sinned. You have forgotten those who walked through valley
and field defying the promise of pain and death to chant cries of war and peace.

SAGE:
My father shakes his head and goes "now if that bunker is full of weapons why they
gonna drop something on it that explodes?"

CHORUS:
Forgive us children. For we have sinned. You have forgotten those who walked
through valley and field defying the promise of pain and death to chant cries of war
and peace.

SAGE:
I ease close. Closer to my father. The burning shell of the bunker stood defying the
assault of C-4, and 10,000 rounds of ammunition. Then it sighed, and fell and fell
and fell.

CHORUS:
Forgive us children. For we have sinned. You have forgotten those who went to
their deaths with eyes quiet pleading to God...

SAGE:
Leaving only shadows and silence.

CHORUS:
To save them from justice.

SAGE:

My mother comes to call us to dinner. She makes her announcement quickly then retreats. Not wanting to be a part of this vigil that leaves the faint smell of smoke and burning flesh clinging to this space that my father and I created in this moment. **(SAGE SLOWLY BEGINS TO DRESS IN HER CLOTHES AS SHE CONTINUES TELLING THE STORY. SHE BECOMES HER FATHER.)** My father wants to believe in goodness. That given the choice most people do the right thing. But my father is a man who grew up in the Depression-era segregated south. He had seen evil live and breath growing like a force unto itself. "Jesus Christ!!! The whole block is on fire! Those people gonna lose everything. Look at the police and the fire trucks blocking the way. They gonna lose everything..." He shakes his head. Sucks his teeth. Goes "humph..." It would take almost 15 years before I would understand the meaning of this vigil. It was a rite of passage. A place where I would understand the meaning of this vigil. It was a rite of passage. A place where I would pass from father's hands into womanhood. A place of charred bone; ash; and silence.

MUMIA:
And you are still here.
You are not alone Sage. There are so many others.

CHORUS:
Lay yourself open to the light of this hearing...

MOVEMENT #9: INSERT GUEST ACTIVIST. THE ARTIST WILL LIT-ERALLY GIVE THE AUDIENCE THE LATEST PER-TINENT INFORMATION ON THE MUMIA CASE... THEY MAY ALSO CHOOSE TO ADDRESS OTHER POLITICAL PRISONERS OR MATTERS OF JUSTICE.

MUMIA:
Resistance...you wear it just behind your eyes. Resistance...you hold the words in your throat. Trying to swallow them into silence. But I hear them. Resistance...you hold it in your hands.

SAGE:
I studied Mumia's hands raised...shackled...reaching...
My daddy's hands raised...reaching...then shackled.

CHORUS:
Resistance...

MUMIA:
You were girl then...passing from your father's hands to become a woman...

SAGE:
With places too raw to give birth to beauty...

CHORUS:
Resistance...

MUMIA:
Will you make beauty with me?

SAGE:
There's been too much loss...

CHORUS:
Resistance...

MUMIA:
Feel it in your hands...

SAGE:
These hands...uncovering no prayers...laying bare no prophecies. These hands have seen too many wars. Me, I'm no savior.

MUMIA:
Your hands are a gift. Their medicine memory and resistance.

SAGE:
How do you believe in hands?

CHORUS:
You begin by saying no! The Stono Rebels...Denmark Vesey...Gabriel Prosser...Nat Turner...David Walker...A chorus of voices all of them saying no...shimmering across the surface of time reflecting and refracting light. A mirror held up to the face of this nation so that it may see itself...clearly.

SAGE:
I've been saying no for centuries.

CHORUS:
We are calling you by your name...

MUMIA:
Give your hands to me...

SAGE:
No! My hands can't be trusted.

MUMIA:
Will you walk away from my life?

SAGE:
There was a faint calling of drums.

CHORUS:
Will our children ever forgive us?

MOVEMENT #10: SAGE FIRST TRAVELS TO 13TH AND LOCUST STS ONE COLD DECEMBER NIGHT...THEN TO A POLICE VAN...THEN TO THE HOSPITAL... THEN A COURTROOM...AND FINALLY DEATH-ROW. ALL OF THIS TRAVEL IS SUGGESTED BY SOUND AND IMAGE.

SAGE:

He laid his hand in mine and I was there that night. The night of his survival.
Lying on his back counting the soft-bass beating of his heart. Counting slow looking up at the starless sky. He tries to remember it.
Remember it all. Heading toward Center City looking for a fare. The slow drive
past 13th and Locust. The crowd gathered in the street. A man staggering...dizzy
in the middle of the street. A flashlight crashing down on the man's head. Was the
man screaming? He can't remember. He only remembers the man's face. It's his
brother. He remembers running toward the sound. His cab is still running. He is
counting slow as his lungs burn with each breath. Feeling a warm trickle of blood
first on his cheek...then his chin. Counting slow as he turns to see the white
police officer lying there dying with him. Looking up at the starless sky wondering
which one of them heaven would claim first. Then he hears sirens. Sees the flash of
red lights. He's counting slow as each blow from the cops' batons ignite new fires
in his chest. Sealing burning breath in his lungs. Sending it to his belly to erupt in
blood. Counting slow...the only prayer he can remember now. His face pressed
against the icy steel floor of the police wagon. Would they stop at the morgue or
the hospital?
Would it matter? Would it stop the burning in his chest? Loose his breath? The
soft-bass beating of his heart drowned out by curses and bright lights. "Let that
nigger cop killer die!!!" "Help our brother!!!" His chest on fire. His breath is raw
heat. Words...screams...sorrow-songs...calling to god...all seared in his throat.
Ashes on his tongue now. He's counting slow. Standing in the courtroom first
accused of murder. Then silenced. No, he could not represent himself. No, he
could not have the wisdom and legal assistance of his friend John Africa. No, he
would not have jury of his peers; competent counsel; or an impartial judge. But he
was counting slow...when they smiled and said death. He knew he would outlast
them. I am a witness. I am a witness. I am a witness.

MUMIA:

"Despite the legal illusions erected by the system to divide and
seperate life, we the caged share air, water, and hope with you, the
not-yet-caged. We share your same breath. As John Africa teaches 'all
life is connected.'" (LIVE FROM DEATH ROW, pp. 51–52)

SAGE:

Breath...air...hope...our lives connected...

MUMIA:

Standing in the middle of Hell. I'm wearing Africa inside me. I'm
wearing Africa inside me when they come to get me.

SAGE AND CHORUS:

Breath...

MUMIA:

To strip me naked. Shackle my wrists.

SAGE AND CHORUS:

Air...

MUMIA:
To take me to wait. To wait for my death.

SAGE AND CHORUS:
Hope...

MUMIA:
My naked feet walking quiet soft footsteps behind a batallion of prison
guards to an empty cell.

SAGE:
Our lives forever connected... Hear my prayer...

MUMIA:
Death speaking in cold whispers against my bare skin.
As my fate was read the first time...

CHORUS:
The Governor of the Commonwealth of Pennsylvania has signed your Death
Warrant today. Effective for the week of August 13, 1995. The
Department of Corrections has set the date of Thursday August 17th to
carry out this order...

SAGE:
You are a fortress surrounded by your warriors.

MUMIA:
And when the judge came speaking death a second time...

CHORUS:
The Governer of the Commonwealth of Pennsylvania has signed your death
warrant todday, effective for the week of October 13, 1999... The
Department of Correction have set the date of Thursday December 2,
1999...

SA1E:
In the fever pitch of battle we cry...

MUMIA:
And when a judge tried to silence me... you... (indicating the
audience)... the truth... with a lie of compromise...
life in prison... what's life in prison to an innocent man? I resist! I resist! I
resist! And I'm still here... standing in the valley of the
shadow of death I'm still here. A fierce warrior for speaking the
truth! A fierce warrior for living the truth! A fierce warrior... I am
the truth and I'm still here! Long long live John Africa!!!

CHORUS:
They will never touch you!

SAGE:
And you are free!

CHORUS:
And you are free!

ALL:
They will never touch you!

SAGE:
It is war that brings me to this place of beauty.

MUMIA:
come dawta . . .

SAGE:
I'm being called. His hands were a gift.

MUMIA:
I need soldiers . . . we need soldiers. Come dawta . . .

SAGE:
I want to hold him in the softest part of me . . .

MUMIA:
This is a song of hands . . .

SAGE:
My hands . . .

MUMIA:
dancing . . . soul-healthy . . . spirit-strong . . . warrior-memory
intact . . . born to live . . . born to lead this father and his father's
father and his father before that to love.

SAGE:
This is a love story. Loosed from bits of concrete . . . the heat of summer
days . . . and sanctuary. Unfolding knatty ringlet by knatty ringlet. This
is a love story. A womb. A beginning . . . a place of departures. He
surrenders me to the edge of light. For the moment I forget the history
of my blood. Then I remember . . . remember it all.

MUMIA:
Can we make beauty my sister?

SAGE:
I slip into a hallowed place . . .
my hands dancing . . . I would save his life . . . I would save my life

MUMIA:
I was in search of a woman who could love like a prayer.

SAGE:
That woman was me.

SAGE AND MUMIA:
This is a love story.

CHORUS:
Now our hands will rest.

THE CHORUS READS THE WORDS OF MUMIA'S LETTER AS IT IS PROJECTED ON THE SCREEN.

AUGUST WILSON AND BLACK AESTHETICS

Sandra G. Shannon

Dear Sandra Shannon
In a speech I delivered on June 26, 1996, to the Eleventh Biennial Theatre Communications Group (TCG) Conference at Princeton University, I issued a call for a conference on the future of Black American theater....As a Montgomery Fellow at Dartmouth College, during Winter Term 1998, I will convene the National Black Theatre Summit—"On Golden Pond," to take place during the week of March 2, through March 7, 1998. This invitation is being sent to you as one of forty invited summit participants. Exploring the complex issues facing Black theater now and in the future requires the efforts of many different people with expertise in a number of different areas and disciplines. To that end the Summit will be unique to theater arts, bringing together individuals from the worlds of American theater, government, education, and business to create a national dialogue that generates proactive and constructive ideas....Thank you in advance for taking time out of your schedule to make the commitment to participate in The National Black Theatre Summit—"On Golden Pond." We look forward to your presence.

Sincerely,
August Wilson

During the winter of 1998 in a bold move to convert his recent rhetoric into action, playwright August Wilson joined forces with Dartmouth professors Victor Leo Walker II and William Cook to undertake a thorough assessment of what ails black theater and to prescribe remedies to fix it. That plan was set into motion by convening an eclectic group of thinkers from all over the United States whose professions and whose passions intersected in various ways with the African theater industry. My invitation to join this distinguished group came in a letter from Wilson in which he explained the impetus behind this subsequent move and provided specifics about the proposed National Black Theatre Summit, "On Golden Pond."

This letter was to become my ticket to a behind-the-scenes orientation to the nuts and bolts of black theater. It was to lead me to an awareness of black theater's role in African American cultural preservation and, toward that end, impressed upon me the importance of my role as critic and educator. My neighbors for the week included an arsenal of theater greats, the likes of whom included Ed Bullins, Ntozake Shange, Robbie McCauley, Paul Carter Harrison, Woodie King, Walter Dallas, Lou Bellamy, the late Beverly Robinson and Don Evans, Sydne Mahone, Vernell Lillie, and, of course, August Wilson. After several days of workshops, breakout sessions, and heated fireside debates, I left the cozy quarters of the Minary Conference Center feeling as if I had been to a revival. This invitation had led me to shift my third-person perspective on black theater to that of one who shared a vested interest in its survival as well as in its future direction. I cared.

As with most high-profile activities, the media came; they saw; they took stock; and they came to various conclusions about our mission. In the months that followed the Dartmouth retreat and conference, quite a few observers raced to put their spin on the entire affair. Some were suspicious of our motives; some were angry about their exclusion; and some were genuinely taken in by the proactive agenda set forth by Wilson, Walker, and Cook. Still others likened our efforts to a second black arts movement while a few questioned exactly what we were doing sequestered out in the woods in the midst of a bitter New England winter.

It has been five years now since I sat down with thirty-nine other lovers of black theater in Ashland, New Hampshire, to devise ways to improve the state of black theater. In the years that followed that revival, several earnest attempts were made to extend the dialogue on its business and aesthetics practices beyond what transpired there and into the larger arts community. In July 1998, Atlanta, Georgia's National Black Arts Festival put our concerns on its agenda and provided yet another forum for strategizing the survival of black theater. In the fall of 1998 and in the spring of 2000 I organized two national symposia on the campus of Howard University (The Ground Together I and II) that examined similar issues about cultural ownership and cultural property from an interdisciplinary perspective.

Since Wilson delivered his shocking and unabridged "The Ground On Which I Stand" speech in 1996, the aesthetic distance made possible by a seven-year time span—as well as reams of reactionary rhetoric; a host of television and radio interviews and public forums; and steadily increasing numbers of articles, theses, dissertations, and books that address his aesthetic manifesto—makes now as strategic a time as any to take a sober, critical look back to assess this moment. In a recent interview, August Wilson gave his take on what has come of the passionate and daring movement that began in Princeton, New Jersey, stopped over in New York at Manhattan's Town Hall, lingered on the campus of Dartmouth College, and ultimately found its way to Atlanta's National Black Arts Festival. When asked during a recent interview, "what do see as the most significant advance of the speech and the subsequent conference at Dartmouth?" he explained

> The African Grove Institute for the Arts (AGIA) came out of that. But the concrete results of black gains—I don't see any, none. I think it's been the opposite. These are not always the things by which we measure. But the important thing is we started with one black LORT theatre, and we don't have any now. Jimandi Productions in Atlanta, a city that is something like 73% black cannot support a black theatre. They closed. It's closed. It's not there anymore. I'm willing to bet that, if you go back and look, after the speech there was less money given to black theatres than before. (Interview, September 2003)

August Wilson and Black Aesthetics demonstrates in less tangible ways how the aesthetic position expressed in the playwright's address speaks to a wide range of multidisciplinary and multiethnic issues. It invites readers to focus their attention more closely upon issues of black aesthetics raised in "The Ground On Which I Stand"—issues that often became marginalized next to the lightning-rod topic of colorblind casting. For the poet, the hip-hop artist, or the dancer, for example, issues of cultural ownership, cultural preservation, and cultural nationalism are equally pertinent. In that sense, Wilson offers a whole new way of viewing the artistic expressions of an increasingly diverse America—and, by extension, a diverse world. After all, what emerges from the numerous reactions to August Wilson's challenging "The Ground On Which I Stand" speech is an urgent need to respect one's cultural and aesthetic grounds: "We may disagree, we may forever be on opposite sides of aesthetics, but we can only share a value system that is inclusive of all Americans and recognizes their unique and valuable contributions."